CULLIS
Club and
country

A centenary tribute

CULLIS
Club and
country

A centenary tribute by

Steve Gordos

Geoffrey Publications

First published in Great Britain in October 2016 by
Geoffrey Publications, Kingswinford, West Midlands

Also by Geoffrey Publications
Those Were the Days, 2007
Crumpled Bits of Paper, 2009
Out of Darkness, 2011
Wembley Wolves, 2014
The Valley Wanderer, 2015

ISBN 978-0-9929826-5-2

Printed and bound by T.J. International Ltd.
Trecerus Industrial Estate, Padstow,
Cornwall. UK. PL28 8RW.

Contents

Acknowledgements

Fortunate enough to have been born in time to savour the days when Wolves were the best team in England, I always felt a debt of gratitude to Stanley Cullis. Thanks to a father who had been watching Wolves since 1908, I learned that the Master of Molineux was as great a player as he was a manager – and he was indeed a great manager.

The centenary of Cullis's birth is an appropriate time to chronicle for Wolves fans old and young the achievements of the man born in Ellesmere Port on October 25, 1916. I am grateful to **Clive Corbett** for encouraging me in this project and making sure it came to fruition. Like me, Clive's love of Wolves had paternal roots. He has a great feeling for the history of Wolverhampton Wanderers and has already made impressive contributions to gold and black literature. Others, too, have been enthusiastically helpful in making this book possible:

Wolves' head of marketing and communications **Matt Grayson** was at once willing to grant access to the club's impressive archives and I am sure he will see that the Cullis centenary is suitably observed. With his vast knowledge of the club's history, **Pat Quirke** is the ideal man for welcoming visitors to the superb museum beneath the stand that bears the name of Stan Cullis. Club historian Pat was only too happy to lead me to a wealth of Wolves archive material housed in an underground home where I could happily spend a week and still not have looked at everything.

Wolverhampton is also fortunate to have the **City Archives** available with a staff ready to help one delve into the past. It too has its Wolves connection housed as it is in Molineux House, whose grounds became the home of the town's team in 1889.

Not for the first time the programme collection of Wolves matchday magazine editor **John Hendley** has been of valuable help. The same can be said of enduring Billy Wright Stand regular **Kevin Jones**, whose support of the club home and away is matched only by his magnificent collection of photos, programmes and memorabilia. Another fan fantastic **David Dungar** has always been a trusty source of information.

Finally, a word of thanks to my former Express & Star colleague **David Harrison** who has covered sport in many parts of the world but has never forgotten his gold and black roots. It was a remark made to him by Cullis that proved a fitting inscription for the magnificent statue of the great man outside the stand which bears his name.

To all others who have been of assistance, many thanks.

Steve Gordos   October 2016

Foreword

To be a great player and great manager with the same football club has fallen to few. Such a man was Stanley Cullis. The year 2016 marked the centenary of the birth of Cullis – the greatest name in the history of Wolverhampton Wanderers. He narrowly missed out on trophies in his playing career but as a manager then proceeded to make Wolves the best club in the land, bringing to a new generation of players the cups and medals that had eluded him.

It irks Wolves fans who remember what the side achieved in the 'Fabulous Fifties' that Cullis is often a forgotten man when it comes to listing the game's finest managers. Yet he deserves his place among the legendary British bosses like Chapman, Shankly, Stein, Ferguson, Paisley and Clough. Apart from winning trophies, his teams played a brand of football that provided fans with entertainment and excitement.

Some have criticised the methods he embraced yet his style of play produced the thing fans loved most – goals. Wolves' style has sometimes been labelled "kick and rush" but no team can win two FA Cups and be champions of England three times playing that way. True, Cullis wanted his teams to play direct football yet he always had time for the gifted player and it was because he integrated skill with a necessary degree of directness, allied to fitness, that his teams were so attractive to watch.

Distinguished sportswriter Tony Pawson said Cullis was "the most explosive and exciting manager of his time." That speaks volumes about the man as his contemporaries included Matt Busby, Arthur Rowe, Ted Drake, Bill Shankly, Tom Whittaker and Bill Nicholson. Pawson added: "Cullis was to be totally absorbed in the game as player and manager and as both he is a colourful part of its history. He was a centre-half imbued with the spirit of attack, neat in his control, bristling with aggression." Of Cullis's attitude toward his players, Pawson said: "Cullis drove them on with relentless impassioned determination. To be near him at a match was to experience total involvement."

It was that passion and total commitment that made Cullis the most significant influence on the history of Wolverhampton Wanderers. His main rival during the period that spanned the 1950s was Busby at Manchester United. In a period of 12 seasons, neatly bookended by Wolves' FA Cup triumphs of 1949 and 1960, each three times won the First Division, as England's top flight was then known. Cullis and Busby believed in finding and encouraging young players and both shunned traditional insularity, being willing to take on the best teams in Europe.

Pawson's opinion of Cullis was endorsed by another legend of British sportswriting – Geoffrey Green. Football correspondent for The Times for many years, Green it was who described Cullis as the "Iron Chancellor." That was the nickname given to Otto von Bismarck who made Prussia the most powerful of German states in the 19th Century, famously saying that Germany would only become one great state through "blood and iron". The academic Green could see a touch of Bismarck in the way Cullis was almost fanatical in wanting to make Wolves the best team in the land and insisted on the same dedication from his players. Bismarck succeeded in unifying the many states of Germany into a powerful empire and Cullis transformed Wolves from the nearly men of football into winners. Green said of Cullis: "A stern disciplinarian and keen student of the game, he was his own man. He did not follow the herd; he had his own clear cut ideas and he stuck to them through thick and thin. A dynamic driving force and physical fitness fanatic he stood no nonsense from anyone."

Jim Holden painted a fine picture of the man in his biography of Cullis, The Iron Manager, while Cullis's autobiography, All For The Wolves, sets out his forthright views and opinions on football. Here, I hope to fill in more of the detail of Cullis's career year by year as first player and then manager. As both he was something special, and a man never afraid to stand up for himself and his colleagues and single-minded in wanting the best for Wolverhampton Wanderers.

Cullis's passion for football was matched by his passion for the club he served for 30 years and is best summed up by a remark he once made to David Harrison, a well-respected sportswriter who worked for the Birmingham Evening Mail, the Wolverhampton Express & Star, Today and the News of the World. Harrison would often act as chauffeur to Cullis when, some years after Cullis's management days were over, they travelled to meetings to elect a Midlands player of the month. Once their conversation touched on Cullis's brief spell as manager of Birmingham City a few years after his departure from Molineux and Harrison wondered why it had not been a great success and received the reply: "In this world you only have one life and I gave mine to Wolves."

Fittingly, that comment appears at the foot of the magnificent statue of Cullis that stands proudly outside the stand at Molineux which bears his name. The words sum it up perfectly – Wolverhampton Wanderers would not have a prominent place in the history of English football had it not been for the life of Stanley Cullis.

Chapter 1   It had to be Wolves

To the eternal good fortune of Wolverhampton Wanderers, the father of Stanley Cullis was a Wulfrunian. Billy Cullis was one of many who had migrated from the town of Wolverhampton to Ellesmere Port as an employee of the Wolverhampton Corrugated Iron Company. When it became apparent that young Stanley had an aptitude for association football and might make it as a professional, his father was adamant it had to be with Wolves. Most other youngsters growing up in Ellesmere Port with dreams of football fame were far more likely to look to the giants on Merseyside, Everton and Liverpool, rather than unfashionable Wolves. Not so Stan Cullis, born in the Cheshire town on October 25, 1916, the youngest of ten children.

Cullis's football ability soon emerged at Cambridge Road School and he later played in the same Ellesmere Port schoolboy side as Joe Mercer who would become a friend and rival as both player and manager. In those days Cullis was seen as an inside forward and Mercer a striker. In time they would find their true role as centre-half and wing-half respectively. Significantly, Cullis was made captain of the team at William Stockton Boys Modern School.

As a youngster, Cullis showed a capacity for learning as well as for sport yet he was not allowed to go to grammar school by his father. He wanted him to be out earning money for the family. Young Stanley soon had a job as an errand boy for a grocer but that did not stop him going to night school to try to better himself. His thirst for learning and for knowledge of many things would stay with him throughout his life. He learned French, Esperanto, book-keeping and short-hand. He made himself an educated man and when, many years later, he came to write his life story there was no need for a "ghosted" autobiography. Cullis wrote it himself and did it very well.

Mercer painted a picture of young Cullis in his book, The Great Ones: "While I was always one for a laugh and a joke, he was a serious boy, always studying something new. He did not share my fanatical desire to become a footballer. No other career would have done for me, but Stan could have taken many other roads and made an equal success. He had the ability to absorb knowledge in a way that I did not. He went to night school and could have gone on to grammar school and probably university. One of a large family, he wanted to improve his social standing and way of life. All the Cullis family were like that; I imagine they got their inspiration from Mrs Cullis who was confined to a wheelchair and was one of the nicest women I have ever met. Stan saw football as an escape from his background. He had an understanding of the game right from the start, but tactics never entered my head in those days. Stan saw everything earlier than me."

When it became clear that young Stan might have what it took to be a footballer, his father allowed him to go for a week's trial with Bolton Wanderers, stressing this was merely to gain experience. Cullis learned many years later that the Burnden Park club were not impressed by him, thinking him to be too slow.

Mercer, being over two years older than Cullis, was first to take a step on the ladder of football success, joining Everton as an amateur after leaving school and getting a job at the local Shell oil refinery. In September, 1932, at the age of 18, he signed professional forms at Goodison and the following Easter he made his First Division debut just a few days before his club beat Manchester City 3-0 at Wembley to win the FA Cup. The following season would see Mercer restricted to games in the Everton reserve and junior teams. Meanwhile Cullis was playing for Ellesmere Port Wednesday and Liverpool loomed large in his life, too. It was there – though at Anfield, not Goodison – that he collected his first footballing honour, a runners-up medal in the Liverpool Hospital Cup.

Cullis followed in Mercer's footsteps by joining a Football League club when he signed for Wolves in March, 1934. He had been recommended to the club by Ellesmere Port referee Joe Forshaw and Cullis maintained in his autobiography that he travelled to the home of Molineux manager Major Frank Buckley and signed without even having a trial. Other sources suggest that he did play in a trial game after his father had written to the club. Whichever was correct, he duly joined Wolverhampton Wanderers.

Once in Wolverhampton, Cullis's digs would be with his aunt and his football would be played mostly for the club's A team in the Birmingham Combination. His starting salary was £2 10s (£2.50) a week with a win bonus of 5s (25p). The shrewd Buckley soon realised that he had not only signed a young man who might make it as a professional but one of great intelligence and presence. Here was captain material if ever there was and Buckley told him so: "Cullis, if you listen and do as you are told, I will make you captain of Wolves one day."

The autocratic manager then ensured Cullis's feet were kept on the ground – literally as well as figuratively – by calling him back from Ellesmere Port during the summer and informing him that he was to be the groundsman's assistant until the new season began. So here was a future captain of the club, weeding the pitch, pulling a roller and sowing seeds along with the lads on the ground staff. Not that Cullis was the sort to keep his head down. After a full season he believed he deserved a rise of 10s (50p) and told the Major so. When the request was turned down Cullis wrote home and soon received a telegram from his father: "Refuse terms. Come home."

When trainer Jack Davies learned what was going on he intervened and a meeting was arranged with the manager and director Ben Matthews. The latter gave Cullis the dire warning that if he went home he would be on the dole. Such threats might have frightened lesser young men but Cullis was made of sterner stuff and informed the director: "Mr Matthews, I shall not starve. I was living before I came to Wolves and no doubt I shall go on living after I leave Wolves." It was brave of him to stand his ground but he was doubtless extremely relieved when they agreed to give him his rise with a warning from the Major: "Make sure you earn it."

In Cullis's early days at Molineux, there was no suggestion that here was a great central defender in the making. Skippering the Birmingham Combination side with an occasional appearance in the reserves, Cullis was seen as a wing-half until a fateful day in December, 1934. Buckley had returned from a trip to Ireland with three players, among them a young centre-forward, Dave Martin, signed from Belfast Celtic. Known as "Boy" Martin he had already been capped by Northern Ireland and great things were expected of him. Buckley decided to show the club's directors in a Tuesday morning practice match the talent he had acquired. As fortune would have it, two of the recognised centre-halves were injured so Cullis, at the suggestion of trainer Jack Davies, was drafted in to mark Martin and he made a very good job of it. Of such simple twists of fate is football fame made.

Apparently, after the game the Major asked one of the directors what he thought of their new centre-forward and was told: "I am more concerned about the new centre-half." As Cullis recalled in his autobiography, All For The Wolves: "This practice game was the turning point in my playing career for, from that day onwards, I rarely appeared in any position other than centre-half-back."

Two of the trio signed in Ireland by Buckley would figure often in the reserves with Cullis – goalkeeper Jimmy Utterson and right winger Jackie Brown. Martin, Utterson and Brown had played in the Irish League side beaten 6-1 by the Football League in September, 1934, and against the Scottish League in Glasgow when Martin scored the Irish side's goals as they went down 3-2.

Despite the discovery of Cullis's centre-half potential, it was not as a central defender that he made his first team debut. Cullis's First Division bow was at right-half on Saturday, February 16, 1935, against Huddersfield Town at Molineux. Playing in a struggling team was not the best of times to get your first taste of top class football and Wolves were beaten for a fifth successive match (one of them an FA Cup tie), this time by the odd goal in five by a side lying 21st in the table. The win lifted Town out of the relegation places. Just 16,519 turned up to see Cullis make a competent debut as reflected by a headline in the Daily Express: "Cullis makes good as a right half-back". The report said: "The success of the home side was Cullis, the reserve right-half making his first appearance in the First Division. Cullis and Shaw were the only home defenders who could be praised."

Though Cullis did all right few would have guessed they were witnessing the start of a great football career. Dave Martin, the man who had played a significant role in the Cullis story, scored Wolves' goals that day with inside-forwards Jimmy Richardson and George Anderson and left-winger Tommy Lang on target for Town. These were the teams:

Wolves: Utterson; Hollingworth, Shaw; Cullis, Smalley, Richards; Brown, Hartill, Martin, Jones, Phillips.

Huddersfield: Turner; Craig, Roughton; Willingham, Young, Wightman; Beaumont, Anderson, Lythgoe, Richardson, Lang.

It was hardly the best of times to make a Wolves debut as they were clearly a side in some disarray. The Express & Star's "Nomad" did not pull any punches in his Monday verdict. He wrote: "Without any fear of contradiction from supporters, I say the team Wolves fielded on Saturday will not keep the club in Division One. Futile and inept are the words I can best employ to describe the display the team put up against Huddersfield at Molineux on Saturday. They were the worst (sic) of two poor sides and for the life of me I cannot see any hope until the attack has been changed and the defence at least tightened up. No excuse can be made for the performance. Huddersfield only had one good half-back on view and that was Young the centre-half. The Wolves players seemed helpless when it came to getting the ball past him. Of understanding in the forward line there was none. Martin as centre-forward gave no inspiration to the rest of the line and he was lacking in initiative, yes, even though he scored two goals." The disgruntled reporter did have a kind word or two for the debutant: "It was a pity that Cullis had to make his Division One debut on such an occasion but he did his best and should be encouraged."

The Yorkshire side's Alf Young had been capped for England three years earlier only to be discarded after just one game. However, he was not destined to be a one-cap wonder and when Cullis a couple of years later had established himself as the most talked-about young defender of his day it would be Young whose place in the England side he would threaten. Also in the news on the day of Cullis's debut was a 19-year-old Scottish centre-forward who scored four times as Sheffield United beat Southampton 6-1 in the Second Division. That player was Ephraim "Jock" Dodds, a craggy striker with whom Cullis would clash several times in wartime internationals.

The 18-year-old Cullis was given two more games at right-half. The first of those was a 5-2 defeat away to West Bromwich Albion as things went from bad to worse, much to the dismay of "Nomad" who did manage to find some encouragement in the displays of Cullis and Bill Morris, the latter being given a first game as a centre-half: "If anything cheerful from the Wolves point of view arose out of the game at the Hawthorns on Saturday it was that in Morris and Cullis the club have a pair of half-backs who will prove the equal of any on the books when they have had more experience. Cullis, indeed, was the best attacking half-back on the field." As Joe Gardiner was chosen at left-half it meant Wolves fielded the three men who had formed the reserve team half-back line for much of the season.

Defeat at West Brom meant Wolves were just above the two relegation places occupied by Leicester with 18 points from 29 games and Tottenham with 23 from 30. Wolves had 24 points from 30 games. If they did not know it before they certainly knew it then – they were in a fight for First Division survival. They would win that fight but Cullis's part in it consisted of just 90 more minutes. He retained his place at right-half when Wolves ended the losing streak by holding fourth-placed Sheffield Wednesday 2-2 at Molineux, after Cullis had conceded a penalty for handball. It seems he was hard done by according to "Nomad" in the Express & Star: "The penalty decision against Cullis was harsh as the ball was kicked against him and it struck him on the arm." Ronnie Starling scored from the spot to cancel out Cecil Shaw's first-half penalty for Wolves and Wednesday then took the lead through Jack Palethorpe. Justice was done in the last minute when Dai Richards's free-kick found Bob Iverson who headed home. In this game Buckley gave a chance at right-back to 20-year-old local lad Jack Dowen and his run of six successive appearances would prove to be his longest in the first team. Many years later Dowen would be among the training staff who served Cullis with distinction. To hold Wednesday was a useful performance – the Yorkshiremen would win the FA Cup that season – but the game ended Cullis's brief taste of top-flight football and, as he recalled in All For The Wolves: "My head was not allowed to swell. On the following Saturday the Major moved me out of the first team – into the third." Tom Smalley took over the right-half spot and helped the club lift themselves to safety.

Buckley may not have considered Cullis quite ready for regular first team football but still believed he was a future captain of the club. He made him skipper of the reserves and stressed that he was to be in charge on the pitch. Buckley backed Cullis to the hilt when he defied a club director during a reserve team match at Blackpool. The director had sent a message from the stand to the trainer, instructing the two inside forwards to switch positions. When Cullis noticed they had done this and was told by one of them why they had done it he immediately told them to revert to their original positions. On his way to the dressing room at the end of the game, Cullis was confronted by the irate director wanting to know why he had countermanded his orders. Cullis was not fazed and told him: "I am captain of this team and I am the one who gives the orders on the field." Next day Cullis thought he had better tell the Major what had happened and the manager told him he had been quite correct in what he had said to the director.

It was during Cullis's spell back in the third team and the reserves that Buckley suddenly got it into his head that the teenager might be able to play as an inside forward, even though he had shown that centre-half was clearly his best position. So when Bryn Jones was on international duty for Wales in their 1-1 draw with Scotland in Cardiff in October, 1935, Cullis was given the task of deputising for him at inside-left. It was a baptism of fire in his new role – away to Derby County who at the time were second in the First Division table and included players like England winger Sammy Crooks and legendary Scottish centre forward Hughie Gallacher.

Wolves lost 3-1 as the Rams chalked up a fourth successive victory. It would have been a tough task for an experienced forward as the man marking him was Jack Nicholas, one of the game's hard men. As Cullis recalled: "Major Buckley, always ready to experiment, thought that my future might be as an inside-forward and he put the theory to the test. He was wrong: I was a complete flop."

After Cullis's dismal attempt to become an inside-left, he returned once again to hone his centre-half skills in the reserves. Frequently a teammate was goalkeeper Jimmy Utterson. Born in Gateshead, he had grown up in Ireland and had joined Glenavon, from whom Buckley signed him on the same "shopping trip" that saw forwards Dave Martin and Jackie Brown signed from Belfast Celtic. So Cullis was among those devastated when on Friday, December 6, 1935, it was learned that Utterson had died in hospital after suddenly being taken ill. The Express & Star reported he had died in the Queen Victoria Nursing Institute, always known locally as the QVNI, where he had been taken for observation two days earlier.

"The cause of death was heart failure," said the paper's front-page report, adding, "Utterson kept goal for Wolves' A team as recently as Saturday last at Market Harborough where he played a particularly good game. This season the majority of his appearances were made in the Central League. Curiously enough, his first league game was against Stoke City at the Victoria Ground and Wolves visit City tomorrow." Some sources maintain Utterson had received a kick on the head against Middlesbrough on September 18 when he deputised for the injured Jack Weare, but the Express & Star report of that game makes no reference to any injury and subsequent editions of the paper list him as being chosen for reserve team games.

Cullis, his reserve team colleagues and indeed all at Molineux were stunned at losing this personable young man. The Express & Star report said: "He was one of the most popular players on Wolves' books, a smile rarely being absent from his lips." The paper's Wolves man, "Nomad", added his own tribute: "Utterson will be greatly missed at Molineux and by all with whom he came into contact. His tall well-built frame and laughing blue eyes made him a conspicuous figure wherever he went. As a goalkeeper he was full of promise. I shall not forget the great game he played on his first appearance for the Wolves at Stoke last season when the Molineux side won their first away game of the campaign. Several times last season he was cheered by supporters of opponents' teams as he left the ground when the game was over. He was gaining with experience the makings of a good player and in two or three seasons he may well have made his mark in the game. It is difficult to believe that he will not be seen on the field again. Utterson had a very likeable personality and made many friends. Football has lost a fine fellow and player and we shall greatly miss him."

A week later came the funeral and Cullis was one of six players who acted as bearers, among them Joe Gardiner, who had been in digs with Utterson, and Jack Weare, who was Wolves' first choice goalkeeper at the time. The coffin was taken to Molineux and placed in the directors' room where a short service took place. After the service the playing staff and officials lined up in two rows as the coffin was carried to the hearse. There were hundreds of people in Waterloo Road and the large crowd outside the cemetery in Jeffcock Road followed the coffin to the grave where another short service was held. It was a heart-rending occasion for Cullis and the other players closest to Utterson.

Chapter 2   A star is born

With Buckley in charge there was always a constant coming and going in the playing staff and at the end of the 1934-5 season centre-half Jack Nelson was transferred to Luton Town. At the start of the 1935-6 season, Bill Morris took over at the centre of defence and that was the way it stayed until a momentous day when Cullis first played at centre-half in the First Division, Saturday, March 7, 1936, against Blackburn Rovers at Ewood Park. Buckley, still not happy with Dave Martin as the solution to Wolves' centre-forward needs, decided to play Morris as leader of the attack. That meant a chance for Cullis to show he could cut it as a central defender in the top flight. Blackburn were bottom of the table and without a win in their previous eight games but they scored the only goal through left-winger Tom Turner five minutes from time. The verdict of "Nomad" in the Express and Star" did not go overboard but clearly Cullis had done himself justice: "Cullis did well at centre-half though he did not give his forwards much support."

Despite the defeat, Cullis had not been daunted by the tough task of marking Rovers' bustling centre-forward Ernie Thompson and stayed in the team for the next match. This meant the Molineux faithful got a look at their teenage central defender a week later in the derby clash with West Brom. If Thompson was a tough opponent, now Cullis would be up against an even tougher one – W G Richardson, an Albion legend and two-goal hero when they had beaten Birmingham in the 1931 FA Cup final. He was having his best ever season and had hit 33 goals in 31 league games. In those days it was the task of a centre-half to mark the opposing centre-forward and Cullis rose to this particular task when a gate of 34,815 witnessed Wolves win 2-0 thanks to goals from Bryn Jones, playing on the right wing that day, and left-winger George Ashall. Now "Nomad" was far more enthusiastic about the new centre-half: "There was no thaw in Wolves defence and Cullis was the pick of the bunch. There was no-one to touch him for tackling well, winning the ball and drawing or beating another man before passing."

Next it was Joe Gardiner's turn to be tried as a centre-forward and he scored in a 2-0 win at Liverpool and stayed up front when Arsenal came to Molineux and were held 2-2, Dave Martin moving from the right-wing in a switch with Gardiner to grab the equaliser two minutes from time. "Nomad" again had no reservations about the home centre-half. "Cullis was the outstanding defender on the field," he said and that was quite a compliment as the Gunners' full-backs, George Male and Eddie Hapgood, and half-back Jack Crayston were all named the following Monday in the England side to face Scotland.

After Arsenal came another five games without a win and Wolves' place in the top flight was far from secure going into the vital Easter period, when there would be three games in four days. Blackburn were anchored on the bottom of the table with 27 points, Villa above them had 31 and then Wolves were one of seven teams on 33. To heighten the drama Wolves would meet Villa home and away over the holiday, starting with a visit to Villa Park on Good Friday. Before 51,000 fans, Cullis and co were beaten 4-2. Cullis had a tough time against Villa's young centre-forward Frank Broome who was twice on the mark. There were three goals in the first ten minutes, left-winger Eric Houghton opening the scoring and Broome restoring the lead after Gordon Clayton had equalised. Former Wolves man Charlie Phillips, signed by Villa a few months earlier, had to leave the field after injuring his knee but the ten-man home side stretched their lead after half-time through Broome and Dai Astley before Clayton grabbed a Wolves consolation.

Morris had again been played as a striker but was then switched back to centre-half to the exclusion of Cullis as Wolves grabbed a home draw with Stoke. Bob Iverson was at left-half for that game, his second as deputy for the injured Tom Galley. However, Cullis was preferred as Galley's deputy for the return game with Villa on Easter Monday which brought a 2-2 draw at Molineux. Villa fans might have harboured hopes of survival but their favourites were destined to lose their remaining two games and finish 21st in the 22-team First Division. Cullis continued as Galley's deputy at left-half for the rest of the season. With four games to play, Wolves were too close to the bottom two relegation places for comfort. Blackburn were still last on 31 points with Wolves one of four teams immediately above them on 35. Fortunately Wolves had a game in hand and they won it impressively, beating Preston 4-2 at Molineux with Bryn Jones hitting his one and only Wolves hat-trick. Two more home games rounded off the season, Wolves drawing 3-3 with Chelsea and then ending in style by beating Middlesbrough 4-0, wonderfully-named winger Billy Wrigglesworth hitting two goals to make him the club's top scorer with 12 league goals..

Dave Martin, who had played his part in the Cullis story, scored two goals against Chelsea and was also on target in the win over Boro to bring his total for the season to ten goals in 16 games. Yet Buckley still did not rate him and sold him to Second Division Nottingham Forest where he became an instant hit, collecting 29 goals from 37 games in his first season at the City Ground. In his place, Buckley signed Tom "Pongo" Waring from Aston Villa but he lasted just a few months before being sold to Tranmere.

If the 1935-6 season had seen Wolves at the wrong end of the table there was no immediate improvement at the beginning of the new campaign. Cullis took no part in the opening nine games, during which a 2-0 win over Arsenal before 53,097 at Molineux gave false hope. When Cullis finally got another first team outing, a slump had started and Wolves had lost three games in a row. Then right-back George Laking was injured and so Bill Morris was switched to his position, allowing Cullis to come into the side.

It was bad luck for Laking but provided an opportunity which would be the making of Cullis. There could have been few sterner tests of a central defender which awaited Cullis on his recall to the side. Wolves faced a trip to Goodison to tackle an Everton team who were a point behind league leaders Derby with a game in hand. Leading their attack was one of the greatest centre forwards in the history of football – Dixie Dean. This would be a rigorous test of Cullis's ability. If that practice game against Dave Martin had been a major step in his career then so was this.

Dean scored the only goal of the game at Goodison when he somehow managed to squeeze the ball through Wolves' defensive wall from a free-kick about a yard outside the penalty area. It was a rare moment of triumph for the great man – Cullis had kept him firmly subdued as the Express & Star confirmed: "Cullis beat Dean every time the home centre-forward had the ball on the floor." Now there was no question Cullis had come to stay. In a struggling team here was a glimmer of light.

When Wolves, in their next game, were beaten 2-1 by West Brom at the Hawthorns in the middle of October they had suffered a fifth successive defeat and slipped into the bottom two relegation places. Admittedly this match saw Wolves deprived of Tom Smalley and Bryn Jones by the international game between England and Wales in Cardiff but the defeat represented a low point in Buckley's attempt to transform Wolves. Leeds and Wolves occupied the bottom places in the First Division, both with seven points from 11 games. Few would have predicted at that point that within a couple of years Wolves would be the most talked-about team in the land with young Cullis the driving force.

It got worse before it got better as the fans turned against the club – or rather Buckley, whose selling policy had caused increasing anger. Wolves lost 2-1 at home to Chelsea on November 7, 1936, and there was a pitch invasion from the terraces. The Daily Mirror reported: "At the final whistle a crowd of about 100 spectators attempted to surround the referee. They were held back by the police and players and eventually the official reached the dressing room in safety. An even larger crowd then surrounded the players' entrance. The police did their utmost to keep the spectators back and although there were boos and jeers no damage was done and eventually the crowd dispersed." Despite what the report said, there had been some damage as one of the goalposts was uprooted. Ostensibly the supporters were upset at refereeing decisions but it was really the culmination of discontent over the manager's transfer policy. The perception was that if the price was right the club would sell any player of promise.

Such a demonstration did not go down well and the angry fans got short shrift from the Daily Express's Arthur Simmons the following Monday: "The scene after the Wolves v Chelsea match at Molineux was deplorable. A section of the Wolverhampton supporters behaved like lunatics. They have a grouch against the directors. They consider the precarious position in the First Division table is due to too many players being transferred. Danger of the team dropping to the foot of the ladder drove sense out of their heads.

The points dropped to Chelsea set them aflame. They demonstrated angrily, bating the referee, then turning on the directors and the manager. I am glad to be able to say the vast majority of soccer fans would scorn to stoop to such stuff, they may be a lot or a little one-sided in their views but they let off steam in harmless shouting. Hooliganism has no place in their partisanship. Foolish chaps who took part in this Wolverhampton row are, I feel certain, now feeling ashamed and very sorry for their lack of control. It is a pity they cannot be held up to ridicule by being spanked in Wolverhampton market place. I am all for decorum, in matters of flesh, but 'trousers down, take that, and that, and that!' would be a fitting corrective." So spoke the voice of reason in the Daily Express!

It was not beyond the realms of possibility that Molineux could be closed for a couple of games as punishment but, luckily for Wolves, the FA were lenient. Wolves escaped with a severe warning from the governing body. Any similar incidents and they would throw the book at them.

A week later, Wolves lost 2-1 at Stoke and slumped to the bottom of the table, on 10 points, the same as Manchester United but with a poorer goal average. It is said it is always darkest just before dawn and so it proved now as Wolves engineered a dramatic change in their fortunes. It started with a 6-1 home win over Charlton, a game which brought a sparkling home debut for right-winger Teddy Maguire, a 19-year-old County Durham lad, who made four of the goals. Four of the next five games also brought victories, with the other match drawn 1-1 at Grimsby. That game brought confirmation of Cullis's progress, "Nomad" writing in the Express & Star: "Cullis gave such a display against Glover, the Welsh international leader, that if the English team selectors had been present they would have had something to think about."

Despite the occasional setback on their travels – they lost 4-0 at Huddersfield, 3-0 at Arsenal and 4-1 at Manchester City – Wolves continued to rattle in the goals at Molineux, reaching a peak when Everton were the visitors, parading not the experienced Dixie Dean but a highly promising 17-year-old centre forward making his debut. His name was Tommy Lawton. He had been bought from Burnley as the eventual replacement for the great Dixie who was rested on this day as the Toffees had a fifth-round FA Cup clash with Tottenham a week later. Lawton would become arguably his country's best ever leader of an attack but on this afternoon he got little change out of Cullis as Wolves won handsomely 7-2. It was the home centre-forward, Gordon Clayton, who took the limelight, hitting a hat-trick as Wolves reached half-time 4-1 up. Lawton did mark his Everton bow with a goal but not through getting the better of Cullis. It was from the penalty spot after Bunny Bell had been brought down by home keeper Billy Gold with Wolves then 5-1 to the good. Clayton finished the game with four goals to his name.

Like Everton, Wolves, too, were on the FA Cup trail by then. It would end in failure but only after they had played eight games in a competition where five can be enough to get a team to the final. It started easily enough with a 6-1 defeat of a Middlesbrough side who were lying sixth in the First Division at the time, seven places above Wolves. All five forwards scored, including Tom Smalley who was being played as a right-winger. Cullis's day was made a little easier when veteran former England centre-forward George Camsell was injured early in the game, reducing Boro to ten fit men. Wolves did it the hard way against Sheffield United in the fourth round, being held to a 2-2 draw at home by the previous season's runners-up and then winning the replay 3-1 at Bramall Lane on a Thursday evening. That night also saw West Bromwich Albion beaten 10-3 at Stoke in a First Division game, the Baggies' biggest ever defeat. The Sheffield replay was a good old-fashioned Cup-tie as Frank Stainton reported in the Daily Mirror: "It was the sort of Cup-tie calculated to make the pulses hammer and the blood run quickly, with incident following incident, almost unendingly." Jock Dodds beat both Cullis and Frank Taylor before firing United into a first-half lead only for Gordon Clayton to equalise soon after half-time. Winger George Ashall hit the winner eleven minutes from time. Stainton also reported: "Cullis got through a heap of work for the Wolves."

Another replay was needed in the fifth round when Wolves drew 1-1 with fellow First Division side Grimsby Town. A kick on the right knee meant Cullis missed the Molineux replay four days later when Wolves romped home 6-2 before a crowd of 56,799. To accommodate Cullis's absence Smalley moved back to centre-half which gave a chance to 19-year-old Dennis Westcott and he marked the occasion with a goal. A centre-forward by nature, he was played on the right wing which was all part of the Major Buckley philosophy. Apart from Cullis, who had proved without doubt that he was a central defender, players, the manager believed, should be able to play in any position. It was a policy that attracted comment from G W Chisholm in the Daily Mirror as Wolves prepared to meet Sunderland for a place in the FA Cup semi-final. The distinguished football correspondent wrote:

"So Wolverhampton Wanderers are going to play their strongest team against Sunderland in the Cup-tie on Saturday. Just what does that mean? Cullis, Bryn Jones, Morris and Ashall, all absent last Saturday, are fit again but before you try to forecast their "strongest team" just sort this out. Galley used to be a half-back. This season he has been inside-right and inside left. Grand inside-right at the moment. Smalley was a wing half-back. This season he has been right-half, centre-half, left-half and outside-right. Done well in them all, too. Wharton has been playing at right-half and centre-half. Ashall has been outside-right and they say he looks like being England's outside-left. Shining there for Wolves since the transformation.

"Thompson had been inside-right and inside-left. Westcott, getting goals galore as reserve team centre-forward, made his debut in the first team at outside-right and scored within seven minutes. All this season! Major Frank Buckley, the manager, holds that a good player can play anywhere. He's telling us, nay, he's showing us. That's the secret of the Wolves' success. Catch them young and bring them up to play anywhere. Result – a solid, compact team of triers."

Sunderland, whose star man was England inside forward Raich Carter, attracted a ground record 57,751 to Molineux to see the sides draw their sixth-round clash 1-1, Bryn Jones scoring for Wolves and right-winger Len Duns for Sunderland. On the same day Third Division Millwall produced an upset by beating Manchester City 2-0 to reach the semi-final. The draw then paired the Londoners with the winners of the Wolves-Sunderland tie but a replay at Roker Park saw the outcome still unresolved after a 2-2 draw before 61,796. Wolves had been desperately close to victory, Tom Galley scoring three minutes from the end. However, there was enough time left for Bob Gurney to grab an equaliser. Len Duns struck for Sunderland four minutes into extra time only for Harry Thompson to tap home a George Ashall centre within minutes. Their efforts finally told on the young Wolves outfit and the second replay, at Hillsborough, saw Sunderland score four times without reply from a Wolves side without Galley. Sunderland were ahead after only nine minutes through centre-forward Gurney. Wolves rallied well but their dream of a place at Wembley ended in the two minutes before half-time when the Wearsiders struck twice, through Carter and Scotland international Patsy Gallacher. A penalty by Charlie Thomson in the second half sealed an emphatic win. As if to emphasise what Mirror man Chisholm had written, Buckley had Smalley at outside-right in the first game, Bryn Jones there in the first replay and then young Westcott for the second.

Wolves still had two league fixtures to play against Sunderland, both scheduled for later that month. Sunderland won by four goals when the sides met at Roker, Patsy Gallacher scoring three in a 6-2 win and the Molineux meeting produced a 1-1 draw. Is there another instance of two teams playing each other five times in the same month? Perhaps only John Motson would know!

With 5-2 home wins over both Grimsby Town and West Bromwich Albion, Wolves wound up the season to finish a respectable fifth in the First Division. The dismal start and the low point of the Chelsea game were suddenly a distant memory. Supporters may still have been baffled by the constant comings and goings but most would concede Buckley was building a team that would see Wolves feature at the right end of the First Division with their imperious centre-half the fulcrum of the side. As Cullis's displays continued to catch the eye it soon became obvious that here was an old-style centre-half, not afraid to hold the ball or to go forward if he saw an opportunity present itself.

This was in stark contrast to the "stopper" centre-half which had come into vogue following the alteration of the offside law in 1925. This decreed that two players, rather than three were required to be between an attacker and the by-line for him to be onside. To cope with the change, clubs started to use the centre half in a purely defensive role, hence the title "stopper", with his job being to win the ball with head or feet and clear it – and to ensure he did not stray from his position. Charlie Spencer was such a player for Newcastle, helping them win the First Division title in 1927, and the Arsenal side of the 1930s used the stopper to telling effect in Herbie Roberts, their centre-half when they were champions four times in five seasons.

The emergence of Cullis therefore warmed the hearts of those who disliked the Arsenal way of playing, highly effective though it was. Ivan Sharpe, winner of a 1912 Olympic football medal who became a much-respected sportswriter, compared Cullis's style to that of Joe McCall, who played for Preston and England before and after the First World War: "McCall had a telling way of driving an accurate pass from midfield to wing man. He was a safe, as well as stylish, player, and also used the short pushed pass, later seen so often in the displays of Cullis."

For his part Cullis had found, if he did not know it already, that Major Buckley was a man who knew how he wanted to run the club and how he wanted his team to play. Looking back many years later, Cullis recalled: "I soon realised that Major Buckley was one out of the top drawer. He didn't suffer fools gladly, and he was a manager who knew exactly what he was doing and where he was going. His style of managership in football was very similar to his attitude in the Army because you didn't try any tricks on Major Buckley. He had a style of his own. Major Buckley implanted into my mind the direct method of playing which did away with close inter-passing and square-ball play. If you didn't like his style you'd very soon be on your bicycle to another club. He didn't like defenders over-elaborating in their defensive positions. Their job, he maintained, was to get the ball to the forwards as quickly as possible."

Buckley, for his part, knew Cullis was something special: "From the start I realised Cullis had personality and perseverance beyond his years which is why he was entrusted with the first team captaincy before he was 20. Stanley Cullis had a mind of his own and was always willing and anxious to listen and learn." Cullis obviously respected Buckley and would soon be sticking his neck out in order to defend the Molineux martinet.

The 1936-7 season ought to have ended quietly with Wolves in good shape and deserving of praise after turning things around. Cullis had reasons to be cheerful, too, having been appointed captain during the season following the transfer of Cecil Shaw to Albion in December. At 20 he was the youngest skipper in the League.

However, the Football Association were about to shatter the happy Molineux mood. They were not best pleased with reports they had received about the way the team had been playing and had taken the matter up with Major Buckley, only to get short shrift, it would seem, in a letter from the manager. Now the FA flexed their muscles and a bombshell letter arrived on Buckley's desk on the morning of Saturday, April 24, 1937. It read: "Having regard to the increasing number of misconduct reports received in respect of your players, it appears that appropriate steps to eliminate the bad influence which apparently prevails among your players on the football field are not being taken by you as manager on behalf of your club. As you have already been informed, the committee is of the opinion that the conduct of players is the responsibility of the club and, or, their appointed authority, whose duty it is to deal with the players likely to bring the game generally, and their club in particular, into disrepute. From the tone of your letter on April 3 it would appear that you condone the offences of your players and therefore I am instructed to inform you that if further reports concerning misconduct by your players are received the disciplinary committee of the Football Association will hold an inquiry to determine what action they will take in the matter." It was signed by FA secretary Stanley Rous.

Buckley would make no comment to the Express & Star, who made the matter its front page lead. The reporter covering the story noted, however, that Buckley appeared greatly surprised by the FA's letter, a surprise which was shared by the directors and the team at St Andrew's where Wolves were playing Birmingham that afternoon. In the next few days the players, led by their young captain, would take matters into their own hands. They wrote to the FA in defence of Buckley and the sending of the letter drafted by Cullis was described by the Express & Star as: "a step unprecedented in the annals of football history." It read: "Dear Sirs, We, members of Wolverhampton Wanderers' Division One team, are at the least amazed at your action in sending a recent letter of caution to our manager, Major F C Buckley. By the tone of your letter it seems apparent to us that you are under the impression that Major Buckley condones and encourages questionable tactics on the part of our players on the football field. We should like to state that far from advocating the rough play we are accused of, Major Buckley is constantly reminding us of the importance of playing good clean and honest football and we as a team consider you have been most unjust in administering this action to our manager. We realise your determination to stamp out rough play but we feel we cannot allow this very unfair censure to pass by without some form of protest. This communication has been inspired by the members of the team and not by any suggestion of any officials at the club who are totally unaware of its existence."

Earlier that week, the club had announced a four-match close season tour on which they would play games in Budapest, Bucharest, Belgrade and Antwerp. The Football League gave approval but that had to be rubber-stamped by the game's ruling authority – the FA. This was their chance to show who was boss and they knocked the tour plans on the head with a letter that read: "In view of the numerous reports of misconduct by the players of the Wolverhampton Wanderers club in the past two seasons the FA council, meeting in London today, decided that the application of the club for permission to play matches on the Continent during the coming close season be not granted." It was later announced that newly-promoted Leicester City would play the matches that Wolves had arranged.

It would have been easy for Cullis to keep his head down. With ambition to play for England he could have been forgiven for not wishing to offend the FA, yet he was not one to let personal ambition prevent him doing what he thought was the right thing. In this instance he believed the right thing to do was to let the FA know what the players felt. It appears no further action was taken by the FA who doubtless felt that banning the proposed tour would teach Wolves a lesson.

Chapter 3   So near yet . . .

As the 1937–8 season unfolded it was clear that Buckley's side could mount a genuine attempt to make Wolves champions of England for the first time. Still among the other contenders were Arsenal, despite the retirement of Alex James, the little Scottish maestro who had been at the heart of their many recent triumphs. The Gunners gave initial notice that they could survive without the great man when they won their opening three games, the last of them being 5-0 against Wolves in front of 67,311 fans at Highbury. This was Wolves' only defeat in their opening six games and it was a match that Cullis missed. He had received a knock in a 2-1 win at Derby three days earlier and failed a fitness test at Highbury. Tom Smalley was drafted in at centre-half but failed to curb home centre-forward Ted Drake who scored two of the goals to take his total to six in the first three games of the season.

In his side's useful start to the campaign, Cullis was outstanding in defence, confident in his ability and a commanding figure. Clearly he was destined for representative honours and the first arrived sooner than expected. The man in possession of the England centre-half berth was Huddersfield Town's skipper Alf Young and the Football League duly chose him as their captain for the prestige game against the Scottish League at Ibrox Park, Glasgow, towards the end of September, 1937. Two days before the game Young cried off through injury and so Cullis was sent for. Still a month short of his 21st birthday, he joined in the team clubmates Tom Galley at inside-right and left-winger George Ashall. Cullis made the most of his opportunity and though the English side lost 1-0, he impressed the 30,000 crowd. The report in the Glasgow Herald said: "Cullis had a splendid game throughout." A report in the Daily Mirror was not quite so gushing: "Cullis at centre-half did not always seem sure of Stewart's whereabouts but at least he kept him away from the danger zone." That was a reference to Motherwell centre-forward Willie Stewart. Jimmy Delaney, already a star with Celtic and destined to become one with Manchester United after the war, scored the goal just before half-time heading home a centre from left-winger Jimmy Caskie which just eluded Vic Woodley in the Football League goal. It was not the greatest of games but the Wolverhampton trio were among the few visitors to emerge with credit.

Teams at Ibrox Park, Glasgow, on Wednesday, September 22, 1937:

Scottish League: Dawson (Rangers); Hogg (Celtic), Carabine (Third Lanark); Robertson (Kilmarnock), Dykes (Hearts), McKenzie (Motherwell); Delaney (Celtic), McKenna (Partick Thistle), Stewart (Motherwell), Venters (Rangers), Caskie (St Johnstone).

Football League: Woodley (Chelsea); Sproston (Leeds), Barkas (Manchester City); Willingham (Huddersfield), Cullis (Wolves), Bray (Manchester City); Matthews (Stoke), Galley (Wolves), Steele (Stoke), Westwood (Bolton), Ashall (Wolves).

Clearly Cullis was pushing Alf Young for the centre-half spot in the England side but Young's injury was a minor one and, fit again, he was the Football League's choice when two weeks after the Ibrox game they beat the Irish League 3-0 at Bloomfield Road, Blackpool. If a look at players in two inter-league matches was not enough for the England selectors, a week later they were able to make yet another assessment in a "trial game". Young was in the Probables side and Cullis in the Possibles in a 1-1 draw at Goodison Park, each centre-forward scoring, Bob Gurney (Sunderland) for the Probables and Albion's W G Richardson for the Possibles. Despite a useful game, Cullis failed to displace Young when the selectors afterwards announced their choice ten days before the scheduled trip to Belfast to face Northern Ireland. However, Cullis was named as a reserve along with Brentford inside-forward Billy Scott, who had been capped against Wales a year earlier. Despite their goals, neither of the centre-forwards was chosen, the vote going to Chelsea's George Mills, who had scored for the Football League in the game at Blackpool but had to miss the trial game.

Cullis may have been delighted to be so close to a cap or disappointed not to be in the team. If it was the latter, his disappointment would not last long. While Cullis was sailing through Wolves' 2-0 home win over Liverpool on the Saturday before the international, Young had the misfortune to sustain an ankle injury in Huddersfield's 2-1 home defeat by table-topping Grimsby. Cullis would receive his first England cap.

The Wolves man was still two days short of his 21st birthday when England took on Northern Ireland at Windsor Park, Belfast. As well as missing the game, Young had an added disappointment as he had been named captain of the side. In his absence, Manchester City full-back Sam Barkas was skipper against an Irish side who were no match for England and lost 5-1 with Cullis's fellow debutant, George Mills, scoring three goals before a crowd of 36,000. The Chelsea man hit a genuine hat-trick – three goals in a row after 10, 20 and 55 minutes. Three minutes later Willie Hall scored from an Eric Brook pass and after 75 minutes Brook was put in by Mills for the fifth goal. Alex Stevenson grabbed an Irish consolation in the last minute. Up against Cullis was Dave "Boy" Martin, the teammate of his at Molineux a couple of years earlier and by then with Nottingham Forest. Martin was given little chance to shine as Cullis made a useful debut in a side who were a class above the opposition.

The match brought another historic moment for Cullis – the first England player to wear the number-five shirt on British soil. Today, numbering of shirts – and shorts – is all part of helping the paying customer to identify players easily. In the late 1930s, there was still opposition to it in some quarters. England had wanted to have numbered shirts at Hampden earlier in the year but the Scottish FA would not agree. However, England opted on their close-season tour to Norway, Sweden and Finland to have numbered shirts and the Irish FA had no objection to shirt-numbering.

Teams at Windsor Park, Belfast, on Saturday, October 23, 1937:

Northern Ireland: Breen (Manchester United); Hayes (Huddersfield), Cook (Everton); Mitchell (Chelsea), Jones (Glenavon), Browne (Leeds); Kernoghan (Belfast Celtic), Stevenson (Everton), Martin (Nottingham Forest), Doherty (Manchester City), Madden (Norwich).

England: Woodley (Chelsea); Sproston (Leeds), Barkas (Manchester City); Crayston (Arsenal), Cullis (Wolves), Copping (Arsenal); Geldard (Everton), Hall (Tottenham), Mills (Chelsea), Goulden (West Ham), Brook (Manchester City).

Tom Smalley had been capped against Wales a year earlier and Tom Galley in the summer tour of 1937. With Bryn Jones a regular in the Wales team, it was clear Wolves' young side had an abundance of quality. In those days league fixtures went ahead as usual on the occasion of Saturday international games but the absence of Cullis and Mills had no obvious effect on their clubs. Chelsea beat Brentford 2-1 at Stamford Bridge to take over from their London rivals at the top of the table and Wolves won 2-1 at Leeds to move into second place. On the same day West Brom lost 6-1 at home to Sunderland and though the Baggies were still mid table at that stage they would slump dramatically to be relegated at the end of the season.

With Young still sidelined it was no surprise that Cullis kept his place for the game against Home International champions Wales at Middlesbrough, a month later. This time the game was played in midweek with Cullis up against Doncaster Rovers centre-forward Eddie Perry, who opened the scoring in the first half. Apart from this, Perry seems to have come off second best against Cullis, one report recording: "Cullis, using his height to advantage, generally mastered Perry, a dashing leader who often promised danger." A breakaway by Bryn Jones, Wales's outstanding player, set up Perry for his goal. England were soon level when Mills failed to control a Stanley Matthews centre. Fortunately, Matthews had followed up and slotted the ball home. Matthews on the right and Eric Brook on the left were in prime form and it was from Brook's centre on 59 minutes that Willie Hall won the game for England.

Teams at Ayresome Park, Middlesbrough, on Wednesday, November 17, 1937:

England: Woodley (Chelsea); Sproston (Leeds), Barkas (Manchester City); Crayston (Arsenal), Cullis (Wolves), Copping (Arsenal); Matthews (Stoke), Hall (Tottenham), Mills (Chelsea), Goulden (West Ham), Brook (Manchester City).

Wales: Gray (Chester); Turner (Charlton), Hughes (Birmingham); Murphy (West Brom), Hanford (Sheffield Wednesday), Richards (Birmingham); Hopkins (Brentford), L Jones (Arsenal), Perry (Doncaster), B Jones (Wolves), Morris (Birmingham).

Cullis had been given a relatively quiet introduction to international football but he had a far busier time when England faced Czechoslovakia at Tottenham, on the first day of December, 1937. Twice England established a two-goal lead only for the Czechs to battle back and equalise. It took a goal from Stanley Matthews in fading light five minutes from time to clinch a 5-4 victory. Cullis could have had clubmate George Ashall in the team with him. When Manchester City's Eric Brook had to withdraw, Ashall was sent for but he was having treatment for a slight knock and unable to join up with the team. The selectors were not prepared to wait to see if he recovered and so his chance of a cap was gone. John Morton of West Ham came in for what proved to be his only England appearance. If Matthews shone at Middlesbrough he was positively dazzling at Tottenham, hitting a hat-trick. He had to move to inside forward following injuries to George Mills and Jack Crayston and took the game by the scruff of the neck. Crayston scored with a shot from outside the penalty area after 11 minutes, only for Antonin Puc to cancel it out two minutes later. Morton scored on his debut to restore the lead and Matthews made it 3-1 on the half-hour, only for Oldrich Nejedly to reduce the lead just before half-time. Matthews again put England two goals ahead but debutant centre-forward Josef Zeman and Nejedly struck to make it 4-4. Then came Matthews's winner with a shot that bounced and deceived veteran Frantisek Planicka in the Czech goal.

Teams at White Hart Lane, Tottenham, on Wednesday, December 1, 1937:

England: Woodley (Chelsea); Sproston (Leeds), Barkas (Manchester City); Crayston (Arsenal), Cullis (Wolves), Copping (Arsenal); Matthews (Stoke), Hall (Tottenham), Mills (Chelsea), Goulden (West Ham), Morton (West Ham)

Czechoslovakia: Planicka (Slavia Prague); Kostalek (Sparta Prague), Daucik (Slavia Prague); Vodicka (Slavia Prague), Boucek (Sparta Prague), Kolsky (Sparta Prague); Riha (Sparta Prague), Kloz (Kladno), Zeman (Sparta Prague), Nejedly (Sparta Prague), Puc (Slavia Prague).

Unexpectedly, Arsenal did not kick on from that early success over Wolves and won only two of their next 12 games and when they were held at home 1-1 by West Brom, they lay tenth in the table with 15 points from 15 games. Wolves were held at home by Charlton on the same day but were third in the table with 19 points, two behind leaders Brentford and with a game in hand.

By then, Arsenal had made a bid to fill the gap left by Alex James by signing Leslie Jones from Coventry City and it would prove a shrewd move, if anything a more successful one than the high profile signing of another Jones the following summer (more of that later). Arsenal suffered the loss of another key player after just 13 games when centre-half Herbie Roberts was injured.

The man who had perfected the role of stopper centre-half under legendary manager Hebert Chapman would not play again but the Londoners found a superb replacement in amateur player Bernard Joy. He had won an FA Amateur Cup winners' medal with Corinthian Casuals and had also been capped once in the full England side, the last amateur to have that honour. Arsenal could still boast stalwarts Male, Hapgood, Crayston, Copping, Drake and Bastin but Jones and Joy would prove vital additions.

Wolves also had their Jones but not much joy when it came to the fourth-round FA Cup clash with Arsenal at Molineux in January. Though Bryn Jones scored, Arsenal triumphed 2-1 before a gate of 61,267. That was almost 22,000 more than had seen the clubs meet in the league a week earlier when Wolves gained vital points from a 3-1 win. Arsenal would surprisingly be beaten 1-0 at home by Preston in the next round of the Cup and they would lose ground to Wolves in the title race, too. When Wolves won 1-0 at Liverpool on February 26, 1938, thanks to a goal from left-winger George Ashall, they took over at the top of the table for the first time that season as Arsenal were held 0-0 at Portsmouth. Things were looking good for Wolves. They led with 38 points from 28 games from Arsenal (37-30) and Brentford (35-31). It was definitely advantage Wolves – but beware the sides of March! Five games that month failed to produce a win and yielded only two points. Wolves lost 1-0 at Grimsby and by the same score at home to Middlesbrough before an emphatic 4-1 defeat at Charlton, where Cullis was an absentee. Tom Galley deputised at centre-half and scored. The other games in March saw Leeds and Stoke hold Wolves at Molineux, drawing 1-1 and 2-2 respectively.

When Ireland unexpectedly beat Wales 1-0 in Belfast it meant that England were assured of winning the International Championship, as the British nations quaintly continued to describe it, not bothered by the fact that the year would see the third staging of the World Cup finals. No, all that mattered was the Home International tournament with its showpiece end-of-season clash between England and Scotland. This would be Cullis's first taste of the unique atmosphere of a clash between the Auld Enemies. For this demanding fixture the selectors decided to give débuts to forwards Micky Fenton of Middlesbrough and Leeds inside-left Eric Stephenson. The Scots had lost to Wales and drawn with Ireland but they rose to the occasion at Wembley as they would so often do in future years, winning by the only goal of what was a dismal game. The score came after five minutes and Cullis was at fault. Milne beat Hapgood on the left and O'Donnell collected the centre. He flicked the ball sideways for Walker to evade Cullis's attempted tackle and send a swerving shot past Woodley.

England hardly sparkled after that setback as the Scots held on for their first win at Wembley in ten years, the previous one being a game that has gone down in football folklore when the Scots won 5-1 and would be forever known as the "Wembley Wizards". There was little chance of the 1938 encounter going down in football history, Henry Rose of the Daily Express describing it as: "The worst international I have seen for years; almost ever."

It reflected particularly badly on the Football League as all but three of the 22 players on view plied their trade there. "Here were the cream of English football," wrote Rose, "total value £100,000, mispassing, miskicking and never at any time settling down to even an apology of the class we rightly expect from them. Some of the players complained the ball was soft. We are used to alibis in boxing, but this is a new one on me." For once, Matthews did not have a great influence on the game, much of that due to a tenacious display at left-back by future Wolves caretaker boss Andy Beattie. After three impressive games for his country, Cullis had faltered and it was scant consolation that he had become the first Wolves man to play at Wembley.

Teams at Wembley Stadium, London, on Saturday April 9, 1938:

England: Woodley (Chelsea); Sproston (Leeds), Hapgood (Arsenal); Willingham (Huddersfield), Cullis (Wolves), Copping (Arsenal); Matthews (Stoke), Hall (Tottenham), Fenton (Middlesbrough), Stephenson (Leeds), Bastin (Arsenal).

Scotland: Cumming (Middlesbrough); Anderson (Hearts), Beattie (Preston); Shankly (Preston), Smith (Preston), Brown (Rangers); Milne (Middlesbrough), Walker (Hearts), O'Donnell (Blackpool), Mutch (Preston), Reid (Brentford).

Cullis's absence from the Wolves team was more damaging than was the absence of the three Arsenal men on the same day. Wolves were beaten 1-0 at Portsmouth with Cliff Parker scoring after just four minutes while the Gunners won by the only goal at Leeds. That meant Arsenal had a three-point lead at the top of the table, though second-placed Wolves had a game in hand. What would become a familiar name among Leeds goalscorers in later years was responsible for the winner at Elland Road – Bremner. However this was Gordon Bremner, making his debut for the Gunners on the right wing. He was no relation to Leeds legend Billy.

Next match for Wolves came six days after the Wembley match – on Good Friday. It saw Cullis get his name on the scoresheet at Molineux but not for Wolves. His own goal mattered little, however, as Wolves hit the Leicester City net no fewer than ten times to post what remains the club's record league victory. Cullis's mishap came nine minutes from time when Wolves were 7–0 up. They won the game 10-1.

Easter was a hectic time for footballers in those days, with three games in four days the accepted norm. After the Friday goal feast, Wolves went without reward the following day as they were held by fellow title contenders Preston in a goalless draw at Molineux and the return game with Leicester on Easter Monday ended 1–1. Yet Wolves' four points from three holiday games was enough to throw the title race wide open as Arsenal had managed only one. They were beaten 2-0 at Highbury by Brentford on Good Friday and then 3-0 in the return at Griffin Park on the Monday, having been held 0-0 at home by Birmingham in between.

Suddenly, Wolves had their championship hopes in their own hands. They and the Gunners were on 46 points but Wolves had a game in hand. Preston's four-point Easter haul meant they too had 46 points and led the table on goal average but had played one more game than Wolves. The Lancastrians also had other matters on their mind – they were in the FA Cup final which in those days took place before the end of the league season. They were due to face Huddersfield Town.

A week before the final Preston lost 3-1 at Arsenal while Wolves won 3-0 at Middlesbrough, so now it was a two-horse race. A week later, on the day Preston were beating Huddersfield 1-0 at Wembley thanks, famously, to a late extra-time penalty from George Mutch, Wolves faltered slightly, being held 1-1 at home by Chelsea. Arsenal edged a point ahead of them thanks to a 1-0 home win over Liverpool. The goalscorer was the diminutive Eddie Carr, enjoying a purple patch in a brief Arsenal career. In the side as deputy for Ted Drake he had scored twice against Preston. However, Cullis and his men could swing things back their way if they won their game in hand – a Monday evening encounter with local rivals West Bromwich Albion.

The game at Molineux was vital for both sides as Albion were fighting to avoid relegation and had to give a debut to 17-year-old goalkeeper Harry Baldwin. Although he was beaten after just 30 seconds, the youngster had a rousing game. The early goal came when right-winger Teddy Maguire centred for left-winger Dickie Dorsett to fire the ball home. With half-time approaching Dennis Westcott took a pass from Bryn Jones, beat centre-half Cyril Davies and scored with a left-footed drive. Albion would not lie down, however, and got back into contention when inside-left Teddy Sandford, who had played most of the season at centre-half, thumped home a shot from 30 yards. Cullis drove his team on and they had a host of second-half chances only for Baldwin to make save after save. While the 2-1 defeat pushed the Baggies towards their inevitable relegation, it meant Wolves' title fate was in their own hands.

So to the final Saturday of the season, May 7, 1938 . . . win at Sunderland and Wolves and their young skipper would be champions of England. Alas the only goal of the game at Roker Park came from Sunderland's England international Raich Carter after just seven minutes. Wolves, as they would at Wembley a year later, failed miserably at the final hurdle. They could not step up their game in the final ten minutes, either, when they had a man advantage following the dismissal of Sunderland's Scottish international left-half Alex Hastings. A report in the Daily Worker said: "Wolves were not a championship side on this display, for the home side were superior in all departments and even after Hastings was sent off for an alleged offence, Sunderland with ten men were still the more dangerous side. Sunderland had 75 per cent of the game and always played better football and were a better combination. The home club were continually on the attack and when Wolves did get going, mainly through Maguire, their best forward, the Sunderland defence generally had the better of the play and Mapson in goal was never seriously troubled."

Down at Highbury, Arsenal took advantage in glorious style as they swept aside Bolton, hitting five goals without reply, two of them from that man Carr as the title rested at Highbury for the fifth time in eight seasons. Not since Villa in the 1890s (five titles in seven seasons) had a club so dominated English football. Their 52 points equalled the lowest ever to take the title in a 42-game season, The Wednesday, as the Sheffield side were then known, having succeeded with that total in 1928-9. There was a huge roar at Highbury when the Wolves result was posted on the scoreboard. At the final whistle the crowd invaded the pitch and things looked like getting out of hand until the leader of the Arsenal brass band got his musicians to play God Save the King, which calmed everything down.

Significantly, there was a brief story in the Daily Express the Monday after Wolves had lost at Sunderland and it would prove spot on. It read: "Wolverhampton Wanderers, who refused to sell Bryn Jones at any price during the season, are believed to have revised their attitude. Negotiations for the transfer of Jones to Arsenal broke down last year. But Arsenal may now resume them." The negotiations certainly were resumed and would be concluded in time for the new season. However, the current campaign was not yet done for Cullis.

There was no time for Cullis to dwell on what might have been. Despite his poor display against Scotland he was named in the touring party for England's internationals against Germany, Switzerland and France. The squad travelled by boat from Harwich to the Hook of Holland and were in good spirits as skipper Eddie Hapgood recalled: "There was Stan Cullis discoursing deeply on various topics – I can't remember if he had taken up Esperanto by then – Ken Willingham, the irrepressible humourist, Don Welsh with his bubbling laugh, and the rest of us." A week after the league season's dramatic climax, the spotlight would switch to Berlin and one of the most infamous occasions in England football history – the day the team appeased the fascist regime by agreeing to give the Nazi salute as the anthems were played.

An urban myth has grown up around Cullis and this game – that he refused to play rather than give the salute. It is the sort of defiant principled gesture one might expect from Cullis but it would seem to be a case of . . . don't let the facts spoil a good story. For the truth was that Cullis had been dropped after the side's dismal showing at Wembley, along with left-half Wilf Copping and the inside trio of Willie Hall, Micky Fenton and Eric Stephenson. The selectors turned again to the experience of Alf Young and Cullis's international career was temporarily on hold. In the autobiographies of three men who played in Berlin, Eddie Hapgood, Stanley Matthews and Cliff Bastin, there is no mention of a refusal to play by Cullis. It is inconceivable to think they would not mention such a gesture of defiance had it been made. Furthermore, Cullis's autobiography has no reference to any refusal.

However, Cullis was in the dressing room before the game when the team were informed they must give the salute. Speaking many years later on the BBC series, Kicking and Screaming, he said: "I, along with other England players, objected to giving the Nazi salute, despite the Football Association informing us that it was only courteous to salute the German people. But at the same time we were informed, in a nice diplomatic way, that if we didn't give the Nazi salute we wouldn't be selected for any future England games." The players were far from happy at being made to give the salute at the request of the British ambassador and that may have got them fired up for the game as they proceeded to dent Hitler's theories of Aryan supremacy by beating Germany 6-3.

In Berlin, Cullis was among the onlookers and would be again in Zurich a week later as an unchanged side were chosen for the match against Switzerland. Perhaps it was an anti-climax after the prestige match in Berlin but England failed to sparkle and were beaten 2-1. They were also up against a rugged Swiss side obviously fired up for the match. Arsenal winger Cliff Bastin did not mince his words when he recalled the game: "The Swiss virtually kicked England off the field. It was quite the dirtiest game that I have been unfortunate enough to play in." The winner came from the penalty spot 17 minutes from time by Andre Abegglen, a player who scored 29 goals in 52 games for his country. Cliff Bastin had also scored from the spot in the first half to wipe out a headed goal by Georges Aebi.

The Swiss penalty seemed harsh on Young as the ball appeared to bounce up and hit his hand. Young had also been guilty of the foul on Mutch which enabled the Scot to give Preston their dramatic Cup Final victory. That, too, was controversial as it looked as if the foul occurred outside the penalty area. Film evidence later seemed to confirm this. Young had been a busy man in Zurich but left-half Don Welsh of Charlton had struggled even more – so cue Stanley Cullis. To bolster the side he was asked to play at left-half in the final match of the tour against France at the Colombes Stadium in Paris. His last half-back outings for Wolves had been three years earlier. The Cullis switch was not the only surprise alteration. It was decided to leave out young Jackie Robinson who had been a success in Berlin but not so effective in Zurich. To replace him, Stanley Matthews was switched to inside-right with Matthews's place on the right wing going to Frank Broome. That enabled Arsenal's Ted Drake to come in to lead the line.

France had been unbeaten that season with four wins and a draw from five games, one of their victories being over England's conquerors, Switzerland. Not surprisingly, there were nearly 48,000 fans packed into the stadium, hoping to see France complete an unbeaten campaign. The ground was soon in virtual silence as the new-look England side led after only five minutes as Broome took a Matthews pass and dribbled through the French defence to score.

After Bastin had hit a post, there were then three goals in as many minutes. Auguste Jordan headed France level from a corner; Drake made it 2-1 only for Jean Nicolas to beat Woodley with a 35-yard effort. Drake restored England's lead before half-time, dashing through on to a Len Goulden pass and just getting his foot to the ball before the French 'keeper. The only goal in the second half came from a Bastin penalty after Drake had been fouled. It was Bastin's 12th goal for England in what proved to be his final international. As for Cullis, he acquitted himself well despite pulling a muscle late in the game. One report said: "Cullis was quite at home in the unusual position of left-half and Matthews played brilliantly at inside-right."

Cliff Bastin wrote of the game some years later: "The England selectors made some rather curious team changes but they were changes with a plan and changes which were certainly effective." Unknowingly the England selectors had set a precedent – two central defenders. Cullis would dovetail with Alf Young while right-half Ken Willingham would play a more attacking role. It was a forerunner of the 1960s England team when Peter Swan wore the number-five shirt and Wolves' Ron Flowers played alongside him in a 4-2-4 formation. Then there was Bobby Moore playing alongside Jack Charlton in the 1966 World Cup-winning team and many years after that John Terry and Rio Ferdinand. Had the selectors of 1938 only known it, they had found a very effective formation.

Teams at the Colombes Stadium, Paris, on Thursday, May 26, 1938:

France: Di Lorto (Sochaux-Montbéliard); Cazenave (Sochaux-Montbéliard), Mattler (Sochaux-Montbéliard), Bourbotte (Fivoix), Jordan (Racing Club de Paris), Diagne (Racing Club de Paris), Courtois (Sochaux-Montbéliard), Brusseaux (Séte), Nicolas (Rouen), Heisserer (Strasbourg), Aston (Red Star Olympique).

England: Woodley (Chelsea); Sproston (Leeds), Hapgood (Arsenal); Willingham (Huddersfield), Young (Huddersfield), Cullis (Wolves); Broome (Aston Villa), Matthews (Stoke), Drake (Arsenal), Goulden (West Ham), Bastin (Arsenal).

Cullis was left to reflect on a season of great disappointments. His team had failed at the final hurdle to become champions of England and he had lost his centre-half place in the national side. Yet at 21 he had achieved much. He was a player rated highly by his fellow professionals and an able lieutenant to the controversial Molineux manager, the flamboyant Major Frank Buckley. Here it should be pointed out that Buckley led the way in encouraging young players. He believed that if they were good enough then they should be in the first team. This willingness to give youth a chance was being shown by Wolves more than decade before Manchester United adopted a similar philosophy under Matt Busby. Yet Buckley rarely gets the credit he deserves for this bold policy.

Chapter 4 Chasing the Double

Buckley's ambition in 1938 was to see the balance of power in English football swing from Highbury to Molineux but he seemed to Wolves fans to be going about it in a strange way – he sold his star forward to the Londoners. Arsenal had become First Division champions when many thought they would struggle following the retirement of their midfield maestro Alex James. Yet manager George Allison and his number-two Tom Whittaker were aware they still needed to replace the Scottish wizard and their eyes had for some time been focused on Molineux and the man who was probably Wolves' most prized asset after Cullis – Bryn Jones. Buckley had often angered fans by his willingness to sell players but had always managed to escape lasting criticism as he unearthed new gems. Now, though, there was unprecedented unrest among the faithful and it was understandable. Buckley had put the club on the football map, they had narrowly failed to become champions of England for the first time in their history and now they were prepared to sell one of the cornerstones of the team to the side who had denied them the title. The protests were long and loud – there was even a fans' meeting – but it was all in vain. Arsenal, despite a late bid from North London rivals Tottenham, duly got their man for what was then a world record fee of £14,000. Buckley spent some of the money on Doncaster winger Stan Burton, a player who had made 196 league appearances for the Third Division North side.

So Cullis would have to lead the team into the new season without the Welshman pulling the strings in midfield. In due course Buckley found the right blend from the remaining talent to see Wolves challenging not just for the league title but for the FA Cup as well. However, by the time they had got their act together, their main rivals had stolen a considerable march on them. Would Wolves have won the First Division if they had hung on to Jones? No-one can say but one suspects they would have given the ultimate champions a far closer run for their money.

Wolves' season began with four successive draws, then a win over Brentford followed by a home defeat by Jones's new club, Arsenal, who had lost their previous three games. In stark contrast, Everton's first six games had brought six straight wins. They were flying and so was their young centre-forward Tommy Lawton. He had scored in each of his side's six wins and it was no surprise when he was given his first representative honour, being chosen along with Cullis in the Football League team to play the Irish League at Windsor Park. It was a welcome diversion from Wolves' low-key opening to the season and it was virtually an England team that had been chosen for the trip across the Irish Sea. Cullis had a relatively quiet evening though the Irish started well and the score was 2-2 when the proceedings came to an unexpected halt ten minutes after half-time.

The heavens opened and fans on the uncovered terracing at one side of the ground sought shelter from the rain by racing across the pitch to the cover of the main stand opposite. As there were at least 2,000 of them, it meant the game came to an abrupt halt. When play resumed the Football League showed their class and rattled in six goals to run out 8-2 winners. Lawton scored four and others came from Jackie Robinson, Don Welsh, Len Goulden and John Morton.

Teams at Windsor Park, Belfast, on Wednesday, September 21, 1938:

Irish League: McCurry (Cliftonville); Adams (Distillery), Fulton (Belfast Celtic); McIvor (Newry Town), Carlyle (Derry City), Walker (Belfast Celtic); Todd (Glentoran), McAlinden (Belfast Celtic), Shearer (Derry City), Duffy (Derry City), McCormick (Linfield).

Football League: Woodley (Chelsea); Sproston (Tottenham), Hapgood (Arsenal); Willingham (Huddersfield), Cullis (Wolves), Welsh (Charlton); Matthews (Stoke), Robinson (Sheffield Wednesday), Lawton (Everton), Goulden (West Ham), Morton (West Ham).

Back in league action, Cullis and Wolves could still not get going and their second six games of the season brought one win and four defeats, each of them 1-0. One of those was at Goodison where Wolves hardly had an ideal preparation. Their train was held up because of some problem on the line and so the team alighted at Edgehill and completed the journey with the help of a taxi and a newspaper van, eventually trotting out seven minutes after the scheduled kick-off time. The match, won by a goal from Tommy Lawton, was a painful one for Cullis who collided late on with Everton's inside-right Stan Bentham, and was knocked out cold. Both players were carried from the field apparently unconscious but eventually recovered. Cullis's mishap got a rough reception from the home crowd, as Ken Abram reported in the Daily Express: "Cullis and Bentham, young Everton inside right, collided head on five minutes from time. Both were taken off, Cullis with concussion and Bentham with a badly cut lip and head. The crowd cheered. It made me wonder what had happened to this British sportsmanship about which we hear such a lot. Some of Cullis's tackles had not pleased spectators, but his accident should have aroused sympathy. That ending marred a well-fought game." The clash with Bentham was the second time in the match that they had collided and Wolves took no chances when the team returned to Wolverhampton. Cullis was admitted to the QVNI (Queen Victoria Nursing Institute) to ensure there was no lasting damage. Many years later Cullis said of the incident: "It was a complete accident which would not produce any serious consequences in a million other instances but I spent seven days in bed suffering from concussion." Had Cullis realised at the time, this was early evidence of his susceptibility to head injuries that would bring a premature end to his career.

Wolves were clearly struggling, and defeat at Middlesbrough on October 29, 1938, meant they were in 18th place with just nine points from 12 games. Derby headed the table with 20 points from 13 games, Everton lying second with 18 from 12. It was a sizeable gap to close in the days of only two points for a win. Significantly, Middlesbrough's next game saw them beaten 4-0 by Everton at Goodison.

Old boyhood rivalries were renewed as Everton emerged as the side to catch with one of the mainstays of their team being Cullis's fellow Ellesmere Port man, Joe Mercer. In contrast to Wolves, Everton had begun the season with those six successive wins but Wolves would also reel off six successive wins – in November – after a significant switch by Buckley. Harry Thompson had been given the task of filling Bryn Jones's boots but the team did not gel until Dickie Dorsett was given the inside-left position, having previously been used at outside-left and right-half. Justifying the Buckley youth policy, the 19-year-old Dorsett and 21-year-old Dennis Westcott proved a mighty effective strike force. In league and cup that season their sum total was 72 goals. Westcott's individual total of 43 from 43 games stood as a club seasonal record until Steve Bull beat it in 1987-8 with 52 from 58.

Before Wolves began their climb up the table, England met Wales at Cardiff but there was no place for Cullis. He, Don Welsh and Jack Morton were the only three members of the Football League team who had posted that emphatic win in Belfast not to be selected for the game at Ninian Park. It was probably a good game to miss as England were soundly beaten by a Bryn Jones-inspired side. The score was 4-2, one of the losers' goals coming, via the penalty spot, from Lawton in his first international. His absence from the Everton side that day had no ill effect. They beat Leeds 4-0 at Goodison helped by a hat-trick from Lawton's deputy, Bunny Bell, the man who had hit nine goals for Tranmere when they beat Oldham 13-4 on Boxing Day, 1935. In Cardiff, England's defence were given the run-around and that meant the end of Alf Young's international career. Cullis was clearly the man to take over at the centre of his country's defence and was duly named in the England team to play a Rest of Europe XI at Highbury four days after the Wales game. The match was to mark the Football Association's 75th anniversary.

A knock in the 2-2 home draw with Liverpool meant Cullis might have to miss the special occasion. He had sustained a slight cut on the inside of his right knee and was treated at Molineux before joining up with the England team two days before the game to face a representative side managed by celebrated Italian coach Vittorio Pozzo. Cullis was fortunate as usually if a player was not able to report to the team at the scheduled time, he would be declared unfit and another would be drafted in. That was what had cost George Ashall his chance of a cap.

It was Pozzo who had coached Italy to World Cup triumph earlier in the year, his side beating Hungary 4-2 in the final in Paris. Not surprisingly, there were five Italians in the Rest of Europe line-up. There was a lower-than-expected crowd of some 40,000, possibly accounted for by a rise in ticket prices. Before the game the sides were introduced to guests of honour, the Duke of Kent and Italian ambassador Signor Grandi, while flags of the nations involved fluttered over Highbury, including the swastika of Nazi Germany. England then virtually strolled to a 3-0 win, the continentals hardly endearing themselves to the fans with their use of obstruction which referee Jimmy Jewell generally treated leniently. Stanley Matthews was again on top form and his pass to Willie Hall set up the first goal on 22 minutes, the inside man firing home from 18 yards. Tommy Lawton then managed to get on the end of a Wally Boyes cross to make it two. There must have been a multi-lingual tactical talk at half-time as the Europeans then tested England's defence only to see goalkeeper Woodley save a Braine shot and Cullis head one from Brustad off the line. The brief storm was weathered and Len Goulden struck in the 72nd minute with a long-range shot to match that of Hall.

John Macadam of the Daily Express made Cullis England's top man and in an article under the banner heading "Cullis was Europe's undoing" the distinguished sportswriter wrote: "Stan blotted Piola out of the game as if he had been a spot of ink on an important letter and found the task so simple that he had also time to set his forwards off with those clinging, sneaky passes that never seemed likely to miss. Cullis, I dare say, never wasted a single ball." Funny how two people can watch the same game and come up with different opinions; thus John Thompson of the Daily Mirror wrote: "Cullis I thought disappointing but Willingham and Copping were the excellent workmen we have long known them to be." Of major concern to the Mirror man was the poor turnout: "The attendance was 40,185, a gate with which Arsenal would not be overjoyed for one of their ordinary league games. I had suspected that this would happen since reading the many letters I received following my attack on this prices scandal when the charges of admission were announced some weeks ago. The man in the cloth cap has made this game. Unless he receives more consideration he can break it." Ticket prices ranged from 7s 6d (37.5p) to a guinea (£1.05). Final verdict from Thompson: "By their convincing victory England have shown that they remain the masters and that the Europeans are still the pupils . . . although extremely promising pupils. The skilful and pretty football which our visitors served up was a joy to watch but came to nothing when confronted by the solid determination and sturdy tackling of the English defence."

Teams at Arsenal Stadium, Highbury, London, on Wednesday, October 26, 1938:

England: Woodley (Chelsea); Sproston (Tottenham), Hapgood (Arsenal); Willingham (Huddersfield), Cullis (Wolves), Copping (Arsenal); Matthews (Stoke), Hall (Tottenham), Lawton (Everton), Goulden (West Ham), Boyes (Everton).

Rest of Europe: Olivieri (Torino and Italy); Foni (Juventus and Italy), Rava (Juventus and Italy); Kupfer (Schweinfurt 05 and Germany), Andriolo (Bologna and Italy), Kitzinger (Schweinfurt 05 and Germany); Aston (Racing Club de Paris and France), Braine (Royal Beerschot and Belgium), Piola (Lazio and Italy), Zsengeller (Ujpest and Hungary), Brustad (Ski of FK Lyn and Norway).

As the European side were chosen only from countries affiliated to FIFA, no player from the Home Nations could be selected as Scotland, Wales and Northern Ireland were, like England, not affiliated at that time though they would come back into the fold after the war. Tommy Lawton reflected many years later that the distinguished guests and the eager fans did not see any wonderful football. "All-in wrestling would be a better description" was the Lawton verdict. "In those days the continentals had not learned how to play the game without kicking, hacking, punching, jersey pulling and obstructing. Nor had they learned on-the-field manners, and when the referee Jimmy Jewell awarded a free kick against Andriolo, the Italian deliberately spat at the official." At least Cullis and co could forget what had gone on when they and the European team attended the lavish banquet at the Holborn Restaurant which followed.

A week later Wolves fans got a chance to see Cullis playing in top company when Molineux staged an inter-league game. A ground of some quality by then, it was the venue for the meeting of the Football League and the Scottish League, with Cullis named in the English contingent. He unexpectedly found a familiar face alongside him when Joe Gardiner was drafted into the team following the withdrawal of Bolton left-half George Taylor because of a groin injury. Arsenal left-back Eddie Hapgood also pulled out and into the defence came young Everton full-back Norman Greenhalgh who only a season earlier had been playing in the Third Division North for New Brighton. Hapgood's absence meant Cullis was given the honour of captaining the team on his home ground.

With Derby inside forward Ronnie Dix the star of the show, the Football League ran out comfortable 3-1 winners with Cullis and Gardiner helping to subdue the Scottish forwards. The Glasgow Herald said the Scottish side "gave a sorry display" and added: "The English were faster on the ball and tackled with more devil and their finishing was vastly superior."

After 18 minutes Matthews's slide rule pass put Wally Boyes clear to beat goalkeeper John Brown with a fierce right-foot shot. After 27 minutes Dix beat two men before firing low past Brown and the inside man struck again a few minutes after the break, again tripping his way past two defenders. A goal soon afterwards from Tommy Walker via the penalty spot was the Scots' only reply.

Teams at Molineux Grounds, Wolverhampton, on Wednesday, November 2, 1938:

Football League: Woodley (Chelsea); Sproston (Tottenham), Greenhalgh (Everton); Willingham (Huddersfield), Cullis (Wolves), Gardiner (Wolves); Matthews (Stoke), Hall (Tottenham), Lawton (Everton), Dix (Derby), Boyes (Everton).

Scottish League: Brown (Clyde); Hogg (Celtic), Hickie (Clyde); Geatons (Celtic), Lyes (Celtic), Paterson (Celtic); Delaney (Celtic), Walker (Hearts), Martin (Clyde), Venters (Rangers), Kinnear (Rangers).

England were due to play Norway at St James' Park the following week and Gardiner could have been excused for thinking he might be chosen to play alongside his club skipper. No chance! Meeting at the Victoria Hotel straight after the game, the selectors, in their familiar perverse way, chose at left-half Doug Wright, of Newcastle, a 21-year-old who had been playing for Southend a couple of years earlier. Gardiner's useful display had not been enough to get him the vote, yet it ought to have been, Wright's choice surely being influenced by the match's venue.

After Norway had been beaten 4-0, newcomer Jim Smith, the Millwall outside left, scoring twice while Dix and Tommy Lawton added others, one report said: "Cullis took chief honours among the half-backs." England were clearly not greatly extended and the score would have been far greater but for some heroics in goal by Henry Johansen. It took the home side 18 minutes to take the lead when Smith headed home a Matthews centre. Ten minutes later Dix had a shot deflected home and Lawton made it 3-0 eight minutes before half-time. There was still time before the break for Smith to make it four, netting after a Lawton shot had hit the bar. The 39,887 fans must have expected more goals but the Norwegians defended gallantly with Johansen getting plenty of chances to defy the home forward line.

Teams at St James' Park, Newcastle, Wednesday, November 9, 1938:

England: Woodley (Chelsea); Sproston (Manchester City), Hapgood (Arsenal); Willingham (Huddersfield), Cullis (Wolves), Wright (Newcastle); Matthews (Stoke), Broome (Aston Villa), Lawton (Everton), Dix (Derby), Smith (Millwall).

Norway: Johansen (Oslo); Lars Martinsen (Oslo), Holmsen (Oslo); Henriksen (Oslo), Eriksen (Skien), Holmberg (Skien); Brynilsden (Lillestrom), Kvammen (Stavanger), Alf Martinsen (Bergen), Isaksen (Oslo), Brustad (Oslo).

When the selectors met after the game to name the team for the following week's clash with Ireland at Old Trafford, they decided to drop both inside forwards, particularly surprising in Dix's case as he had sparkled for the Football League at Molineux and had impressed at St James' Park. Into the side came Tottenham's Willie Hall and Leeds man Stephenson who had played in the dismal Wembley defeat at the hands of Scotland the previous year. However, the third change would have brought great pleasure to Cullis. Chosen at left-half was Joe Mercer, his Ellesmere Port schoolboy pal. Mercer had played before on the left of defence for Everton but had for some time been playing at right-half as they mounted their challenge for the First Division title with Cullis's Wolves in hot pursuit.

There was soon cause for more Cullis pride. When full-back Sproston had to withdraw through injury on the eve of the game, Bill Morris was called on to replace him. Morris had been playing at centre-half for Wolves when the claims of Cullis to the position could not be resisted. So Major Buckley switched Morris to right-back and the West Bromwich-born player took to the new role as if to the manner born. His baptism into international football would prove a gentle one in a match that proved historic. Cullis and Morris had a relatively quiet afternoon in Manchester as Tottenham's Hall, despite being no great goalscorer for his club, wrote his name into football history by rattling in five goals, including three in the space of three minutes. Despite Hall equalling a record individual total for his country, the star of the proceedings as England triumphed 7-0 was Stanley Matthews, clearly at the height of his powers.

Teams at Old Trafford, Manchester, on Wednesday, November 16, 1938:

England: Woodley (Chelsea); Morris (Wolves), Hapgood (Arsenal); Willingham (Huddersfield), Cullis (Wolves), Mercer (Everton); Matthews (Stoke), Hall (Tottenham), Lawton (Everton), Stephenson (Leeds), J R Smith (Millwall).

Northern Ireland: Twoomey (Leeds); Hayes (Huddersfield), Cook (Everton); Brolly (Millwall), McMillen (Chesterfield), Browne (Leeds); Cochrane (Leeds), Stevenson (Everton), Baird (Huddersfield), Doherty (Manchester City), J Brown (Birmingham City).

It was the second visit to Old Trafford in four days for Cullis, the first one being when Wolves beat Manchester United 3-1. That put Wolves in 12th place in the table, on 13 points – nine behind leaders Derby and second-placed Everton. The top two had both lost 1-0, Derby at Charlton and Everton at struggling Birmingham who were destined to be relegated at the end of the season. It was around this time that Wolves chairman Arthur Oakley addressed a meeting of the Wolverhampton Amateur League and commended his club's young skipper to the assembled players. "I am holding up Cullis as a pattern to you," said Oakley. "He attends Wolverhampton Technical College two or three nights a week and he is trying to master several languages. I hope you will show the same spirit and attempt to improve your minds. It is the man who uses his brains who goes a long way in football."

The Christmas period was always busy in those days and Wolves, like other clubs, played three times in four days, the first being Christmas Eve when leaders Derby were held to a goalless draw at Molineux. On Boxing Day and the next day, Wolves gained emphatic victories over Grimsby, 4-2 at Blundell Park and 5-0 at Molineux when only the brilliance of veteran keeper George Tweedy prevented an absolute rout. The holiday rush of action left Derby still at the head of the table on 33 points, with Everton on 30 and Wolves 27. The two chasers both had a game in hand on the leaders.

If the assault on the league title was well under way, that on the FA Cup would soon gain momentum as Wolves were favoured with a home draw in each round leading up to the semi-final. It began with a routine 3-1 win over Bradford Park Avenue, continued with a 5-1 dismissal of Leicester City and by the time Liverpool came to Molineux in mid-February for the fifth round clash the cup run had captured the fans' imagination. The chance that their side might reach Wembley always galvanised supporters in those days and Molineux was packed as it had never been packed before or since. A record gate of 61,315 saw Wolves win 4-1 and set up a sixth-round clash with title rivals Everton. Cullis was not at his best and with Wolves 2-0 up he gave Liverpool some hope by handing off centre-forward Willie Fagan who scored from the resultant penalty. Second half goals from Alex McIntosh and Dickie Dorsett saw Wolves through but John Macadam in the Daily Express, said: "Cullis had the poorest day I have seen him have." Star man for Liverpool was their right-half, a veteran Scot by the name of Matt Busby.

Wolves and Everton had been due to meet in the league on the day of the fifth round so the re-scheduling of that game in midweek would serve as a rehearsal for the Cup game – and what a rehearsal! Wolves brushed aside Everton 7-0. Major Buckley liked his side to play on heavy pitches and that certainly applied to Molineux that day as Everton centre-forward Tommy Lawton recalled: "We ran up against the Molineux ground at its worst that afternoon. It was a beautiful day, in fact the weather had been perfect for the preceding four days, but we ran on to a water-logged pitch. The well-known Wolverhampton water cart had been at work. And did those Buckley water babes put us through our paces!" Lawton was not Cullis's direct opponent that day as he played at inside-right with Bunny Bell at centre-forward.

It was the Cup win over Leicester that prompted one of the city's MPs, Montague Lyons, to raise in Parliament the issue of Wolves having "monkey gland" injections to help them feel fitter and stronger. Major Buckley, always willing to test new ideas, had first tried them himself and felt much healthier and so thought it was worth trying on the players. Only young reserve goalkeeper Don Bilton and Dickie Dorsett refused to try them. Montague Lyons's call for an inquiry into the matter was rejected by the Speaker of the House of Commons and eventually the fuss would die down. It seems bizarre that a man named Lyons, a fan of the Foxes, should raise the subject of Wolves and monkeys!

In All For The Wolves, Cullis wrote: "Whether or not monkeys came into the picture I do not know. The injections, which were something quite new in football, were nothing more potent than an immunization against the common cold, and certainly I do not think they ever helped or hindered me." He added that several players had not completed the course as it appeared to be having no effect on them. While Cullis was dismissive of the affair, Tommy Lawton was not so sure. He said that before the Molineux game he had seen Cullis and, knowing him from the England side, had said hello. "He just walked past me, eyes glazed and ignored me. Well there was no doubt in my mind they were on those monkey pills or something like." Of course, what Lawton perceived as a pill-fuelled trance may just have been Cullis being super focused on the matter in hand. We will never know.

Without doubt, Buckley was a man ahead of his time and had also recommended the use of a psychologist in football, a thing now routinely accepted in modern sport. Cullis attended the surgery of one in Wolverhampton on several occasions. He said it was a matter of trying to build up his confidence through an analysis of his worries and problems. Cullis felt he had few of those at that time as things were going well for him but reckoned visits to the psychologist had definitely helped another Wolves player who had lost his form

A week before the sixth-round Cup showdown, both clubs won away from home, Wolves 2-0 at Liverpool and Everton 2-1 at Leeds so that with 12 games to play, the First Division was now a two-horse race, the Merseysiders having 42 points and Cullis's men 40. So both entertained hopes of being the first side in the 20th Century to win the Football League and Cup in the same season – the magical Double. As in the league meeting, the pitch was again tailored to what Buckley felt best suited his team, namely a muddy surface as Lawton testified: "We knew what to expect in the cup-tie. Fate was again against us. During a week of scorching weather the water cart had been in use all the week – and then it rained all Friday night and the Saturday morning of the match. So the groundsman was sent out to fork the ground, which he did only too well." Lawton felt he was hard done by: "I was sent through down the middle, just how I like it. But, in the act of shooting a desperate hand came out, clutched my jersey and the ball ran loose to the giant Wolves goalkeeper Scott. A quick clearance, Dennis Westcott picked up the ball and, beating four of our defenders, he ran through to score the all-important first goal. Dennis got another later on and we were out of the Cup." Everton centre-half, TG "Tommy" Jones, looking back many years later, testified to the state of the Molineux pitch: "We went down by coach to Wolverhampton from Harrogate, and when we got there the ground was a sea of mud. We were on our bottoms more than we were on our feet, to be quite honest."

Cullis recalled the Everton trainer being led a merry dance when, having seen the state of the pitch, he sought to have a longer stud put on the players' boots: "In those days the players would have a stud and then they would implement another stud on top if it was heavy ground. The trainer was deputed to go down and put another piece of leather on the boots. But when he asked the secretary of the Wolves who had they key of the boot room, the secretary said he didn't know. The trainer went to the groundsman and he asked him where the key was. He didn't know. I don't know how many people he asked until he finally ended up in Major Buckley's office. He asked Major Buckley for the key to the boot room and eventually Major Buckley gave him the key after this fella had practically gone on his knees to ask for it. After that, Everton had the rule changed so that clubs would not be able to water the pitch during a period of the season."

Watering the pitch was something Cullis would favour as a manager and not everyone thought the practice a bad one. No less a figure than Raich Carter, a gifted inside-forward for Sunderland and England, wrote in his autobiography Footballer's Progress: "I am all in favour of watering football pitches and would like to see the practice made compulsory. In the first place it reduces the risk of serious injury. If a player takes an awkward toss on a soft ground he will probably get away with it. But on an iron hard ground that same fall can quite easily mean a broken limb, keeping the player out of the game for weeks and possibly shaking his confidence for good. In the second place, good football needs a yielding pitch. A light ball on a hard ground is extremely difficult to control. It becomes almost impossible to keep the ball low and pass accurately."

Had Lawton but known it, that Molineux defeat before a crowd of just under 60,000, would be a blessing in disguise. It meant Everton then had only one thing on which to focus – the First Division title. Wolves, like sides before them and after them, would wilt under the weight of chasing twin targets. Not that there were any immediate signs of that as four days after they reached the Cup semi-final, Wolves played Middlesbrough and brushed them aside 6-1. It was no mean feat against a team lying fourth in the table. The win meant Wolves had won seven and drawn one of eight league games and were breathing down the neck of the leaders. In a 19-game run they had lost only once. Yet Everton were refusing to wilt and on the same afternoon beat Leicester 4-0. Alas for Wolves, the wheels were about to come off their title bid as they lost three successive away games – 3-2 at Birmingham, 5-3 at Stoke and 4-2 at Preston. The Cup was now the only realistic prospect.

Chapter 5 Flop of the favourites

A week before the semi-final against Grimsby Town, Cullis skippered what was believed to be the youngest team in the club's history with a 16-year-old on each wing – Alan Steen and Jimmy Mullen. Steen was a scorer as Manchester United were beaten 3-0 and it was to Manchester that Wolves travelled seven days later for the Cup semi-final.

Three days before the clash with Grimsby Town, Cullis was allowed by Buckley to go to a dinner in Chester, staged by the company who had once employed him as a youngster. The Daily Mirror told the tale: "Once a grocer's boy earning a few shillings a week, now the highest priced soccer player in the world, such is the romance of Stanley Cullis, famous English international, captain of the Wolves (favourites for the FA Cup) and one of the greatest centre half-backs in the history of the game. Cullis was the guest of honour at the staff dinner last night of a well-known dairy company. He had been allowed the night off to be among old friends at this Chester gathering. He sat at the top table but when asked to make a speech declined – he was too shy! Stan told me: 'When I left school at the age of fourteen I worked as a grocer's lad at one of the firm's branches at Ellesmere Port for three years. I have enjoyed meeting all my old friends at Liverpool, Ellesmere Port and Chester and have been showered with good wishes for our success on Saturday.' Stan said he thought Wolves had a good chance of going to Wembley. After the dinner he travelled back to Wolverhampton by train and will make up for any loss of sleep tonight. It is known that the Wolverhampton club, who transferred Bryn Jones to Arsenal for £14,000, wouldn't accept £15,000 for Cullis. Any club who wants his services might have to write a cheque for £17,000 or £18,000 – a record that would undoubtedly stand for a long time." As well as showing that Cullis had not forgotten his roots, the report also reveals just how highly he was rated. Today he would be a millionaire super star.

What is still an Old Trafford gate record, 76,962, witnessed a one-sided semi-final. Grimsby goalkeeper George Moulson, making his debut as deputy for England international George Tweedy, a flu victim, was injured after 20 minutes in a collision with Dickie Dorsett. Moulson, a future Republic of Ireland international, was carried off with concussion and later detained in hospital overnight. By then Wolves were a goal up and they eased their way into the final 5-0 against the ten men with Dennis Westcott scoring four times. Poor Grimsby, they had faced Wolves three times that season and conceded 14 goals, managing just two in reply. In contrast, the other semi-final at Highbury saw Huddersfield leading Portsmouth 1-0 until 12 minutes from time when Pompey scored twice, through Jock Anderson and Cullis's former teammate Bert Barlow.

Delight at reaching Wembley for the first time was tempered somewhat for Wolves by those three successive away setbacks in the league. With six games to play they then trailed Everton by eight points with a game in hand. In the days of only two points for a win it would take a dramatic collapse to swing the balance towards Cullis and his men.

The centre-half would briefly have to forget the chase for club success and turn his attention to the call of his country. As far as Scots were concerned the biggest game of the season in those days was the annual clash with England. Cullis had played so badly in the fixture at Wembley a year earlier that he had been dropped. Now he had the chance to atone and to help England's quest for a rare victory on Scottish soil. They had not won at Hampden Park for 12 years. Cullis was by that time established as the best centre-half in the land and his clubmate Bill Morris would join him in the England team as full-back Bert Sproston was injured. An epic encounter saw England triumph, coming from a goal down to grab a late winner.

A report of the match in the Glasgow Herald made the key to victory the England half-back line of Huddersfield's Ken Willingham, Cullis and Joe Mercer. It said that as a constructive force they were magnificent and added: "Cullis was everything that we in Scotland had expected him to be. We do not have his like. A massive figure, at first sight cumbersome, Cullis was extraordinarily nimble on the ball, and once he had Dougal in subjection he was an inspiration to his side as he shunned defence and braved everything in attack. That was what Scotland lacked – a leader, a driving force from behind."

It was Morris who gifted Scotland the lead on 21 minutes. He was unaware 'keeper Vic Woodley had come out of goal and his intended pass back merely let in Jimmy Dougal to put Scotland ahead. It was Dougal's only appearance for his country and after that early boost he never got a look-in against Cullis. The centre-half began the move which led to left-winger Pat Beasley putting England level just after the hour. Cullis brought the ball out of defence then found Len Goulden whose centre eluded Jimmy Carabine and was flicked on by Tommy Lawton to Beasley who made no mistake. Beasley was making his debut as deputy for the man originally chosen, Eric Brook, who had withdrawn through injury. Stanley Matthews, who had tormented the Scots all afternoon, conjured up the winner with two minutes to go. His pinpoint centre was powered home by the head of centre-forward Lawton to clinch a famous win. Skipper Hapgood, not usually the most demonstrative of men, danced a jig of delight when the final whistle sounded.

Teams at Hampden Park, Glasgow, on Saturday, April 15, 1939:

Scotland: Dawson (Rangers); Carabine (Third Lanark), Cummings (Aston Villa); Shankly (Preston), Baxter (Middlesbrough), McNab (West Bromwich); McSpadyen (Partick Thistle), Walker (Hearts), Dougal (Preston), Venters (Rangers), Milne (Middlesbrough).

England: Woodley (Chelsea); Morris (Wolves), Hapgood (Arsenal); Willingham (Huddersfield), Cullis (Wolves), Mercer (Everton); Matthews (Stoke), Hall (Tottenham), Lawton (Everton), Goulden (West Ham), Beasley (Huddersfield).

One could say that Cullis and his teammates had done the England shirt proud that day but that would be only half true. In the second half several of them did the Queen's Park shirt proud! After a first half played in steady rain, a change of strip was needed by some but England had not brought a second set of jerseys with them. There was no way that would happen today but way back then it was the Hampden Park-based amateur club who came to England's rescue and they were able borrow their shirts for the second half.

Without Cullis and Morris, Wolves had beaten Charlton 3-1 at home and, as Everton were held at home 0-0 by Preston, were technically still in the title race. Everton had a six-point lead with three games to play and a better goal average so it needed Wolves to win their remaining fixtures emphatically and for Everton to lose all theirs. It was not going to happen and a week after the joy of Hampden Park, Cullis came down to earth when Wolves were held 0-0 at Burnden Park, Bolton, to ensure the title would go to Goodison and not Molineux. It mattered not that Everton had been beaten at Charlton.

Wolves had paid the price for their poor start to the league campaign but had still a chance of glory with the FA Cup final against Portsmouth due the following Saturday. Again it would be disappointment and one of the biggest Wembley upsets has been well documented. Wolves had been chasing the First Division title and were the most talked about team in the land while Portsmouth were 15th in the table with relegation not beyond the realms of possibility. Before the game, Buckley had to decide whether to give a place to Jimmy Mullen, who had played in the semi-final. In the end, the manager decided that, at 16, Mullen might find the occasion too much and so decided that the experienced Stan Burton would get the vote. What seemed a safe choice did not turn out well as Burton on the right wing and the talented Teddy Maguire on the left were below their best on the big day, looking hesitant in contrast to their usual direct style of play. Mullen's role was restricted to helping another youngster, Billy Wright, pack the team's brand new shirts, shorts and socks into the kit hamper.

Major Buckley's men, the hottest favourites in years, froze on their big day and Pompey players knew they were on to a winner when before the game they saw an autograph book signed by Wolves players with the signatures looking decidedly shaky. Of course, in those days, people usually signed their name so it could be read by others. Today it would be much harder to tell if a signature was done with an unsteady hand!

John Macadam, in the Daily Express, was one of the reporters who referred to the signatures. He said one of the Portsmouth party told him: "Most of the signatures were shaky. One of them was almost indecipherable. I told our boys 'They're licked already.' Our boys felt on top as they walked out to wait for the King." Macadam wrote: "You could see it, too. Cullis, usually the coolest man on any field, was fidgeting with the ball as he waited. And in the first ten minutes he was still nervy." Wolves were way below their best, yet in those opening minutes they had chances to take the lead. Dennis Westcott broke clean through but sent his shot wide and on another occasion the ball flashed across the Pompey goal with no Wolves player able to get the final touch. What surely cannot have helped Wolves' cause was the decision to travel down to Wembley on the morning of the big game. A long train journey was never going to be the ideal way to build up to a match of such importance.

To add insult to injury, the opening goal on 31 minutes was scored by Bert Barlow, who had played in the opening three games of Wolves' season before being transferred to Pompey. It came when Jock Anderson drew Cullis and Frank Taylor away from the goalmouth before centring to Barlow who placed his shot with pace and accuracy past Alex Scott. If that goal owed much to Portsmouth's skill, the second, just before half-time, owed something to Wolves' mistakes. Cullis seemed to mistime his intended interception of a Worrall centre and when Anderson turned the ball in he was aided by Scott's premature lunge at the ball. An even greater comedy of errors led up to the third goal barely a minute into the second half. Tommy Galley tried to backheel the ball near the halfway line but Bill Morris failed to reach it. Parker took advantage and squared to Barlow whose shot carried little weight. Scott appeared to have the shot covered, then fumbled the ball, attempted to grab it on the line only for Parker to poke the ball home. The game was up even though Wolves, urged on by Cullis, rallied to make it 3-1. It was his pass into the Portsmouth penalty area that eventually resulted in a cross from the right which Dickie Dorsett put home. It was but a token gesture and Portsmouth came back to score the best goal of the game with Fred Worrall's centre being met at the far post by Cliff Parker who nodded the ball past Scott. With 22 minutes still to play, the final scoreline might have been even more embarrassing but Portsmouth, who included another Molineux cast-off, Guy Wharton, at left-half, appeared to "take matters in a more leisurely style", as one report put it.

Teams at Wembley Stadium, London, on Saturday, April 29, 1939:

Portsmouth: Walker; Morgan, Rochford; Guthrie, Rowe, Wharton; Worrall, McAlinden, Anderson, Barlow, Parker.

Wolves: Scott; Morris, Taylor; Galley, Cullis, Gardiner; Burton, McIntosh, Westcott, Dorsett, Maguire.

"Not for eleven years at least has any team been so strongly fancied to win the trophy as were Wolverhampton Wanderers," wrote J T Bolton in the Sunday Times, "but they were more thoroughly outplayed as far as the real art and craft of the game are concerned than has any side been since the final ties were first played at Wembley." He added: "The genius of Cullis was notable at times but he has played more convincingly, and the wing half-backs of Wolverhampton were not nearly as persistent as those of Portsmouth." Stanley Halsey reckoned in the Daily Express that Buckley had tried to lift his team during half-time with not just words but with a drop of bubbly, too: "Gland-groomed Wolves, revived with champagne of classy vintage at half-time, were made to realise that after all it's the football that matters in football. And Portsmouth had all the football. I picked up a champagne bottle on the floor of Wolves' dressing room after the game. It was empty. But players had only a sip each at half-time to give them that little extra kick for part two of the game. And that was the only real kick they got out of the entire final. Portsmouth, with tough lively tackling that made the Wolves look lamb-like, tepid and tame, cornered all the play that mattered."

John Thompson, the Daily Mirror man, painted a verbal portrait of Cullis after the game: "A dejected figure is Cullis as we drive back together from the stadium. 'You don't know what a blow this is,' he says. And to a friend he remarks 'Tell mum not to worry.' Like the good sportsman that he is, he pays tribute to his opponents. 'It was a good game, fairly refereed, and we were beaten by a better team in which I thought Walker played particularly well,' he says. 'What a difference the first goal must make in a final. If we'd had the encouragement of scoring when we were on top in those first ten minutes I think the result might have been different. Still, it's all in the game, and Portsmouth easily deserved their win. Perhaps . . .' And with the determination typical of him Stanley Cullis builds up a new ambition from the wreck of the old."

Bear in mind that in those days winning the FA Cup was often more cherished by fans than winning the league title. So the disappointment among the Wolves faithful would almost certainly have been greater than when their favourites missed out on the First Division championship. It had been 31 years since the cup was won by Wolves and 18 years since they had reached the final. Yet the fans had still been given a team to stir the blood and they turned out in great numbers to welcome them back from London on the Monday afternoon after the final. The players had stayed at the Dorchester Hotel after Wembley and perhaps it would have been better if they had stayed in a London hotel the night before the big game. In summing up 1938-9, the Express & Star headlined the article by "Nomad" with "Wolves' glorious but imperfect season". The writer said: "Surely this succession of honours just missed cannot go on. Wolves' supporters will be fully entitled to expect the club to go one better next time and already Major Buckley is laying down his plans with the intention of bringing a major honour home next season."

"Nomad" also wrote: "The season, however, has not ended without Wolves writing yet more football history – they are the first club to finish runners-up in both the cup and league championship". Alas, he was ill-informed as Wolves were in fact the third club to collect that dubious honour, it having befallen Huddersfield in 1928 and Arsenal in 1932.

A much-asked question, then and in subsequent reflections on one of the biggest FA Cup final upsets ever, is whether Buckley got it wrong in not playing Jimmy Mullen. A telling verdict on Stan Burton's display at Wembley came five days later. He was sold to West Ham for £6,000 in time to play in the Hammers' last Second Division game. He thus became the first player to play in an FA Cup final and afterwards in a league game for a different club in the same season. Mullen may well have done well if Buckley had let his heart rule his head but it is still doubtful if the youngster would have made a difference to the result. Too many experienced players, Cullis among them, were not at their best at Wembley.

Chapter 6 Captain of England

There were two games to play after the final and Wolves beat Leicester 2-0 away before drawing at home 0-0 with Sunderland. The team who had let in four goals at Wembley had thus kept three clean sheets in their last three league matches which made their Cup Final display all the more baffling and frustrating. Mullen was on the left wing for those last couple of games. Clearly he was the future but it was a future that would be put on hold. He was also in the side for the opening three games of the 1939-40 campaign before it was brought to an abrupt halt by the declaration of war on Germany.

Before hostilities began, England made one last summer tour with Cullis and Bill Morris in a party of 15 players, accompanied by Arsenal trainer Tom Whittaker, for games against Italy, Yugoslavia and Romania in the space of 12 days. Wolves also had Teddy Maguire and Tom Galley chosen for the tour but Maguire had to withdraw through injury while Galley was dropped from the squad because he had not yet re-signed for Wolves. By the time he did agree terms it was too late and he was not reinstated. Dickie Dorsett was another who did not immediately sign on again. Brentford winger Leslie Smith replaced Maguire in the England party and Charlton's Don Welsh took Galley's place. There had been much discussion at Government level as to whether the trip should be made, with fears that any trouble at one of the games might spark an international incident. Once the go-ahead had been given Cullis and the rest left from Victoria Station, London, before travelling by ferry from Dover to Calais. The journey to Italy was completed by train and at stops along the way the players were greeted by enthusiastic people who gave them flowers. There was time for sightseeing before the international, including a trip to Lake Como. The warm welcome would banish thoughts of war – if only briefly.

Italy presented a tough first test for the tourists. They had a year earlier won the World Cup for a second time and fielded ten of the team who had beaten Hungary 4-2 in the final at the Stade Colombes in Paris. England quickly silenced the 55,000 fans inside the San Siro Stadium when Tommy Lawton headed home a Stan Matthews cross. Italy bounced back well and Amedeo Biaviti beat Vic Woodley to level before the break. It was a fine goal but the same could not be said of that which gave Italy the lead in the second half. Centre forward Silvio Piola, scorer of two goals in the World Cup final, could not quite reach Gino Colaussi's cross and so promptly punched the ball home before following through to hit full-back George Male. With, England expecting to be awarded a free kick, German referee, Dr Bauwens, signalled a goal. There were chants of "Viva Ribbentrop" and "Viva Goering" from the crowd. Up in the royal box Italy's Crown Prince was asking FA secretary Stanley Rous to accompany him on to the pitch to inform the referee the goal was illegal.

Rous had politely to persuade him that it was not a good idea. England, with Male virtually out of action, were not fazed and battled back for a 2-2 draw. After 77 minutes Matthews's centre brought a shot from Len Goulden which was blocked only for Willie Hall to score from the rebound. Justice had been done.

Teams at the San Siro Stadium, Milan, on Saturday, May 13, 1939:

Italy: Olivieri (Torino); Foni (Juventus), Rava (Juventus); Depetrini (Juventus), Andriolo (Bologna), Locatelli (Ambrosiana); Biavati (Bologna), Serantoni (Roma), Piola (Lazio), Meazza (Ambrosiana), Colaussi (Triestina).

England: Woodley (Chelsea); Male (Arsenal), Hapgood (Arsenal); Willingham (Huddersfield), Cullis (Wolves), Mercer (Everton); Matthews (Stoke), Hall (Tottenham), Lawton (Everton), Goulden (West Ham), Broome (Aston Villa).

Next stop was Belgrade and the Yugoslavs were just as welcoming as the Italians had been. One newspaper's greeting typified the attitude towards the visitors: "Illistrovani Sport cordially welcomes the England football team to Belgrade. How cordially it is difficult to put into words. For years we have waited for the moment when the chosen representatives of the 'Home of Football' would measure themselves at their full strength against our eleven, which, at least in enthusiasm for the game, yields nothing to them. As true sportsmen, we think less of the result of the game itself, but it is natural that on this occasion, when we are faced with the most dangerous opponents the world provides, we should be anxious to give of our best and prove the strength of our young Yugoslav football. We know that our guests and opponents, also as true sportsmen, ask neither more or less. We wish them a pleasant stay in Belgrade and a hard match, which will provide fine football for tens of thousands who have come to see the greatest match of their lives."

It certainly did prove a hard match, played in searing heat with water buckets placed around the pitch so the players could try to keep themselves cool. England were soon reduced to virtually nine men. Stan Matthews had jarred his hipbone in the game in Milan but was declared fit only to feel his leg give when he first tried one of his trademark shuffles. Matthews was a passenger after only five minutes and then skipper Eddie Hapgood tore an ankle ligament. Things got worse when Yugoslavia scored after 15 minutes through Svetislav Glisovic but England managed to hold out until half-time without conceding another goal. Four minutes into the second half Tommy Lawton and Frank Broome combined for the latter to score. England continued to create chances but were defied by goalkeeper Ljubomir Lovric, a teenage law student making his international debut. There was high praise for Cullis in one match report: "When Hapgood was slowed up by his injury, Cullis rose to the occasion in fine style and he was the outstanding man in the English defence." However, the home side won the game on 62 minutes when Cullis failed to cut out a long pass which found left-winger Nikola Perlic, who hammered the ball past Vic Woodley.

Teams at the Stadion Beogradski on Thursday, May 18, 1939:

Yugoslavia: Lovric (Jugoslavija); Dubac (Beogradski), Pozega (Vojvodina); Manola (Beogradski), Dragicevic (Beogradski), Lechner (Beogradski); Glisovic (Beogradski), Vujadinovic (Beogradski), Petrovic (Jugoslavija), Matosic (Beogradski), Perlic (Jugoslavija).

England: Woodley (Chelsea); Male (Arsenal), Hapgood (Arsenal), Willingham (Huddersfield), Cullis (Wolves), Mercer (Everton); Matthews (Stoke), Hall (Tottenham), Lawton (Everton), Goulden (West Ham), Broome (Aston Villa).

As they turned their thoughts to Romania, the tired England party were treated to a relaxing 14-hour trip down the Danube. Cullis and the rest made sure they were up at 4am to see the famous Iron Gates Gorge. On reaching Romania the players and officials were feted once more. At Turnu-Severin, two bands played God Save The King but, much to the amusement of the tourists, one played much faster than the other and so finished earlier. There were more diversions to come as England were taken to see Romania's oilfields and to Pelash Castle, summer residence of King Carol. On the day before the game there was a trip to see a circus and there was even time to do some shopping. By then Cullis had received news of destiny fulfilled. He had been named as captain of his country.

Eddie Hapgood's injury meant he would not face the Romanians and Cullis was the obvious choice to take over the captaincy, even though he was, at 22, older than only two other members of the side and even though full-back George Male had previously deputised as skipper on six occasions. Hapgood addressed a players' meeting before the game, urging them to make sure they ended the tour with a victory. Wolves man Morris deputised for Hapgood, while Wilf Copping, Don Welsh and Leslie Smith came into the side at the expense respectively of Willingham, Hall and Broome. Len Goulden, who had been switched to inside right, scored after five minutes. Welsh was pulled down just outside the penalty and from the free kick fired in a shot which Dumitru Pavlovici could only parry to Goulden who made no mistake. Welsh got the second goal early in the second half. Lawton sent a pass out to Broome, who was standing limping and lame near the touchline. Broome pulled the ball down with his left foot and coolly placed it to the far post where Welsh rose to head home to secure a 2-0 victory.

In the Daily Express, reporter John Macadam said the game, watched by King Carol, had contained more fouls than he could remember in any previous international. He went on: "Tall, lanky Langenus, the Belgian referee, kept up a constant obbligato on his whistle, and if he had blown for everything he saw he would never have had the thing out of his mouth. Trouble is this continental temperament, allied to the fact that continental referees allow tackling and obstruction of players who are nowhere near the ball – and it's no good expecting our fellows to keep on turning the other cheek.

"They didn't, by any means, and the result was a second half that would not have been out of place in a Third Division "Derby" cup-tie. Our players were kicked, hacked, pushed and elbowed. One Rumanian (sic) brought his foot up behind after a perfectly fair tackle by Joe Mercer. Young Leslie Smith was flying through once when a defender picked him up bodily and hurled him to the ground. He seemed surprised when a foul was awarded against him. But there is no point in outlining all the petty and vicious fouls that took place. It is enough to say that our men went out there to play football, and they were never given the chance." Macadam added: "Cullis was the outstanding Englishman. For the first time since we left home we saw him at the full peak of his Wolverhampton form. He allowed the very fast Rumanian centre forward no rope at all."

In his autobiography, Football Ambassador, Hapgood said of the game: "The England side played brilliant football, with Stan Cullis and Len Goulden outstanding." What Hapgood does not mention is that the Romanians did not take kindly to being outclassed and the game could have boiled over. Cullis, as aware as anyone that there must be no trouble, made sure his teammates did not retaliate to some rough treatment.

Teams at the Stadionul ANEF in Bucharest, on Wednesday, May 24, 1939:

Romania: Pavlovici (Ripensia); Burger (Ripensia), Sfera (Venus); Cossini (CS Rapid), Juhasz (Oradea), Demetrovic (Venus); Orza (Venus), Ploesteanu (Venus), Bodola (Venus), Reuter (Timisoara), Dobay (Ripensia).

England: Woodley (Chelsea); Male (Arsenal), Morris (Wolves); Mercer (Everton), Cullis (Wolves), Copping (Arsenal); Matthews (Stoke), Goulden (West Ham), Lawton (Everton), Welsh (Charlton), L Smith (Brentford).

Tired, battered and bruised, the England party returned home. Cullis had captained his country at a young age and was acutely aware of the honour. Eddie Hapgood was nearing the end of his career and there was only one man who could succeed him as skipper of the national side – Stanley Cullis. He and his Wolves team should have been on the brink of great things but the impending war changed all that.

Chapter 7   Historic substitute

When war was declared on Germany at the beginning of September, 1939, Cullis, a territorial soldier, did not hesitate to volunteer for Army service. Surprisingly, he failed a first medical examination by a doctor who must have been unaware that he was checking the fitness of an England footballer. In fact this was not just any footballer but England's first choice centre-half and their skipper in the last full international of peacetime. There were even suggestions Wolves may have pulled strings to get him excused but these were quickly quashed when he again applied and a different doctor, appraised of the situation, passed him as fit first class and did not even bother to examine him.

Naturally, the demands of the Army took precedence over those of football, though the Government were anxious for the game to continue as a morale-booster in dark wartime days. In the 1939-40 season Cullis played just eight times for Wolves as well as three guest appearances for Aldershot, a club who would benefit greatly from the wealth of football talent who saw service at the local Army barracks.

While the Government were happy to encourage football, the game had to take second place to the situation in the country. So outside considerations often dictated what sides were chosen. England's selectors decided to restrict the choice of players for the first international, a couple of months after war had been declared, to players based in the south, so the centre-half spot went to John Oakes of Charlton. It was his only England call-up. A side skippered by Eddie Hapgood, with the Arsenal defender Leslie Compton given a game at centre-forward, drew 1-1 with Wales in Cardiff on Armistice Day, 1939.

Exactly a week later the teams met again, this time at the Racecourse Ground, Wrexham, and England restricted selection to men based in the Midlands and North. There was no such restriction on the Welsh and several players had to travel on the morning of the match, some of them arriving only just in time for kick-off as the Glasgow Herald reported: "Players like Astley, Bryn Jones and Hopkins stepped off the train only half an hour before the game and carried their bags among the stream of enthusiasts making their way to the ground." With no Hapgood in the side, the captaincy of his country was given to Cullis for a second time in his career and once again he led his team to victory, though it was a close-run thing. Fielding the pre-war half-back line of Willingham, Cullis and Mercer, England won 3-2, after a goalless first half, thanks to goals from Villa's Jackie Martin, Jack Balmer of Liverpool and an own goal from the Wales skipper, Everton centre-half TG "Tommy" Jones. Dai Astley, the Blackpool centre-forward, scored both goals for Wales.

The scoring came in a hectic 15-minute spell, Astley's double strike putting the Welsh ahead. Then Jones sliced an attempted clearance into his own net. That sparked England's revival and within a minute Martin had levelled. The winner followed soon afterwards, Balmer slamming home an Eric Brook centre.

Teams at the Racecourse Ground, Wrexham, on Saturday, November 18, 1939:

Wales: Sidlow (Wolves): Hughes (Birmingham), Smith (Chelsea); Burgess (Tottenham), T Jones (Everton), Witcomb (West Bromwich); Hopkins (Brentford), Redfern (Derby), Astley Blackpool), B Jones (Arsenal), Cumner (Arsenal).

England: Swift (Manchester City); Sproston (Manchester City), Crook (Blackburn); Willingham (Huddersfield), Cullis (Wolves), Mercer (Everton); Matthews (Stoke), Martin (Aston Villa), Lawton (Everton), Balmer (Liverpool), Brook (Manchester City).

Cullis missed the game against Scotland in aid of the Red Cross Fund at the beginning of December, a match which England won 2-1 at St James' Park, Newcastle, despite starting the match with only nine men. Manchester City pair Sam Barkas and Eric Brook sustained minor injuries when their car was in collision with another at Dishforth and so Newcastle duo Joe Richardson and Tommy Pearson were drafted into the England side, an unexpected honour for the latter – he was a Scot! Getting to games was never easy as Cullis would soon find out.

Before the year was out Cullis would create a piece of Wolves history – the first substitute used at Molineux. He was named in a Football League XI to play an All-British XI in another game in aid of the Red Cross Fund. However, he was delayed on his way down from Ellesmere Port where he had spent Christmas with his family, so former Wolves man Dicky Rhodes came to the rescue. He had left the club a few years earlier for Sheffield United and then saw service with Swansea before joining Rochdale. Fortunately he was back in Wolverhampton and able to step into the breach. Rhodes held the fort for about 15 minutes but once Cullis had arrived and quickly got changed, the historic substitution was made. The Football League won the game 3-2.

Under the headline "Cullis car dash to help in Football League victory" this is how the Express & Star told the story: "At 1.55pm yesterday, 20 minutes before the kick-off at the Red Cross match between the Football League and an All-British XI at Molineux Grounds, Sergeant-instructor Cullis, Wolves and England centre-half, chosen for that position in the League side, was 16 miles away in Stafford. However, at 2.30, a quarter of an hour after the start, Cullis, following a 50-miles-an-hour dash from Stafford in a stranger's car, was able to take over his place from Dicky Rhodes.

"The stranger in the story was a 62-year-old native of Cheadle who acceded to Cullis's request for a lift to Wolverhampton. The Wolves player did not tell him of his predicament only that he wanted to go to the match and it started at 2.15. Naturally conversation was difficult with the car going at that speed but Cullis was able to learn the benefactor's age and town. The request for a lift was necessary because Cullis, after travelling from Ellesmere Port to Chester by road and by train via Shrewsbury to Stafford, discovered to his dismay he would never get to Wolverhampton in time for the match if he waited for a connection. Cheers greeted Cullis's appearance on the field."

The game served up some scintillating football, Peter Doherty giving the British side a first-half lead on 36 minutes when he headed home after Wolves 'keeper Alex Scott could only push out a Frank Broome centre. It should have been 2-0 a minute into the second half when centre-forward Jock Dodds eluded Cullis to get first to a Broome centre only to turn the ball wide. The rest of the scoring came in the last 21 minutes, starting when Blackburn's Len Butt ran on to a Joe Gardiner pass to equalise. Two minutes later, with the light starting to fade, Huddersfield winger Pat Beasley restored the British side's lead only for Tommy Lawton to head a second equaliser four minutes later from a Cliff Bastin centre. Eight minutes from time Butt, only in the side after Arsenal's Bryn Jones had withdrawn, ran on to a Bastin pass and beat Liverpool's South African goalkeeper Arthur Riley who had previously come to his side's rescue on several occasions. Before the end it was Alex Scott's turn to show his goalkeeping prowess as he denied Broome to preserve the Football League's 3-2 lead.

Teams at Molineux Grounds, Wolverhampton, on Thursday, December 26, 1939

Football League XI: Scott (Wolves); Hayes (Huddersfield), Hapgood (Arsenal); Gardner (Burnley), Rhodes (Rochdale), sub Cullis (Wolves) 15 min, Gardiner (Wolves); Matthews (Stoke), Martin (Aston Villa), Lawton (Everton), Butt (Blackburn), Bastin (Arsenal).

All-British XI: Riley (Liverpool); Cook (Everton), Cummings (Aston Villa); Dearson (Birmingham), Harper (Barnsley), Witcomb (West Brom); Broome (Aston Villa), Mutch (Preston), Dodds (Blackpool), Doherty (Manchester City), Beasley (Huddersfield).

In January, 1940, Cullis was named as skipper of an Army XI against an England XI at Crystal Palace and it gave him the distinction of having captained both England and a team playing against his country. The Army side were beaten 4-3. Soon afterwards, Cullis was named in a British Army side to travel to France to play the French Army in three games to entertain troops. It meant a sea trip and Cullis was not the best of sailors but he thought he had found the answer when he suggested to Tommy Lawton and Matt Busby that they invest in some anti-seasickness tablets as the other two were fellow sufferers.

Let Lawton take up the story: "On the train going down from Victoria, Stan Cullis came up to where Matt Busby and I were sitting and said that as all three of us were notoriously bad sailors he had obtained a sea-sickness remedy which 'positively could not fail'. Cost of the three pills was a guinea (£1.05), but both Matt and I agreed that if they did all that was claimed for them we wouldn't mind paying a guinea each! We three waited until we had got aboard before swallowing the pills and then settled down below to a game of cards. With the passing of time, our apprehension decreased and our spirits correspondingly rose. We acclaimed Stan as a life-saver, we joked and went into fits of laughter at the thought of some of the other weak-stomached members of the party suffering at the hands of King Neptune. Then, after about an hour and a half of this jollity and chaff, Stan said: 'We ought to be there by now. Let's go up and look at France.' In the distance we could see shaded lights of a blacked-out harbour. 'Calais,' I exclaimed gaily. 'No,' said a voice from the darkness, 'Dover, we are still in the harbour.' I'll draw a veil over the rest. We hadn't moved from our berth. When we did, Matt, Stan and I dead-heated for the ship's side."

If the sea trip was a rude awakening for Cullis, there was greater pain waiting on the other side of the Channel. In their opening game the British Army were held 1-1 by the French Army and with the Brits leading through a Maurice Edelston goal, there was a familiar story for Cullis – a head injury. French forward Henri Hiltl had weaved his way through the British defence before firing in a shot which had "goal" written all over it had it not hit the Cullis forehead. He was knocked out cold. He was able to resume in time to see Hiltl head the French side level. That was the final score but the British had been given a testing afternoon as John Macadam reported in the Daily Express. He said 30,000 French fans had come expecting to see a typical British show of pluck and skill: "Instead they saw what looked like a tired-out team lacking in craft and initiative licked by the Frenchmen who had as many tricks as a barrow load of monkeys and as much courage as the Maginot Line. I have never seen a Continental team play with the dash and cunning of these French soldiers."

A few days later there was more woe for Cullis as the French Army were beaten 1-0 in Rheims. He was hit by a flying tackle from a French player and shot up in the air and came down with a thud on the back of his head. He was carried off unconscious but gamely came back ten minutes into the second half, though only able to operate as a somewhat dizzy left-winger, Don Welsh having moved to centre-half. Despite not being 100 per cent, Cullis still went close to a goal when he got on the end of a cross from Albert Geldard. Alas, there was no storybook ending to his gallant display and he skied the ball over the bar. The British goal came when Eric Stephenson headed in a Denis Compton centre.

There was plenty to cheer for the British soldiers in a crowd of 15,000 and John Macadam noted that while the French soldiers cheered on their team with "Allez", the Tommies responded with "Get on with it!" Cullis recovered for the final game of the trip, the British Army beating the French 2-1 in a rugged encounter at Lille that earned praise from John Macadam: "Not a man of them shirked his task. Mercer and Cullis and Copping gave and took knocks that looked like murder." All the goals came in the first half, Stephenson wiping out the opening one by Hermant for the French before Mercer swept home a Denis Compton cross for the winner.

Back on home soil and recovered from the bruising three games in France, Mercer, Cullis and Copping were named to face Wales at Wembley, but Cullis's old Ellesmere Port pal chose to play for Everton in their Lancashire Cup semi-final against Liverpool at Goodison Park. The FA were far from pleased and a telegram was sent commanding Mercer to play but it was ignored. Everton won the tug-o-war for his services, Ken Willingham being drafted in. Cullis was fit to take his place in the England side and lock horns again with his old teammate Bryn Jones. The Arsenal man may have been missing from the Molineux representative game when Cullis made his historic substitute appearance but he was very much in evidence as Wales were granted their first ever game at the home of English football. The Welshmen, playing before a crowd of only 40,000, rose to the occasion and it was Jones who scored the only goal of the game. It came just before half-time after he beat three men on the edge of the penalty area before sending a swerving shot past goalkeeper Sam Bartram. Wolves were well represented with Cyril Sidlow in goal for the victors while Dennis Westcott led the England line in place of Tommy Lawton. It was the centre-forward's first game for his country and fellow debutants were Charlton's Bartram and Arsenal winger Denis Compton, a man better known for his prowess as a Middlesex and England batsman. It was definitely not England's day. Westcott was fouled by Welsh skipper Bert Turner five minutes from time and referee Jimmy Jewell pointed to the penalty spot. Willie Hall stepped up to take the kick and sent his shot wide. Justice was done as Wales reaffirmed the superiority they had held over England in the latter half of the 1930s.

Teams at Wembley Stadium, London, on Saturday, April 13, 1940;

England: Bartram (Charlton); Bacuzzi (Fulham), Hapgood (Arsenal); Willingham (Huddersfield), Cullis (Wolves), Copping (Leeds); Matthews (Stoke), Hall (Tottenham), Westcott (Wolves) Goulden (West Ham) D Compton (Arsenal).

Wales: Sidlow (Wolves); Turner (Charlton), G Williams (Millwall); Green (Bradford), Davies (Nottingham Forest), Witcomb (West Brom); Hopkins (Brentford), Dearson (Birmingham) Astley (Blackpool), B Jones (Arsenal), L Jones (Arsenal).

Less than a month later and Cullis was back at the scene of the memorable 1939 win over Scotland – Hampden Park. There was no England victory this time but a creditable 1-1 draw with Cullis apparently acquitting himself well in stark contrast to long-serving skipper Eddie Hapgood who seems to have been given a veritable run-around from tricky right-winger Jimmy Caskie. The report in the Glasgow Herald positively revelled in the fact, writing: "Little Caskie, Scotland's will o'the wisp right winger, was a rare tonic for war-strained nerves at Hampden. He had the spectators splitting their sides with laughter at his dribbling antics, and his immediate opponent, the stately Hapgood of England, must have found it very difficult to keep his dignity and his temper. But, to his credit Hapgood contrived to do both despite the ridiculous figure he cut on occasion when he was quite miraculously toppled over by the little fellow. Caskie was an entertainment in himself." As for Cullis, the report confirmed that he was still a man at the peak of his powers: "As was the case at Hampden in April of last year, one felt real admiration for the English half-backs. Cullis was a pillar in defence and Willingham and Mercer, especially in the second half, inspired many a raid on Dawson's charge." Don Welsh, the Charlton inside-left, put England ahead soon after half-time, powering his way through the Scottish defence before placing a shot into the corner of the net. Cullis was hard done to when it came to the equaliser 14 minutes from time, being brought to the ground by Derby centre-forward David McCulloch who hooked the ball through to Jimmy Dougal who scored. Even the Glasgow Herald report rated the Scots lucky to get away with it: "If Hapgood's tackling and that of his colleagues was scrupulously fair for the most part, as much could not be said for more than one Scottish player. Indeed one's native loyalty was severely strained by this aspect of the game, especially when the referee contrived to close his eyes to a foul by M'Culloch (sic) on Cullis which left Woodley exposed and unable to prevent Dougal scoring the equalising goal with a fine right-foot drive."

Although 68,000 tickets had been sold for the match, only 62,341 fans turned up. Rumours ran around the city that a German radio announcer had said that the match would never go beyond half-time . . . so many stayed away. "Not that they missed much football," wrote John Macadam in the Daily Express, "but they did miss one of the big international thrills of my time . . . Don Welsh had bored his way through everything to wake the game up at the beginning of the second half and scored a lovely goal." A limit on excursion trains meant few Englishmen were in the crowd and it must have been an intimidating atmosphere with the Scottish fans raised to a fever of excitement by pre-match community singing led by legendary entertainer Sir Harry Lauder.

Teams at Hampden Park, Glasgow, on Saturday, May 11, 1940:

Scotland: Dawson (Rangers); Carabine (Third Lanark), McClure (Hearts); Shankly (Preston), Baxter (Middlesbrough), Brown (Hearts); Caskie (Everton), Walker (Hearts), McCulloch (Derby), Venters (Rangers), Dougal (Preston).

England: Woodley (Chelsea); Sproston (Manchester City), Hapgood (Arsenal); Willingham (Huddersfield), Cullis (Wolves), Mercer (Everton); Matthews (Stoke), Martin (Aston Villa), Broome (Aston Villa), Welsh (Charlton), Smith (Millwall).

Cullis was at this stage of the war playing much of his domestic football with Fulham as Wolves decided they could not field a team during the 1940-1 season. He played nine times for Fulham in the South Regional League and six times in the London Cup. He also made eight appearances for Liverpool that season. The previous season had seen him turn out occasionally for Wrexham.

It was while "guesting" for Fulham that Cullis again crossed swords with the men from north o' the border and this time at St James' Park, Newcastle. Captaining the team in the absence of Eddie Hapgood, he had a much more difficult day than he had at Hampden thanks to the twin menace of Rangers centre forward Jimmy Smith and Clyde inside-left Dougie Wallace, scorer of two goals. England were ahead in seven minutes. After Lawton's header had been partially cleared, Newcastle winger Ralph Birkett was on the spot to ram the ball home. Ten minutes later the Scots were level when Smith's shot was punched up in the air by Sam Bartram only for Joe Bacuzzi to nod the ball into his own net. Tommy Lawton restored the lead but close to the interval Wallace levelled the scores again and he hit the winner in the second half with a powerful drive from the edge of the penalty area. Star man for Scotland was 'keeper Jerry Dawson but the strike duo were not far behind as the Glasgow Herald reported: "Apart from the display of Dawson, Scotland found most satisfaction in the understanding between Smith and Wallace. As expected the pair stood up well to their powerful opponents, and Cullis, at centre-half, one may venture to say, had his most uncomfortable international experience in trying to quell the enthusiastic Rangers leader." According to the paper, Cullis was caught napping when Wallace scored in the 77th minute to give Scotland their 3-2 win: "Wallace's winning goal was a superb effort. He pounced on a rebound from Cullis and Bartram never saw his full-blooded shot." The game brought what would prove to be a lone England appearance for Liverpool winger Alf Hanson. The son of a Norwegian mariner, he was born "Adolf Hansen" and was the brother of Bolton goalkeeper Stan Hanson.

Teams at St James' Park, Newcastle, on February 8, 1941:

England: Bartram (Charlton); Bacuzzi (Fulham), Mountford (Huddersfield); Willingham (Huddersfield), Cullis (Wolves), Mercer (Everton); Birkett (Newcastle), Mannion (Middlesbrough), Lawton (Everton), Goulden (West Ham), Hanson (Chelsea).

Scotland: Dawson (Rangers); Hogg (Celtic), Beattie (Preston); McDonald (Celtic), Dykes (Hearts), Brown (Rangers); Milne (Dumbarton), Walker (Hearts), Smith (Rangers), Wallace (Clyde), Caskie (St Mirren).

The wartime motto of "Keep calm and carry on" was exemplified by a special game played at Stamford Bridge in early March when an Allied Armies XI were assembled to play the Army who were skippered by Cullis. Not only was it special to get such a game on at the height of the Blitz, but it was memorable for Cullis as he did something he had not done for his club – he scored a goal. It helped the Army win 8-2, with Don Welsh hitting a hat-trick and Denis Compton scoring twice. Ex-England, Sunderland and Arsenal star Charles Buchan, by then a respected journalist, wrote of the game: "I am sure it will go down as one of the most astonishing ever played, not that the result mattered a scrap. Its significance rested in the fact that during the greatest war of all times and in the midst of visits from enemy bombers dealing death and destruction, it was possible to gather together a team of sportsmen from conquered countries in Europe, good enough to match their skill against the best England could produce. Only a few thousand (10,794) were privileged to watch the game, but millions of people throughout the world heard a description of play through the medium of the BBC. It was broadcast in several languages and came as a tonic to British people and sympathisers all over the globe." The match had been promoted and facilitated by Chelsea vice-president, A V Alexander, First Lord of the Admiralty, using his football and forces connections. The Allied Armies side consisted of players of six nationalities – Dutch, Norwegian, Czech, Polish, Belgian and French.

Defiant in playing and watching the game, the players and fans were reminded – if they needed it – of the danger always lurking. On the front of the programme was a notice: "In the event of an air raid warning the ground exits will be opened so that those who wish to leave can do so. Play will proceed unless the spotter reports enemy activity in the vicinity. Cover is provided at the rear of the main stand." Keep calm and carry on, indeed!

Having discovered the knack of goal-scoring, Cullis found the net again twice soon afterwards. First it was for Fulham in a London Cup game at Aldershot, when his side lost 4-2. That was just a week after the Stamford Bridge game. He was also on target in an amazing game at Anfield in April, 1941, which produced sixteen goals. Cullis was in an All-British XI who were beaten 9-7 by a Football League XI in a game to raise money for the Lord Mayor of Liverpool's War Fund. Tommy Lawton scored three and Dickie Dorsett two for the winners, while Matt Busby was also a scorer for the losing side.

The Anfield game unexpectedly brought the first representative chance for Billy Liddell, a teenage winger who would become a Liverpool legend. He had gone along as a spectator because he wanted to watch a star-studded match but when League goalkeeper Alf Hobson of Chester was injured just before half-time Liddell was asked if he would go on as substitute. Hobson had been a late replacement for Frank Swift who was unable to get military leave. Cullis's Molineux teammate Tom Galley went into goal and left-winger Alf Hanson dropped back to left-half. Within minutes Liddell had his name on the scoresheet to put the League 5-3 ahead. Cullis's goal had come early on to make it 2-2. Liddell recalled: "The spectators enjoyed a feast of goals as well as a brilliant display of football at its best largely because there was nothing at stake and every player did his utmost to entertain the paying customers."

Cullis was again skipper when England faced Wales at Nottingham, in a game that was a personal triumph for Charlton centre-forward Don Welsh who scored all four goals for the home nation in a 4-1 win. It was a new-look team that Cullis led out before a crowd of 13,000. There was no Matthews in this game and England fielded a new right-wing of Millwall's Fred Fisher, on the wing, and Maurice Edelston of Fulham at inside-right. Other newcomers were Sunderland 'keeper Johnny Mapson, Middlesbrough left-back George Hardwick, Tottenham left-half Vic Buckingham and Sheffield United inside-left Jimmy Hagan. A dozen years on and Cullis and Buckingham would be managers of Wolves and Albion respectively as they went neck and neck in an epic race for the First Division title. Dai Astley had a similar experience to that of Cullis on Boxing Day, 1939, arriving late for kick-off. His car was delayed in traffic so Bob Davies of Forest played for the first ten minutes until Astley, then playing for Blackpool, could be substituted. England led 2-0 at the break and eventually won convincingly despite fielding their six debutants. Albion's Dai Witcomb scored Wales's goal.

Teams at the City Ground, Nottingham, on Saturday, April 26, 1941:

England: Mapson (Sunderland); Bacuzzi (Fulham), Hardwick (Middlesbrough); Britton (Everton), Cullis (Wolves), Buckingham (Tottenham); Fisher ((Millwall), Edelston (Fulham), Welsh (Charlton), Hagan (Sheffield United), J Smith (Millwall).

Wales: Sidlow (Wolves); Hughes (Birmingham), Williams (Charlton); Burgess (Tottenham), Turner (Charlton), Witcomb (West Brom); Hopkins (Brentford), R Davies (Nottingham Forest), sub Astley (Blackpool) 10 mins, Perry (Doncaster), B Jones (Arsenal), Dearson (Birmingham).

With Hapgood back as skipper, England gained revenge for the defeat by Scotland at Newcastle when they won 3-1 at Hampden Park, where Cullis was the outstanding player, closely followed by his half-back partners Harry Goslin of Bolton and his old pal Joe Mercer. Newspapers were much smaller than in pre-war days and space was at a premium so the big game was allotted just a short single column story in the Glasgow Herald.

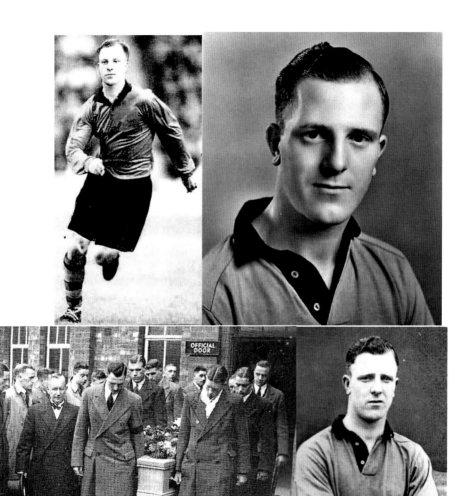

Top left: Starting out – the young Cullis in action for Wolves

Top right: An early portrait of a young player of high promise.

Bottom left: A sad day as Cullis helps to carry the coffin of goalkeeper Jimmy Utterson, who died suddenly in 1935.

Bottom right: An established player and leader of the Wolves pack.

Top left: Cullis spins the coin before kick-off in the FA Cup sixth round second replay at Hillsborough in March, 1937, watched by Sunderland skipper Raich Carter and referee George Twist. Sunderland won 4-0.

Top right: Determination on the face of Wolves' young centre-half in action.

Bottom left: A proud man in England shirt and cap. He played five times for his country in 1937-8.

Bottom right: England skipper Eddie Hapgood has just introduced the England side to the Duke of Kent before the game against the Rest of Europe at Highbury in 1938.

Top left: Ready for action –Wolves' skipper takes to the field.

Top right: Proud moment for Cullis as he introduces his team to the King George VI before the 1939 FA Cup final. Teddy Maguire is the man shaking hands with the monarch.

MIddle: Jock Anderson makes it 2-0 for Portsmouth in the 1939 FA Cup final with Cullis a worried onlooker as the shot beats Alex Scott.

Bottom right: Cullis heads clear during Wolves' ill-fated 1939 Wembley Cup Final.

Stan Cullis – The Wolves' Captain says:

"THE BEST HAT I'VE EVER HAD"

Smart, yet most comfortable and in just the shape I wanted. I shall certainly insist on a Ward's Hat next time and every time." writes S. Cullis.

Ward's Hats, famous throughout the world for comfort and smartness, are obtainable at all good hatters and outfitters.

WARD'S HATS

Nearly a Century of Hat Making

Top: The trilby hat was already a favoured Cullis headgear as this advertisement from the 1939 FA Cup final programme confirms.

Middle left: Captain of his country. Cullis introduces Deputy Prime Minister Clement Attlee to Jimmy Hagan before a wartime international at Wembley. On Hagan's right are Stanley Matthews and Raich Carter. **Middle right:** A legendary wartime England half-back line – Cliff Britton, Cullis and Joe Mercer.

Bottom: Looking forward to the 1946-7 season which would prove to Cullis's last as a player. Cullis joins in enthusiastically as ever during a training session on the Blackpool seafront. In the background is full-back Lawrie Kelly.

Top: The Wolves side who chased title glory in 1946-7. Back (left to right): manager Ted Vizard, Galley, McLean, Williams, Crook, Wright, trainer Jack Smith, secretary Jack Howley; front: Hancocks, Pye, Westcott, Cullis, Forbes, Mullen.

Bottom: Programme for the banquet staged to honour Cullis and Billy Wright, Wolves men who captained their country. Back at Wembley again, this time as manager, leading out his team for the 1949 FA Cup final.

Top: Cullis smiles as the Duke of Edinburgh jokes with Wolves skipper Billy Wright before the 1949 FA Cup final.

Middle: A memorable goal by Sammy Smyth at Wembley which clinched Cullis's first trophy, thanks to a 3-1 triumph over Leicester City in the FA Cup final.

Bottom: The 1949 FA Cup winners. Back (left to right) Crook, Pritchard, Williams, Shorthouse, Springthorpe; front: Hancocks, Smyth, Cullis, Wright, Pye, Dunn, Mullen.

Top: Do I have to drink it? Cullis does not seem to relish taking a sip out of the FA Cup at the banquet after their 1949 triumph despite encouragement from legendary broadcaster Brian Johnston and Billy Wright.

Bottom: Ready for the 1952-3 season, this squad included a new Cullis signing, John Taylor from Luton Town, but the inside-forward failed to make the grade at Molineux and soon moved on. Back row (left to right): Taylor, Flowers, Williams, Chatham, Gibbons, Sims, Slater, Wright; seated: trainer Joe Gardiner, Hancocks, Swinbourne, Shorthouse, Short, Wilshaw, Mullen, Cullis; in front: Pritchard, Smith, Stockin.

Top left: Planning tactics – Cullis busy in his office at Molineux.

Top right: Dennis Wilshaw who sometimes crossed swords with Cullis but was top scorer when the First Division title was won in 1954.

Bottom left: Watched by Billy Wright, Cullis addresses fans at Molineux after the Football League championship trophy had been presented following the second leg of the 1954 FA Youth Cup final.

Bottom right: A proud Cullis, with help from club secretary Jack Howley, at last has his hands on the Football League championship trophy.

There was still room enough to sing the praises of Cullis: "England were pleased to be on terms with Scotland at the end of the first half of the war charities match at Hampden Park, Glasgow, on Saturday, but after the interval there was a remarkable change in their fortunes. Then the 75,000 spectators were treated to a refreshingly vigorous display of half-back co-operation by Goslin, Cullis and Mercer, who began to carry the ball through to their forwards with devastating effect. This trio, in effect, won the game for England. Scotland had no dominating force to compete with Cullis, a really great centre half-back." Archie Muirhead endorsed the opinion in the Daily Express: "England has never had such a masterful half-back line in my recollection. Goslin, Cullis and Mercer, solid in defence and clever in attack, were the real match-winners."

Venters struck first for Scotland but Don Welsh fired England level just before the break. Len Goulden headed home a Wilf Mannion centre to make it 2-1 on 70 minutes and two minutes from time Welsh tricked his way past centre-half Dykes before firing home from 20 yards. Mannion had made his England debut in the game at Newcastle but with Newcastle's Ralph Birkett as his partner. Now he teamed up with Stanley Matthews and the pair formed a doubly dangerous right wing.

Teams at Hampden Park, Glasgow, on Saturday, May 3, 1941:

Scotland: Dawson (Rangers); Carabine (Third Lanark), Shaw (Rangers); Shankly (Preston), Dykes (Hearts), Brown (Hearts); Gillick (Rangers) Walker (Hearts), Smith (Rangers), Venters (Rangers), Caskie (St Mirren).

England: Swift (Manchester City); Bacuzzi (Fulham), Hapgood (Arsenal); Goslin (Bolton), Cullis (Wolves), Mercer (Everton); Matthews (Stoke), Mannion (Middlesbrough), Welsh (Charlton), Goulden (West Ham), D Compton (Arsenal).

For the final international of the season, against Wales at Cardiff, Goslin and Mercer were not available so Cliff Britton and Vic Buckingham formed the half-back line with Cullis as an England side showing six changes won 3-2. Maurice Edelston was originally named but chose to put club before country. He opted to play for Reading, the team managed by his father, Joe, and helped them land the London Cup with a 3-2 win over Brentford. In front of a 20,000 crowd in Cardiff, Wales rose to the occasion and took a two-goal lead thanks to goals from Fulham inside-forward Viv Woodward and 19-year-old Cardiff centre-forward Billy James. England rallied well and Don Welsh was again a scorer while there were two goals for newcomer Jimmy Hagan, the Sheffield United inside-right.

Teams at Ninian Park, Cardiff, on Saturday, June 7, 1941:

Wales: Sidlow (Wolves); Hughes (Birmingham), Turner (Charlton); Dearson (Birmingham), T Jones (Everton), Witcomb (West Brom); Rogers (Newcastle), Woodward (Fulham), James (Cardiff), B Jones (Arsenal), L Jones (Arsenal).

England: Bartram (Charlton); Bacuzzi (Fulham), Hapgood (Arsenal); Britton (Everton), Cullis (Wolves), Buckingham (Tottenham); Kirchen (Arsenal), Hagan (Sheffield United), Welsh (Charlton), Goulden (West Ham), Finch (Barnet).

It was in 1941 that Frank Butler of the Sunday Express was asked to name his six most valuable players and he put Cullis at the top, even ahead of Stanley Matthews who was at the height of his powers. The Stoke winger told Butler that Cullis was one of his motivations during training: "The thought of being on the end of a crunching tackle from Stan Cullis focused my mind totally."

Chapter 8   England's glory

The 1941-2 season would see Cullis make nine league appearances for Fulham and just one for Wolves as well as playing in the first three of England's five internationals. First, though, would come a trip to Northern Ireland where Cullis figured in the first two of three games the Army played in Belfast. An Ireland XI, including Cullis's old Molineux teammate Dave Martin, were beaten 4-1 with Jimmy Hagan grabbing a hat-trick and then the Ulster Army were defeated 6-1. Cullis's partners in the halfback line for both games were Everton duo Cliff Britton and Joe Mercer. The game Cullis missed brought a 5-0 win over the Irish League, Don Welsh scoring four times. Soon afterwards, the Britton, Cullis and Mercer trio were in action for the Army when they beat a Scottish XI 2-1 at Dumfries. The three were well attuned to each other's play and would in time go down as one of football's greatest half-back lines.

When Scotland came to Wembley in October, 1941, at the start of a new season, Goslin and Mercer teamed up once more with Cullis and the trio resumed where they had left off at Hampden five months earlier, though the score of 2-0 did not reflect England's superiority. Welsh scored his ninth goal in five internationals and Hagan, now teamed up on the left with Denis Compton, scored the other. Star performer, however, was diminutive blond-haired Middlesbrough inside-forward Wilf Mannion. Cullis was happy to play the role of a stopper centre-half for once in order to curb the menace of Rangers' big marauding centre-forward Jimmy Smith. Confirmation of the half-back line's role came in the Daily Express report of the game: "Mercer and Goslin so soon got the measure of the Scottish wings that they could take trips up among the forwards and Cullis so dominated the rear spaces that Hapgood was often tackling and feeding near the halfway line without danger to his goal." The second half was goalless but only thanks to the brilliance of Jerry Dawson in the Scotland goal. Before kick-off the teams had been introduced to guest of honour Winston Churchill. Perhaps the Prime Minister paused a little longer when he came to shake the hand of Cullis, recognising in the Wolves man the same steely determination to succeed.

Teams at Wembley Stadium, London, on Saturday, October 4, 1941:

England: Marks (Arsenal); Bacuzzi (Fulham), Hapgood (Arsenal); Goslin (Bolton), Cullis (Wolves), Mercer (Everton); Matthews (Stoke), Mannion (Middlesbrough), Welsh (Charlton), Hagan (Sheffield United), D Compton (Arsenal).

Scotland: Dawson (Rangers); Carabine (Third Lanark), Beattie (Preston); Shankly (Preston), Dykes (Hearts), McDonald (Celtic); Caskie (Everton), Walker (Hearts), Smith (Rangers), Wallace (Clyde), Williams (Clyde).

England were able to field almost an unchanged side when they took on Wales at St Andrew's three weeks later, Maurice Edelston coming in for the unavailable Mannion. The Welsh gave England a much tougher time on a ground which was a strange choice of venue as Birmingham had not been fully operational that season. Perhaps it was handier for Welsh fans and the game saw all tickets sold for an attendance restricted to 25,000. England led 2-0 at half-time thanks to goals from Jimmy Hagan after 14 minutes and Edelston a minute before the break. Wales hit back in the second but their only reward was an Idris Hopkins goal on 62 minutes. England kept Liverpool goalkeeper George Poland busy but Wales went closest when Don Dearson missed a penalty.

Teams at St Andrew's, Birmingham, on Saturday, October 25, 1941:

England: Marks (Arsenal); Bacuzzi (Fulham), Hapgood (Arsenal); Goslin (Bolton), Cullis (Wolves), Mercer (Everton); Matthews (Stoke), Edelston (Fulham), Welsh (Charlton), Hagan (Sheffield United), D Compton (Arsenal).

Wales: Poland (Liverpool); Turner (Charlton), Hughes (Birmingham); Green (Charlton), T Jones (Everton), Witcomb (West Bromwich); Hopkins (Everton), James (Cardiff), Dearson (Birmingham), L Jones (Arsenal), Cumner (Arsenal).

On the same day Wolves, having resumed playing activities after the previous season's blank, managed their first win of the season after five defeats and a draw, beating Walsall 1-0 at Molineux thanks to a goal from Tom Galley. He and Dickie Dorsett were in the side as they were on Army leave.

Wolves colleague Frank Taylor was chosen with Cullis when the Army in England met the Army In Scotland at Ibrox, Glasgow, the following month. The Scots, who were beaten 3-1, included Andy Beattie at left-back and Matt Busby at right-half. Back in Aldershot a week later Taylor and Cullis were given a much busier afternoon by the RAF who, skippered by Eddie Hapgood, won 5-2.

Over 60,000 fans were at Wembley in January, 1942, when Cullis played in the third international of the season. There was some doubt whether the match would go ahead as it had been snowing for virtually four days. Proceeds of the match went to the Clementine Churchill Red Cross Aid to Russia Fund and the wife of the Prime Minister was guest of honour. The teams were presented to her and then she went to a microphone and announced to the crowd that her husband was flying home having signed the Atlantic Charter after a secret meeting with US President Franklin Roosevelt.

It was decided to play with snow left on the pitch and the lines marked out in blue. With Tommy Lawton available and Joe Mercer out because he had broken two fingers playing for Everton against Blackburn the previous Saturday, Don Welsh was conveniently switched from centre-forward to left-half as England won comfortably 3-0.

The crowd cheered loudly after Mrs Churchill's announcement and most of them were cheering again within a minute of the kick-off. Jimmy Hagan gave England a 50-second lead. Scoring for a third successive international, Hagan ran on to a Wilf Mannion pass and was too quick through the snow for the Scottish defence. England had to wait until the second half before Lawton in the 52nd and 67th minutes beat goalkeeper Jerry Dawson who had made several fine saves to keep his team in contention. First Lawton headed in a Denis Compton centre and then he nodded home a Stan Matthews corner. The Glasgow Herald reported: "On the whole the Scots were by no means disgraced but their movements were slow and indecisive compared with the fast swinging tactics of the English." Frank Butler in the Sunday Express said the Willingham-Cullis-Welsh half-back line was not as smooth working a machine as Goslin-Cullis-Mercer but added: "It was however more than good enough to hold up a rather subdued Scottish attack." In the final minute Scotland centre-forward Torry Gillick came off second best in a collision with Cullis and goalkeeper George Marks and had to leave the field on a stretcher. The diminutive Gillick was really a winger and would always be favourite to come off second best in a challenge with the England pair. He was catapulted into the air and was eventually carried from the field on a stretcher. He was taken to a Wembley hospital suffering from concussion and was detained for a few days before being declared fit to go home.

Teams at Wembley Stadium, London, on Saturday, January 17, 1942:

England: Marks (Arsenal); Bacuzzi (Fulham), Hapgood (Arsenal); Willingham (Huddersfield), Cullis (Wolves), Welsh (Charlton); Matthews (Stoke), Mannion (Middlesbrough), Lawton (Everton), Hagan (Sheffield United), D Compton (Arsenal).

Scotland: Dawson (Rangers); Carabine (Third Lanark), Beattie (Preston); Shankly (Preston), Dykes (Hearts), Busby (Liverpool); Caskie (Hibernian), Walker (Hearts), Gillick (Everton), Black (Hearts), Johnston (Rangers).

February brought more representative games as Cullis helped an Army XI beat the Belgian Army 4-0 at Aldershot. The Army were then held 1-1 by the RAF at the same venue a few days later. However, Cullis's season was about to come to an abrupt and painful halt. Head injuries had been a problem for him, but he had usually made a fairly quick recovery. Now he sustained an injury that would mean a lengthy spell on the sidelines. Playing for Fulham at Portsmouth in March, 1942, he was injured after 20 minutes and at hospital later was told he had broken his right fibia. Fulham had taken an early lead but trailed 2-1 when Cullis broke his leg. They finished 9-1 losers but, more important, the services of the influential centre-half were lost to his temporary club and to his country. Cullis missed the final two international games of the season, with Coventry City's George Mason playing at centre-half as England were beaten 5-4 by Scotland at Hampden Park, Bill Shankly hitting the winning goal, and 1-0 by Wales in Cardiff. It was the only occasion during the wartime programme that England lost successive internationals.

Not that Cullis would have been totally concerned with England's fortunes at Ninian Park. His attention was probably also focused on the Hawthorns where on the same day Wolves beat Albion 4-1 in the first leg of the League War Cup semi-final. A 3-0 win at Molineux a week later in the second leg ensured a final date with Sunderland. Tom Galley had taken over the captaincy as well as the centre-half place and it was he who received the trophy as Wolves won the two-leg final thanks to a 2-2 draw at Roker Park and a 4-1 win at Molineux. Major Buckley had two more-than-useful guest players in his line-up – Cullis's England teammate Frank Broome and Manchester United's Wolverhampton-born forward Jack Rowley, who scored twice in the second leg.

When he had recovered fitness after his broken leg injury Cullis would manage only five games for Wolves in 1942-3 but turned out 17 times for Aldershot. In September, he again visited Belfast where the Army suffered a 3-2 defeat at the hands of an Irish FA side who included two legends of Irish football – Johnny Carey and Peter Doherty. Cullis then helped the Army beat the Army in Ulster 5-3 but stepped down when the Army beat the Irish League 3-2. Wolves winger Jimmy Mullen played in all three games.

While Cullis was available again, there was no immediate improvement in England's fortunes despite the arrival of a combination which would go down in football history. When half-back lines were a key feature in teams one of the best remembered was that formed by Cullis with Cliff Britton and Joe Mercer. Although they had several times played together for the Army and for Aldershot, the line's reputation is based on a mere eight games together for England. However, it is a reputation that has endured. The first of their England appearances together was not exactly a roaring success as it brought a goalless daw against Scotland at Wembley in October, 1942. Britton was by then 33 and Mercer 28 but still as effective as they had been in the Everton side who denied Cullis and Wolves the First Division title in 1939. There were also legendary names in the Scotland half-back line, Bill Shankly and Matt Busby, but their centre-half was a newcomer, 19-year-old Willie Corbett of Celtic. The Glasgow Herald confirmed: "It was at half-back the Scots, like their opponents, were best," and it said of Corbett: "His cool demeanour suggested he will retain the position for a long time." Sadly, that proved to be his only international appearance, his chances not helped by the fact he was serving in the Royal Navy which may have limited his availability.

In the nine-goal thriller at Hampden the previous season, both Jock Dodds of Scotland and Tommy Lawton of England had hit hat-tricks but it was a different story this time. "With Lawton and Dodds – two of the most dangerous centre-forwards of modern times – on either side, it seems incredible that no goals were scored," wrote W F Smith in the Daily Herald, adding that Cullis "gave as perfect a centre-half display as I ever expect to see."

Frank Butler in the Sunday Express said Cullis held Dodds as tightly as Corbett held Lawton, adding: "There is no doubt that Cullis has fully recovered from that broken leg." The menace of Stanley Matthews, a perennial scourge of the Scots, was curbed by Scotland's left-back and left half, Andy Beattie and Matt Busby. The winger did thread a pass through for Denis Compton to find the net but the referee said "No goal" much to England's annoyance. Compton was adamant afterwards that he had timed his run perfectly and was on side when Matthews made his pass.

Teams at Wembley Stadium, London, on Saturday, October 10, 1942:

England: Marks (Arsenal); Bacuzzi (Fulham), Hapgood (Arsenal); Britton (Everton), Cullis (Wolves), Mercer (Everton); Matthews (Stoke), Edelston (Fulham), Lawton (Everton), Hagan (Sheffield United), D Compton (Arsenal).

Scotland: Dawson (Rangers); Carabine (Third Lanark), Beattie (Preston); Shankly (Preston), Corbett (Celtic), Busby (Liverpool); Waddell (Rangers), Walker (Hearts), Dodds (Blackpool), Bremner (Arsenal), Liddell (Liverpool).

Three internationals without a win would become four when over 25,000 turned up at Molineux to see the game against Wales. It was a rare chance for home fans to see Cullis in action as he had played most of his club football with Aldershot that season. Another bonus for Wolves fans was the call-up of Jimmy Mullen to the England side for the first time, though he was part of strange-looking line-up. The selectors had dispensed with traditional inside forwards and instead fielded an attacking trio of Fulham's Ronnie Rooke, Tommy Lawton and Tottenham amateur Jackie Gibbons – all three of them centre-forwards. It began well enough with 19-year-old Mullen speeding down the left wing before providing a centre from which Lawton scored after 11 minutes. Frank Butler wrote in the Sunday Express: "The experiment of playing three centre-forwards did not come off. Matthews and Mullen were too often neglected."

England did not build on that early boost and it soon became clear that the lack of a creative midfielder like Hagan was having an effect. Horace Cumner equalised on 25 minutes and scored again after 57 minutes to give Wales a 2-1 win. It crowned an amazing recovery by the Arsenal man. A Royal Marine, he had been injured five weeks earlier when a hydrogen container on his ship exploded and badly burned him. He was not long out of hospital but declared himself fit to play. Molineux already had happy memories for Cumner as he made his league debut there as deputy to Cliff Bastin, early in the 1938-9 season, and scored the game's only goal to give the Londoners victory. It was only a month later that Cumner was awarded the first of three full caps for Wales.

Teams at Molineux Grounds, Wolverhampton, on Saturday, October 24, 1942:

England: Marks (Arsenal); Hardwick (Middlesbrough), Hapgood (Arsenal); Britton (Everton), Cullis (Wolves), Mercer (Everton); Matthews (Stoke), Rooke (Fulham), Lawton (Everton), Gibbons (Tottenham), Mullen (Wolves).

Wales: Poland (Liverpool); Turner (Charlton), Hughes (Birmingham); Dearson (Birmingham), T Jones (Everton), I Powell (Queen's Park Rangers); Hopkins (Brentford), Lucas (Swindon), Lowrie (Coventry), B Jones (Arsenal), Cumner (Arsenal).

If the Britton-Cullis-Mercer combination had looked useful at Wembley it was not so effective at Molineux. In the new year they would again line up against the Welsh and then it would be a different story. First, though, Cullis would play in a few more representative games. He and Jimmy Mullen were in the Army side who beat the Civil Defence 8-2 at Millwall. The Civil Defence forward line included W G Richardson of Albion and Arsenal legend Cliff Bastin. A week later Cullis helped an FA XI beat the RAF 4-3 at Stoke. That familiar centre-forward opponent, Jock Dodds, scored twice for the losers. The swashbuckling Blackpool striker was again a scorer at Leeds on Boxing Day when the Britton, Cullis and Mercer combination helped the Army beat the RAF 3-1. In January, the Met Police were the opposition when Cullis was invited to skipper his own side at Chichester. The Stan Cullis XI beat the Police 5-1. Soon afterwards Cullis played for Aldershot when they created a record by fielding a side composed entirely of guest players – Herod (Stoke), Marsden (Bournemouth), Royston (Plymouth), Britton (Everton), Cullis (Wolves), Taylor (Bolton), Geldard (Bolton), Hagan (Sheffield United), Lawton (Everton), Gallacher (Bournemouth), Cunliffe (Hull). It benefited Aldershot little – the team were beaten 6-3 by West Ham at Upton Park.

Scottish football fans got a taste of things to come when the Army in England beat the Army in Scotland 7-0 at Hampden Park in February, 1943. Britton, Cullis and Mercer were at the heart of things while Jackie Robinson and Dennis Westcott provided the goals, scoring four and three respectively. The Glasgow Herald said the Scots were "hopelessly outclassed" and the report added: "The game was too one-sided to be satisfying but the crowd of over 30,000 had compensation in the brilliant all-round display of the victors." Cullis captained the side and soon he would be skippering his country on a regular basis as successor to Eddie Hapgood.

Arsenal legend Hapgood was in the final stages of his RAF commission at Cosford, near Wolverhampton, and football would soon take second place to the demands of war. At 34 he was at the veteran stage but his selection for his 13th wartime international – against Wales at Wembley on February 27, 1943 – brought a significant landmark.

With 30 caps before the war, his total England appearances was then 43, passing the record set by Bob Crompton the Blackburn full-back between 1902 and 1914. Crompton's caps total was many years later amended to 41 after one of the games he played in was no longer recognised as a full international. This did not happen until well after Billy Wright had also been given a presentation by the FA to mark his 43rd game for England.

The Wales game proved a testing one for Cullis even though England won 5-3. He was up against Coventry City centre-forward George Lowrie, who was quite a handful and scored three times. Fortunately his opposite number, Wolves man Dennis Westcott, was also on form and also grabbed a hat-trick, Raich Carter scoring the other England goals. This proved to be Hapgood's farewell England appearance.

Teams at Wembley Stadium, London, on Saturday, February 27, 1943:

England: Marks (Arsenal); Bacuzzi (Fulham), Hapgood (Arsenal); Britton (Everton), Cullis (Wolves), Mercer (Everton); Matthews (Stoke), Carter (Sunderland), Westcott (Wolves), Hagan (Sheffield United), D Compton (Arsenal).

Wales: Poland ((Liverpool); Turner (Charlton), Hughes (Birmingham); Dearson (Birmingham), T Jones (Everton), I Powell (Queen's Park Rangers); Hopkins (Brentford), Lucas (Swindon), Lowrie (Coventry), B Jones (Arsenal), Cumner (Arsenal).

Two months after the game against Wales, Cullis's status as successor to Hapgood was confirmed when he was named captain for the return game with Scotland which turned out to be a stark contrast to the Wembley stalemate. It also turned out to be Cullis's most painful international appearance. Thousands who had trudged to Mount Florida, the Glasgow area where Hampden Park is situated, were disappointed as the gates were closed half an hour before kick-off. The official attendance of 104,000 was the highest for a wartime game up to that date and it was reported that many more fans had managed to scale the stadium walls to get inside. All this when the police had originally set a limit of 75,000. The Scottish fans were worked up into a fervour but England deflated the atmosphere in the best way possible – by scoring twice in the first nine minutes. This was how the Glasgow Herald saw it: "Scots' memories of Saturday's international are likely to be confined to the scenes reminiscent of pre-war enthusiasm which were witnessed before and after the Scotland v England match at Hampden. The Boys' Brigade display and the usual ceremonies raised the enthusiasm of the huge crowd, setting the stage for what might have been a memorable international. Scots, however, will prefer to forget the complete eclipse of their side in the game itself in which the dominance of the better-balanced and smarter English team stifled the famous 'roar' almost from the start. England were by no means flattered by their 4-0 victory."

What was not in that match report was any reference to an incident which left Cullis briefly in agony. As the players lined up for a free kick just outside the England penalty area, a Scotland player grabbed Cullis where it hurts and the centre-half collapsed. He was carried to the touchline while his teammates protested to referee Peter Craigmyle but the culprit got away with it, for the rest of the game at least. Cullis, recalling the incident many years later, said: "I was standing in the wall when this big forward backed into me. Suddenly he reached behind him . . . and grabbed. I must have leapt two feet in the air. No, I mean it, it was serious. I had to wear a special bandage for two years after that, from morning until night." After the game, Cullis was interviewed by both Scottish FA and Football Association officials and his torn shorts were handed over as a prime piece of evidence. It transpired that the culprit was Clyde's South African-born centre-forward Dougie Wallace and he was told by the Scottish FA that he would never be chosen for his country again – and so it proved.

A spectator at the game was a 12-year-old Malcolm Finlayson who was not aware of the incident until chatting to Cullis many years later. Cullis told him how he had chased after Wallace for the rest of the game, trying to exact some retribution. Not blessed with a great turn of speed in normal circumstances, Cullis had been slowed down even more by his injury and never did manage to clobber his assailant. Little did Finlayson know, as he watched Cullis in action, that 13 years later the man at the centre of England's defence would sign him from Millwall to be successor to goalkeeper Bert Williams in the Wolves side. The Wallace incident went unnoticed by Finlayson but he was impressed by Cullis: "What I remember about that game was that he was dribbling away in the penalty area and playing all these short balls. He would have crucified Billy Wright or Bill Slater if they had done that for Wolves."

England were off to a flying start when Raich Carter scored from 15 yards after only three minutes. The inside-right struck again after nine minutes and the game was virtually over. There were a couple of scares for the visitors, Willie Waddell and Alex Venters hitting post and bar respectively. Cullis's clubmate Dennis Westcott made it 3-0 five minutes into the second half and Denis Compton grabbed the fourth goal four minutes later to clinch England's biggest win on Scottish soil since the sides had staged the world's first ever international in 1872. It was the first occasion the Compton brothers had appeared together in England colours, full-back Leslie joining left-winger Denis.

Teams at Hampden Park, Glasgow, on Saturday, April, 17, 1943:

Scotland: Dawson (Rangers); Carabine (Third Lanark), Shaw (Rangers); Shankly (Preston), Young (Rangers), Kean (Hibernian); Waddell (Rangers), Buchan (Blackpool), Wallace (Clyde), Venters (Rangers), Liddell (Liverpool).

England: Swift (Manchester City); Hardwick (Middlesbrough), L Compton (Arsenal); Britton (Everton), Cullis (Wolves), Mercer (Everton); Matthews (Stoke), Carter (Sunderland), Westcott (Wolves), Hagan (Sheffield United), D Compton (Arsenal).

Despite his injury Cullis was able to play for the Army when they were held 2-2 by the RAF at Stamford Bridge where the airmen's powerful forward line included Stanley Matthews, Raich Carter, Ted Drake and Peter Doherty. Britton and Mercer were alongside Cullis but their opponents had a more-than-useful middle line in Stoke's Frank Soo, Arsenal's Bernard Joy and Spurs' Ronnie Burgess.

England were not as impressive as they had been at Hampden when they played their return match with Wales at Cardiff, and were held 1-1. The menace of Matthews was kept in check by that tenacious Birmingham full-back Billy Hughes. Cullis again had a busy afternoon against Lowrie who was on target again to give the home side the lead after just eight minutes. The centre-forward was close several times later in the game but Frank Swift made some acrobatic saves. Unexpectedly in the opposite goal was a Cullis clubmate, Cyril Sidlow, brought in when George Poland was laid low by influenza. Sidlow took his opportunity well and stopped everything that came his way until the equaliser eight minutes from time, another Wolves man, Dennis Westcott, being put through by Jimmy Hagan and firing home from 20 yards. Poland's illness proved costly as Sidlow remained first choice for Wales in subsequent wartime games.

Teams at Ninian Park, Cardiff, on Saturday, May 8, 1943:

Wales: Sidlow (Wolves); Lambert (Liverpool), Hughes (Birmingham); Dearson (Birmingham), T Jones (Everton), I Powell (Queen's Park Rangers); A Powell (Leeds), Murphy (Bradford City), Lowrie (Coventry), B Jones (Arsenal), Cumner (Arsenal.

England: Swift (Manchester City); Hardwick (Middlesbrough), L Compton (Arsenal); Britton (Everton), Cullis (Wolves), Mercer (Everton); Matthews (Stoke), Carter (Sunderland), Westcott (Wolves), Hagan (Sheffield United), D Compton (Arsenal).

England had fielded an unchanged side for the first time in a wartime game and, in contrast to the selection process of peacetime football, the national side were being run like a club side, their "manager" being Stanley Rous, secretary of the Football Association, with Cullis acting as his assistant.

Rous testified to the effectiveness of the arrangement: "Picking the team was no problem. There were many very fine players in the game and I had my own ideas who should play – and if I had doubts then the captain and the senior and more experienced professionals were there to be asked." Joe Mercer confirmed Rous's view: "Throughout the war, players played for the team, not to please the selection committee. We often knew immediately after one game which of us would be playing in the next. Mr Rous would talk to whoever was captain, usually Stan Cullis or later myself, and then say who he wanted for the next game. It may sound a bit casual but it gave us all a feeling we were being dealt with by someone who knew us, not by a committee of people we might never see."

The success of the England team with Rous their manager in all but name and Cullis as his first lieutenant ought to have signposted the way to run the national team. However, even after the appointment of Walter Winterbottom as coach after the war, the FA would continue with a selection committee and there was never going to be any continuity with that system. Winterbottom did his best to try to introduce it but it would not be until the appointment of Alf Ramsey that the England team had a manager in the true sense of the word. Cullis talked about it in Brian James's book, England v Scotland, saying: "Not only did we have fine players, but we saw an awful lot of each other. These same players, or most of them, played together several times a week – for the units and the regiments, the division, the corps, the Army – as well as for England. Without quite realising what we were doing, I suppose, we built an international side like a club team and that was a very important part of the success. It has never ceased to amaze me that we did not carry this on after the war, that we went back to the old way of having a selection committee chopping and changing. It wasn't that they didn't know, they had been told the value of the system we had stumbled on by accident because of the war. It was a great opportunity lost."

Raich Carter, who served in the RAF along with George Hardwick, Eddie Hapgood, Frank Soo and Stanley Matthews, also highlighted the value of the fact England were drawing their side mostly from two sources – the Army and the RAF: "We were turning out together – mostly the same players – far more frequently than we had ever been able to do in internationals. We became used to one another's play, developed into a team working together and our standard improved immeasurably. The same thing was happening in the Army where Swift, Britton, Cullis, Mercer, Compton and Lawton were playing regularly. Thus when the England team for internationals was selected, it was drawn half and half from the RAF and the Army. It was a question of merging these two halves together instead of eleven individuals from clubs all over the country. The result was that the England team of this period was in my opinion one of the best ever sides."

Chapter 9   Trio triumphant

It says much for the Welshmen that they had got the better of England over their previous four matches – two wins and a draw – but they would get a rude awakening in the first international of the 1943-4 season.

Britton, Cullis and Mercer were playing most of their club football with Aldershot during the 1943-4 season which must have helped develop an understanding that was transferred to the international field. However, Mercer was not available because of service duties when the Army side lost 4-2 to Ireland in Belfast. Don Welsh deputised for Mercer alongside Cullis and Britton and things looked to be going well when the Army led 2-1 in the second half. Then Leeds winger David Cochrane had a purple patch and his hat-trick gave the Irish a rousing win. Mercer was also unavailable for the season's opening international – against Wales at Wembley. Frank Soo of Stoke took his place in a side who were just too good for their opponents this time, winning 8-3, Cullis having a big say in the game plan that brought victory. This was how he explained it:

"As captain I had quite a big say in strategy then because there was no manager. I heard before the game that Wales were going to put two men on Stanley Matthews. As a result I decided we would attack on the left through Denis Compton instead of on the right through Stan. We won handsomely but the newspapers gave me a right rollicking and asked how I'd dared treat Stanley Matthews like that. They insisted the spectators had gone to watch Matthews, not me, and demanded that I be forced to give up the captaincy. Then I had a letter from Stanley Rous which said 'You will remain as captain'. It was nice to know I had the backing of the people that really mattered."

Interestingly, Matthews was not in on the plan as he explained in his autobiography Feet First Again: "If Stan had made any pre-match plan to starve me that day he certainly did not confide his secret to me. Cullis was one of the best skippers I ever played under. He gave the whole team a superiority complex before we went on the field. It was almost as good as starting the game with a goal in hand and whatever tactics he chose were OK by me." Frank Butler summed up the fans' frustration, writing in the Sunday Express: "Biggest surprise – and disappointment to an 80,000 record-breaking wartime Wembley crowd – was England's 'Starve Matthews' policy as counter-blow to the Welsh plan to crowd out the Wizard of the Dribble. Cullis considered the tactics completely fooled the Welsh defenders. 'With Hughes and Burgess watching Stan all the time, Carter, Welsh and Hagan had tons of room in which to move. Result was the Welsh half-backs had no time to help their attack.'"

The match was also notable for a substitution forced upon Wales in the first half when Ivor Powell was injured. The Welsh did not have a reserve available but England did – Stanley Mortensen. So the Blackpool goalgetter became an honorary Welshman for the day, running to the dressing room to change out of his uniform and don the Wales colours. Mortensen did not get his name on the scoresheet but Cullis could not prevent Lowrie having a say in the proceedings. He scored twice to take his total to six goals in three games against England. Charlton centre-forward Don Welsh scored three of England's goals, there were two each for Raich Carter and Jimmy Hagan and one for Compton.

Teams at Wembley Stadium, London, on Saturday, September 25, 1943:

England: Roxburgh (Blackpool); Scott (Arsenal), Hardwick (Middlesbrough); Britton (Everton), Cullis (Wolves), Soo (Stoke); Matthews (Stoke), Carter (Sunderland), Welsh (Charlton), Hagan (Sheffield United), D Compton (Arsenal).

Wales: Sidlow (Wolves); Lambert (Liverpool), Hughes (Birmingham); Dearson (Birmingham), T Jones (Everton), I Powell (Queen's Park Rangers) sub Mortensen (Blackpool); A Powell (Leeds), Murphy (Bradford City), Lowrie (Coventry), Burgess (Tottenham), Cumner (Arsenal).

The match provided a lone England appearance for goalkeeper Alex Roxburgh a full-time fireman in Blackpool. He had impressed just a couple of weeks earlier when he kept goal for a Civil Defence side against an RAF side who included Matthews, Raich Carter, Ted Drake and Mortensen. Even though he conceded six goals (Carter 4 Mortensen 2), Roxburgh made save after save to keep the result down to 6-0. Roxburgh had played for Blackpool in the last full season before the war.

Three weeks after the Wales game came the match which really cemented the Britton-Cullis-Mercer legend. They were supreme as Scotland were blown away at Maine Road, 8-0 – the biggest margin of victory over the Auld Enemy. Despite his three goals against Wales, Welsh made way for Tommy Lawton and what looked a surprise decision was fully vindicated. It took 14 minutes for England to open the score, through Jimmy Hagan, but by half-time they led 5-0 thanks to a Lawton hat-trick and a goal from Raich Carter. England seemed to ease up in the second half but Lawton scored his fourth, Hagan his second and even the eternal provider, Stanley Matthews, got on to the scoresheet. The winger beat several players in a run from the halfway line before rounding the goalkeeper to tap the ball home. It was a triumph for England and the Glasgow Herald report recognised that: "England gave a superb display as a team and as individuals. They bewildered the Scots by inter-changing positions without the slightest weakening of team craft. Matthews, the Stoke outside-right, was again 'the terror of the Scots'. He had a hand in nearly all the goals.

"He dribbled, swerved and outpaced the Scots' defence and had the 60,000 crowd in a ferment of excitement, and capped the afternoon's wizardry by scoring the best goal of the game. Scotland were outclassed and the players seemed to know it. They had none of the English qualities – experience, craft and pace. In physique, too, the team was no match." Not one often for superlatives, Cullis reckoned: "This was the finest football I have ever seen."

That view was confirmed by Frank Butler in the Daily Express: "It is unlikely that when the war is over these wartime internationals will be given official recognition but the fact remains that while in the last war international football was abandoned, in this war England has produced perhaps its finest team of all time." Butler also provided confirmation that the "starving" of Matthews had been a one-off plan by Cullis to beat the Welsh: "Unofficial and untrue rumours had it that there was jealousy among the players. This suggestion was blown sky high on Saturday when Matthews was waited on by the other ten players, including Swift, the goalkeeper, who often threw the ball to Matthews's feet."

Teams at Maine Road, Manchester, On Saturday, October 16, 1943:

England: Swift (Manchester City); Scott (Arsenal), Hardwick (Middlesbrough); Britton (Everton), Cullis (Wolves), Mercer (Everton); Matthews (Stoke), Carter (Sunderland), Lawton (Everton), Hagan (Sheffield United), D Compton (Arsenal).

Scotland; Crozier (Brentford); Carabine (Third Lanark), Miller (Hearts); Little (Rangers), Young (Rangers), Campbell (Morton); Waddell (Rangers), Gillick (Everton), Linwood (St Mirren), Walker (Hearts), Deakin (St Mirren).

The injury Cullis suffered playing for Wolves against Everton at Goodison Park five years earlier came back to haunt him when he played for the Army in England against the Army in Scotland on the same ground. It was a case of déjà vu on December 4, 1943, when he was carried from the field on a stretcher. He had been struck in the throat by a shot from Jock Airlie just before half-time and was unable to carry on. Cullis recalled in his autobiography, All For The Wolves: "I was standing on almost the identical piece of turf where I had collided with Bentham. Again I was carried off with even more serious consequences for I spent five days on the danger list in a Liverpool hospital and, altogether, I was on my back for nearly a fortnight." It was yet another warning and Cullis would eventually have to take notice. The English Army side included seven men who figured in England's big win in Manchester but the Scots looked like producing an upset when Aberdeen's South African winger Bill Strauss gave them a first-half lead and Bury inside-left Archie Livingstone's shot, diverted in by Les Compton, made it two in the second half. However, Tommy Lawton struck for the English soldiers with ten minutes to go and in the last few seconds Jack Balmer of Liverpool made the final score 2-2. Balmer would figure prominently in the Cullis story four years later.

Around the same time that Cullis was recovering from his injury there was a report in the Daily Express aimed at quashing rumours of Wolves boss Frank Buckley moving to Notts County. He told the paper: "I am not interested. I am under contract here." The paper reckoned Buckley had been on £1,500 a year in 1938 but that fee had been substantially increased, probably to £2,500. Buckley was still going about his business of running the club and had signed Emelio Aldecoa, a Spanish youngster who had been at Molineux that season. Despite the denials, the wheels were in motion to lure Buckley away and in March, 1944, came confirmation that the man who had made Wolves a football force was off after nearly 17 years.

There were over a hundred applications for the Wolves vacancy. Cullis was not among them but there is every reason to suppose that it had occurred to the Wolves board that he would be an ideal candidate, steeped in the traditions Buckley had established and an ideal man to continue the good work that, before the war, had made the club the talk of English football. For the moment, those thoughts were banished and the club turned to Queen's Park Rangers boss Ted Vizard. As a winger for Bolton and Wales, he had been a fine player before turning to management with Swindon Town in 1933. He had not made any great impact with the Wiltshire club before switching to QPR in 1939.

Just before 1943 ended had come the news that Lieutenant Harry Goslin had been killed in action with the Central Mediterranean forces. Goslin was serving with the 53rd Field Regiment Royal Artillery in Italy. He was wounded by shrapnel and wood after a mortar bomb exploded in the tree which he had made his observation point. The Bolton half-back had three times been in the same England side as Cullis during the war and was aged 35. He was the Bolton skipper and had made his debut for them in 1930.

Cullis had recovered from his Goodison injury by the new year and joined Britton and Mercer in an FA XI who met the RAF at Bristol. On this occasion they found Ted Drake and Stanley Mortensen a lively strike force as the airmen ran out 4-2 winners. Both were on target while Brentford winger Leslie Smith scored twice. Eddie Hapgood was named skipper of the FA side as the game was in his home city but he was given a harrowing afternoon by Smith who was deputising for Stan Matthews. Typical of the hit-and-miss nature of wartime matches, three of the FA side only just made the start. Cullis and Joe Mercer missed their train in London and Maurice Edelston failed to board it at Reading. FA trainer Arthur Rowe, the former Spurs defender, volunteered to play despite his dodgy knee as efforts were made to find replacements. Fortunately, the missing trio arrived just in time to make the kick-off. Spurs keeper Ted Ditchburn was a star performer for the RAF side and his display was good enough to earn him an England call-up to face Scotland in the first international of the new year. It was a similar story for Smith whose sparkling performance earned him the left-wing spot in preference to Denis Compton.

Cullis, who that season again played 17 times for Aldershot and just twice for Wolves, soon forgot that rare taste of defeat at Bristol and turned his attention to the clash with Scotland. Matt Busby was back to skipper the Scots, at Wembley in February, 1944, but the result was little better than at Maine Road. England won 6-2 before a crowd of 80,000 who included the King and Queen, Princess Elizabeth, King Haakon of Norway and General Montgomery. There was little indication at half-time that another rout was on the cards. The score was 1-1, Jock Dodds having equalised a Jimmy Hagan goal but the turning point came three minutes into the second half when West Ham's Archie Macaulay tried to head clear a Les Smith shot but merely deflected the ball past Joe Crozier. That sparked England into life and goals followed from Lawton, Hagan, Raich Carter and Joe Mercer with the only goal of his international career. Dodds scored a second for Scotland in the closing minutes. According to the Glasgow Herald, once in the lead England then played: "some of the devastating football, with brilliant team-work, which characterised them in recent years." It added: "The Scots played with unstinted courage but class told." The Yorkshire Post report confirmed that once back in the lead England "for a long period excelled all round." It added: "This was attributable largely to the manner in which the England half-backs, ably led by Cullis, took control of the play." Clearly, Cullis was in charge of a special side.

Teams at Wembley Stadium, London, on Saturday, February 19, 1944:

England: Ditchburn (Tottenham); Scott (Arsenal), Hardwick (Middlesbrough); Britton (Everton), Cullis (Wolves), Mercer (Everton); Matthews (Stoke), Carter (Sunderland), Lawton (Everton), Hagan (Sheffield United), L Smith (Brentford).

Scotland: Crozier (Brentford); Kilmarnock (Motherwell), Stephen (Bradford); Macaulay (West Ham), Kirton (Stoke), Busby (Liverpool); Flavell (Airdrie), Stenhouse (St Mirren)), Linwood (St Mirren), Dodds (Blackpool), Duncannon (Rangers), Caskie (Everton).

After conceding 14 goals to England in two games, the Scots were hoping to restore some pride when the teams met for a third time that season, but now on Scottish turf. Wolves full-back Frank Taylor joined his skipper in the team at Hampden Park and he and fellow full-back, Leslie Compton, were given quite a grilling in the opening 20 minutes. Cullis and goalkeeper Frank Swift kept the Scots at bay until Jimmy Caskie's weakly-hit shot bounced and swerved into the net to set off the famous Hampden Roar from the 133,000 fans. The noise was soon silenced when, two minutes later, Raich Carter slipped a Swift goal-kick to Tommy Lawton and when he was 20 yards from goal the centre-forward unleashed an unstoppable shot. A few minutes later Lawton struck again and Carter's long range effort made it three goals in the space of 15 minutes.

It was a ding-dong and sometimes heated struggle in the second half as Lawton recalled: "Les Compton and Taylor who started the match with a big 'if' against their names, stood up well, while Cullis was at his brilliant best. Stan likes a fight, but he too must have had his fill long before the final whistle." Dodds did just once get the better of Cullis. As they jumped to a Caskie centre he managed to divert the ball via Cullis's head into the net. Tommy Walker headed against the bar but England held out to win 3-2. A report in the Glasgow Herald noted: "The Scots also made the mistake of playing too sedulously to their centre-forward when it was obvious that Dodds had not the guile to circumvent the English captain Cullis." The report added: "Swift played a grand game in England's goal; his backs were often rescued by the generalship of Cullis and Mercer." If you have not a dictionary at hand, sedulously means diligent in application or persevering!

Frank Butler was even more lavish with his praise of Cullis in his Sunday Express report: "Outstanding for England was their skipper Stan Cullis, playing the game of his life, holding Dodds for 90 minutes. Cullis's performance was all the better when it is remembered he had suggested he should drop out of the team. He had been inoculated in the left arm and had been ill with vaccine fever. He feared the arm would be knocked." It was a rough, tough encounter as confirmed by Butler: "It appeared to me the Scots were carried away by that Hampden roar – a war cry if ever there was. To put it mildly, they got 'stuck in' to their opponents in the second half. When Stan Matthews was sent sprawling, Horatio Carter's indignation led him to say something to a Scottish player. The crowd, there to see Scotland win, barracked Carter from then on and this great player was put out of his stride. Then Leslie Smith was toppled over but Leslie was so upset he pushed McDonald away. An old Scottish international left the ground with me and was shaking his head. 'Scottish football has deteriorated,' he said. 'It used to be Scotland who claimed to play the best football.'"

Teams at Hampden Park, Glasgow, on Saturday, April 22, 1944:

Scotland; Crozier (Brentford); McDonald (Celtic), Stephen (Bradford); Macaulay (West Ham), Baxter (Middlesbrough), Busby (Liverpool); Delaney (Celtic), Walker (Hearts), Dodds (Blackpool), Duncannon (Rangers), Caskie (Everton).

England: Swift Manchester City); L Compton (Arsenal), Taylor (Wolves); Soo (Stoke), Cullis (Wolves), Mercer (Everton); Matthews (Stoke), Carter (Sunderland), Lawton (Everton), Hagan (Sheffield United), L Smith (Brentford).

Football seemed to matter little when it was learned of the tragedy that had befallen winger Jimmy Delaney, the man who had given Cullis's clubmate Taylor a testing afternoon. Butler explained: "Poor Delaney, while he was staging a great comeback, his 18-month-old son was dying. His sister phoned a message which Jimmy received at the end of the match and an hour after he got home the baby died."

With Cliff Britton unavailable, Frank Soo was drafted into the team but Britton was back two weeks later when England met Wales at Ninian Park, and this would be a final outing for the famous half-back trio he formed with Cullis and Mercer. The match had fired the enthusiasm of Welsh fans, hoping to see the man of the moment, Stanley Matthews, and they were far from pleased when it was learned he would not be in the England side. He had been given permission to play for Blackpool against Aston Villa in the second leg of the League North Cup final. There was still a record Welsh wartime gate of 50,000 and Wales proved a tougher proposition than the Scots. They were eventually beaten 2-0, Lawton scoring after 27 minutes with a typical snap shot from 20 yards and Les Smith adding a second seven minutes after half-time.

Cullis was a busy man, particularly in the first half but earned praise from the Sports Editor of the Daily Worker: "Cullis as usual was masterful for the visitors. It was his grip on Lowrie when Wales had the advantage in the opening half that prevented Wales taking the lead." The game saw a first international call-up, as Matthews's deputy, for Albion winger Billy Elliott. Also making his international debut was Wolverhampton-born forward Jack Rowley who had spent much of the previous season on loan to Wolves during which time he remarkably scored all eight goals when Wolves beat Derby County 8-1. As for Matthews, his presence in the Blackpool side could not prevent them losing 4-2 before 55,000 at Villa Park to give Villa the cup 5-4 on aggregate.

Teams at Ninian Park, Cardiff, on Saturday, May 6, 1944:

Wales: Sidlow (Wolves); Barnes (Arsenal), Lambert (Liverpool); Dearson (Birmingham), R Davies (Nottingham Forest), Burgess (Tottenham); Hopkins (Brentford), Lucas (Swindon), Lowrie (Coventry), W Davies (Watford), Morris (Birmingham).

England: Ditchburn (Tottenham); L Compton (Arsenal), Scott (Arsenal); Britton (Everton), Cullis (Wolves), Mercer (Everton); Elliott (West Bromwich), Carter (Sunderland), Lawton (Everton), Rowley (Manchester United), L Smith (Brentford).

So ended the international career of Stanley Cullis, his final season as England skipper seeing all five games won. His posting to Italy meant it unlikely he would be able to play for his country. Frank Butler reported in the Daily Express: "The odds are heavily against the finest footballing centre half this country has had for years being available for the coming season." The Daily Mirror, under a headline "All-star soccer team breaks up", said that Cliff Britton, Jimmy Hagan and Leslie Compton were likely to be out of contention and the report added: "Stan Cullis, centre-half and captain – the man around whom this all-star team was built – will be hardest to replace for Cullis has been the pivot in every sense of the word."

In ten wartime games as England's skipper Cullis had led his team to eight wins and only one defeat. He had missed only four of the wartime games played by England up to that stage and his wartime appearance total of 20 would be bettered only by Stan Matthews (24) and Joe Mercer (23). More important, Cullis had been given a good measure of responsibility by Stanley Rous and had warmed to the task of motivating players and deciding upon tactics. He would no doubt have taken much pleasure in seeing the captaincy stay in Ellesmere Port, so to speak, when the following season it passed to Mercer.

During his wartime football career, Cullis had helped England play some superb football and though the games may not have been full internationals, they should not be undervalued. The great Bill Shankly, who faced England seven times in wartime games, had no doubts: "This was a great England team. They had wonderful players in the side and just as many waiting to get a game. Take the side that beat us 8-0 at Manchester. If I had been picking a team at the time from the best players in the country, I would have picked that same side. I wouldn't have picked myself to play against them – Scotland had no chance!"

While England had many great players in the team – men like Hapgood, Cullis, Mercer, Matthews and Lawton – there was no star treatment. They certainly did not meet at a hotel before a game and have a coach laid on to take them to the ground, as Cullis testified: "You got there the best way you could. In other words, it was left to you to decide how you would get to Wembley. Some players were lucky – they had friends who had a car. Others got the train. I can recall standing in a queue which was about a mile long from Wembley Stadium. The spectators who recognised us were nudging each other and informing their friends that so-and-so who'd been playing that day for England was having to take his turn in the queue. You waited the same as anybody else. It was pointed out that it was our responsibility to get to the ground and away from the ground and I wasn't conscious of any England players being very upset about having to stand in a queue to get back to London, for instance."

In September, 1944, there was news from Burma that Eric Stephenson, by then a major in the Gurkha Rifles, had been killed in action. The Leeds inside-forward had twice been in the same England side as Cullis before the war and was in the Army party, skippered by Cullis, who played those three games in France in early 1940.

Any chance of Cullis continuing playing for Wolves or England during the 1944-5 season was ended when the demands of the Army took precedence. He was promoted to Company Sergeant Major and, as the Allied invasion of Italy had been successful, was posted to Bari. Among his tasks was to organise a football team to play the Yugoslav Partizan side which had been handing out several defeats to the British forces. He was allowed to choose from throughout the forces which gave him access to such players as his old clubmate Bryn Jones and a 22-year-old Preston winger by the name of Tom Finney. Cullis duly produced the goods as the Yugoslavs were beaten 7-2 at Bari before a large crowd. He had tasted success in his first venture as a manager and in Italy were sown more of the seeds of a managerial career that would help him collect the trophies that had eluded him as a player.

Chapter 10 Frustrating finale

Cullis was able to make thirteen appearances for Wolves in the Football League (South) during the 1945-6 season. While the First Division was still on hold, the FA Cup was able to resume and ties were played on a two-leg basis. However, it was still all a question of which players were available at the time. Tom Galley, for instance, played centre forward and scored three goals as Lovells Athletic were beaten 8-1 at Molineux in the second leg of the first-round tie. There were also two goals in that game for Billy Wright who, at that stage of his career, was regarded as an inside-left. Cullis's only Cup appearance that season was in the first leg of the fourth round clash with Charlton when the Londoners won 5-2 at The Valley. The match was a testing one for him as Wolves survived the setback of an earlier goal by home winger Chris Duffy and led 2-1 at the break thanks to two goals from centre-forward Ray Chatham. Things looked good for the visitors, especially as England inside-forward Bert Brown was a passenger from the tenth minute. However, Brown came out for the second half like a man inspired and guided Charlton to an impressive win thanks to goals from Duffy, Les Fell, Bill Robinson and Arthur Turner.

Stan Halsey, in the Daily Express, said it was a "memorable and mighty Cup battle, a game of glittering football, astounding goals and exhausting excitement." He went on: "Smiling Stan Cullis rose above the game and swept his young team into a breathless attack on the Charlton goal. Every chance was taken at flashing speed and twice the Charlton crowd roared when centre-forward Chatham converted the tiniest openings into spectacular goals that swept away Duffy's early lead. Then the second half – no more the limping Brown but a Brown that scudded through the Wolves defence, ever with the ball at his feet. And Cullis? Something had happened. The mighty England centre-half was played almost to a standstill. Four times Wolves' young goalkeeper Williams was prostrate as the ball hit the back of the net and the Charlton victory rose into great certainty that crushed one of the fastest, cleverest sides to visit The Valley."

It emerged that Brown had been given an injection in his knee at half-time by trainer Jimmy Trotter and manager Jimmy Seed explained how they had made it a miserable day for Cullis: "Stan Cullis was too much for our centre-forward Turner. He's got the measure of any man in England has Cullis but not two men. At half-time I told inside-right Robinson to get up with Turner and stay there. Wolves' left-half Crook is young. He wouldn't dare take Stan's share of the field; he was not likely to poach his famous captain's territory and that's how it worked out. Cullis had two men against him and even he could not manage it." Halsey asked Wolves boss Ted Vizard what he thought about his team losing by three goals when they had played so well. "The more I think about it the less I have to say," was the manager's only comment

What Vizard did think about was Cullis's place in the side – and he dropped him. Roy Bicknell was named for the return leg four days later when Wolves were held 1-1 at Molineux and thus went out 6-3 on aggregate. The report in the Daily Express said: "Wolves supporters will never cease to wonder why Bicknell the reserve centre-half was preferred to Cullis." Ironically, Bicknell would make no further first-team appearances and would join Charlton a year later. Soon there was talk of Cullis linking up with his old boss Buckley at Notts County until Vizard was quoted in the Daily Express of February 8, 1946: "I have had a heart-to-heart with Cullis this morning and I see no reason why Cullis cannot settle down in Wolverhampton and be happy." Columnist Frank Butler commented: "The story about Notts County is a little off the beam because Frank Buckley, the County manager, is the first to realise that there is not enough gold in them thar Nottingham hills to buy the old England captain."

There is no smoke without fire, though, and Butler went on: "The Major did in fact make one of his rare journeys to Wolverhampton on January 9 when Lovells Athletic were playing in the second leg of the cup-tie. His idea was that Cullis should finish his playing career at Nottingham and then take over as Buckley's successor. Cullis should get into the managerial side of the game as soon as possible. Wolves can help him. If not this season, in the coming seasons."

County were not the only club eyeing up Wolves' skipper. He was also being wooed by Hull City – and he was tempted. They had an ambitious chairman in Harold Needler and had just moved to a new ground, Boothferry Park. The Tigers' manager, Ernest Blackburn, had been in charge for ten years but he had parted company with the club to become the first football sacking after the war. So Hull were looking for a new boss, someone young and ambitious who might not have managerial experience but had the football ability, character and presence to raise the profile of the club. Cullis was an ideal candidate. Needler wanted Cullis to be the club's manager and a meeting was arranged, after which Cullis informed Wolves chairman James Baker of the approach. In his autobiography, Cullis recalled that Hull had offered him "a handsome salary and a fine house." He added: "I was very tempted to accept the post. In fact, my mind was made up." Baker and his board were taken aback. Cullis was one man they did not want to lose, confirmation that they saw him as the future manager of Wolverhampton Wanderers. They asked him to meet them as a matter of urgency. While Vizard had brought some useful players to the club, he was considered not strong on discipline and there was a feeling among the directors that a tougher regime was needed to get the best out of the players and to weed out any bad influences in the dressing room. Cullis would fit the bill and the board would do their utmost to keep him at Molineux, knowing that one day he would take over the managerial reins.

Baker and his directors responded to news of Hull's approach with an offer to make Cullis part of the off-field set-up at Molineux after his playing days were over, which would no doubt be sooner rather than later. There must also have been a nod and a wink to Cullis that he would one day be boss. Whatever was said to Cullis it was sufficient to persuade him to tell Mr Needler: "Thanks – but no thanks!" Having failed to get Cullis, whom should Hull appoint as manager in 1946 but Major Buckley. He had stayed at Notts County for little over two years.

The injuries and knocks suffered when heading the heavy footballs used in his day must have taken their toll on Cullis. He seriously considered giving up the game. Cullis, however, decided to play at least one more season by which time he would be 30. Could Wolves resume where they had left off in that final pre-war season? That was the big question when the Football League resumed activities on August 31, 1946. With Buckley gone and Ted Vizard as manager, the club no longer had an autocratic figure at the head of affairs. Yet, once the war was over and a resumption of league football loomed, the Welshman, appointed in June, 1944, made some signings that would serve Cullis well in the latter's early years as a manager. First, in September, 1945, Vizard persuaded Walsall goalkeeper Bert Williams to come to Molineux, fending off the interest of Chelsea. Two more future legends arrived in May, 1946. Vizard paid a club record fee of £12,000 for Notts County centre-forward Jesse Pye who had scored for England in their win over Belgium in a Victory International at the start of the year. He also paid a bargain £4,000 to Walsall for Johnny Hancocks, the Oakengates-born little winger with the big shot. Already on the books were two players who had played in Victory and wartime internationals respectively, Billy Wright and Jimmy Mullen. They would prove to be two of the greatest contributors to the wonderful Molineux moments that lay ahead.

Given a last Army posting to Friedrisktad in Norway, Cullis was still able to play in Gothenburg in the opening match of Wolves' five-match Swedish tour in late June, 1946. Beaten 3-0 by a Gothenburg Alliance XI, Wolves did not create a good impression and a niggly game culminated in Dickie Dorsett being sent off. Having seen the ball cleared, Dorsett was running back up field when he collided with home defender Bertil Sernros, who then dropped to the ground. The referee had no hesitation in sending Dorsett off. Little did Dorsett know it but this was the beginning of the end of his Molineux career. Wolves' directors announced afterwards that Dorsett, who had played alongside Cullis in he 1939 FA Cup final, would not be allowed to play during the rest of the tour.

"The Pilgrim" was on tour with the team and it is a sign of the attitudes that prevailed in those days that – unbelievably – he was allowed to use the N word in his report, writing: "Cullis worked like a ****** and gave of his best but he was so hard-worked that he looked tired in the last quarter of an hour."

Afterwards Cullis returned to Norway while the tour saw Wolves beat Sundsvall 7-1, draw 2-2 with Gavie and lose 3-1 to Djurgarden. The final match brought a 3-2 win over Malmo, Ray Chatham scoring the winner nine minutes from time but there was more trouble for Wolves. Tom Galley was sent off though he appeared more sinned against than sinning. A Malmo player kicked him and Galley aimed a kick in retaliation but he alone was dismissed. Afterwards fans gathered outside the ground to jeer the Wolves players as their coach departed and stones were hurled at it. Director Arthur Oakley said at the banquet held later that evening: "On behalf of the club I apologise to the referee and linesmen." Alas for Wolves, it did not end there. The FA held an inquiry and instructed the club to write to their opponents apologising for the behaviour of their players, sending copies of the letter to the FA and to the British Consul General in Gothenburg. It was accepted that Galley's offence was trivial but Dorsett was given a 28-day suspension.

Unlike nine years earlier, there was no suggestion of a players' letter, orchestrated by Cullis, going to the FA to plead their case. The players just kept their heads down – they must have known that they had not brought much credit to their club.

Things looked good for Wolves as a gate of nearly 51,000 turned up at Molineux on the opening Saturday of the 1946-7 season and saw Arsenal hammered 6-1. Inside-right Jesse Pye hit a hat-trick on his First Division debut while centre-forward Dennis Westcott scored two, picking up where he had left off in 1939. It was a false omen and after a goalless draw at Grimsby Town Wolves lost four games in a row, Cullis being absent for three of them. It was the side's worst run of the season and this, as well as the faltering run-in was a key to why the First Division title eluded Cullis for a third season in a row. Dorsett played in the game at Grimsby but it would prove to be his last for Wolves. On September 16, he was transferred to Aston Villa where he would serve the remainder of his suspension. After the events in Sweden his days had been numbered as far as the Wolves hierarchy were concerned but Dorsett still had much to give. He was a Villa regular for seven seasons

One of the reasons for Cullis's absence from those early fixtures was to ensure he was fit to play in a game at the City Ground, Nottingham, that was effectively an England trial. Neil Franklin of Stoke seemed to have made the centre-half position his own in the national side, having played in all six Victory internationals in 1945-6 yet, somewhat surprisingly, Cullis was again in the selectors' thoughts for the first two full internationals since 1939 – against Northern Ireland and the Republic of Ireland. The Nottingham match saw Cullis and Billy Wright in an FA XI who drew 2-2 with a Combined XI, who had Johnny Hancocks at outside right. The FA XI's blushes were spared only by a late equaliser from Wilf Mannion in a match which also served as a testimonial for former Spurs and England inside-forward Willie Hall who had had to have his left leg amputated.

After the game the England selectors, Arthur Drewry, Wolves director Arthur Oakley and FA treasurer Harry Huband, retired to a hotel room in Nottingham and would later make no comment on what the England side would be. When a few days later they did announce the team, there was no place for Cullis, nor for Notts County's highly-rated Leon Leuty who had been centre-half in the Combined XI at the City Ground. The selectors, quite sensibly, stood by Neil Franklin with the only defenders among the reserves being Blackpool full-back Eddie Shimwell and Charlton half-back Don Welsh. It was now clear, if it had not been before, that Cullis's England career was at an end but the good news for Wolves was that Billy Wright would win the first of his 105 caps – against Northern Ireland in Belfast

Of the main contenders for the First Division title, Manchester United, the side managed by Cullis's wartime pal and Scottish rival Matt Busby, were off to a flyer, reeling off five wins in a row. Wolverhampton-born Jack Rowley, who had guested for Wolves several times during the war, scored in each of those five victories which included a 5-0 success over Liverpool at Maine Road, where United had to be based due to the wartime damage to Old Trafford. That setback did not deter Liverpool who promptly went on an unbeaten 12-match run which took them to the top of the table. What would prove a key signing for the Merseysiders had been made when manager George Kay paid Newcastle £12,500 for Albert Stubbins. The centre-forward, who had played in the Geordies' opening three games, arrived in time for Liverpool's fifth game of the season and scored on his debut, a 3-1 win at Bolton. Stubbins's arrival was timely as in the four games before that, Liverpool had been forced to play defender Bill Jones at centre-forward. Stubbins would form a lethal twin strikeforce with Jack Balmer, each scoring 28 league and Cup goals during a memorable season. Stubbins became a cult figure on Merseyside and has the unusual claim to fame of being the only footballer among the host of people on the iconic cover of the Beatles' Sergeant Pepper album.

Liverpool cemented their first place with a 4-2 home win over Arsenal but then got a double setback at the hands of rivals Blackpool and Wolves. A week after losing 3-2 to the Seasiders, Liverpool were knocked from top spot as Cullis and co silenced the vast majority of a 52,512 crowd at Anfield with a stunning 5-1 victory. Centre-forward Dennis Westcott scored four times, his goals coming before half-time. Jimmy Mullen added a fifth in the second half, with the home side's only reply a Jack Balmer penalty. "They had played perfect football and there was not one of them that did not look good enough to play for England," said a report in the Daily Mirror. The writer should have checked his facts, though, as full-back Angus McLean was Welsh and inside – left Willie Forbes Scottish. A week later Westcott repeated his four-goal feat when Bolton were beaten 5-0 at Molineux and the Wolves striker thus headed the First Division's top scorers with 22 goals, followed by Balmer on 18.

Cullis and his men then ploughed on at the top of the table with their only setback a 4-1 defeat against a struggling Brentford side at Griffin Park, where two goals in the first five minutes seemed to rattle Wolves in general and their centre-half in particular. Frank Butler in the Daily Express did not paint a very edifying picture: "That great player and captain Stan Cullis allowed himself to get involved in arguing with the referee and with Idris Hopkins of Brentford and his game suffered. It was the roughest match I have seen this season. I don't remember having seen so many deliberate fouls in one afternoon. Referee P W Poulter (Hemel Hempstead) can be criticised for not taking a firmer hand when the trouble started. There was continual booing – mostly directed against Cullis – and having seen several players kick each other after the whistle and others shaping up to each other in threatening stance I was surprised the referee did not take more drastic action."

The Brentford result was totally against the form book. After this win the relegation-bound Londoners won only one of their remaining 17 games and that against bottom-of-the-table Leeds. However, Wolves still topped the table. Then came the "Big Freeze". The severe winter of 1947 has gone down as one of the worst in history and, as it disrupted life throughout the country, it also meant the football season would be extended to the end of May, plus one final fixture in the middle of June. Wolves were without a game for three successive Saturdays in February but normal service resumed with a 1-0 win at Leeds and a 3-0 home win over Stoke and it looked certain that Cullis would bow out – if bow out he would – as captain of the champions of England. However, a week after the Stoke game, Cullis found himself in hospital.

In the game against Middlesbrough on the second Saturday in March, Cullis, for the umpteenth time in the game headed the sodden ball and was clearly in a daze afterwards. He stayed on until four minutes from time when Dennis Westcott equalised Harold Dobbie's goal to earn a 1-1 draw. Then Cullis collapsed and was carried off. He was unconscious for fifteen minutes but recovered sufficiently to join the team for the homeward train journey. However, he was clearly unwell and unfit to continue and so was taken to Sheffield Infirmary. Recalling the incident, Cullis said: "The ball had become heavy and covered with ice from the frozen pitch and, in the course of an exciting match, I was constantly heading it." At Sheffield he saw a specialist who had treated heavyweight boxer Bruce Woodcock and knew all about the damage that could be done by constant blows to the head. He did not mince his words and told Cullis that he could play on for a few years but it would be far wiser to give up. The Wolves skipper may not have quit immediately but he obviously took the advice on board. When eventually discharged, Cullis had missed two league games – a 2-0 home win over Charlton and a crucial 2-0 defeat at Sheffield United.

Stoke had stirred themselves after that Molineux defeat with an eleven-game unbeaten run which gave them a glorious chance of the title. Their ambitions were not helped, however, by the restlessness of the great Stanley Matthews, who eventually was granted his wish to join Blackpool. It was the last thing manager Bob McGrory needed at a crucial time in the season.

As so often happened in a league campaign, Easter was a vital period with teams playing three games in four days. Wolves were beaten twice and what looked like a one-horse race was suddenly heading for a photo finish. On the Saturday before Easter Day Wolves were beaten 3-1 by Manchester United at Maine Road before no fewer than 66,967 with left-winger Jack Rowley scoring twice and Dennis Westcott, inevitably, replying for Wolves. On Easter Monday, Cullis and co faltered again, this time against Derby County at the Baseball Ground, despite Westcott giving them the lead. Centre forward Jack Stamps scored both goals, one of them a penalty, in the Rams' 2-1 win. A Jesse Pye hat-trick helped Wolves gain revenge with a 7-2 win when the sides met again at Molineux the following day and it looked as though they were over a mere blip in their inevitable progress towards the title. Manchester United had enjoyed a six-point Easter with home and away wins over Leeds after the Wolves match. Stoke, too, collected maximum points, beating Huddersfield at home and Grimsby home and away.

Blackpool had spoiled Liverpool's holiday with a 3-2 win at Anfield, Stan Mortensen scoring twice, and the Seasiders were still in the picture but not real title contenders as they were running out of games. After the hectic Easter fixtures Wolves led the table having played 35 games and collected 48 points, followed by Blackpool (39-47), Manchester United (35-46), Stoke (35-44) and Liverpool (35-44).

Few would have predicted it, but Liverpool would drop only one more point in their remaining seven league games. First, though, they had to try to keep their Double hopes alive, having been held to a goalless draw in the FA Cup semi-final at Ewood Park, Blackburn, by Second Division promotion chasers Burnley. The replay on Saturday, April 2, attracted 72,000 to Maine Road and underdogs Burnley ushered out the Merseysiders thanks to a goal from centre-forward Ray Harrison. There was a ban on midweek games and the FA Cup took precedence over league fixtures. It just so happened that the game in Manchester was on the day Wolves were scheduled to meet Liverpool in the league at Molineux. Having hammered seven goals past Derby County, Wolves would have been in buoyant mood for the visit of their title rivals. However, the game was postponed. Fate had decreed it would become the dramatic finale to the playing career of Stanley Cullis.

While Wolves fans warmed to the displays of their skipper, opposition crowds had taken to giving him a tough time. John Thompson picked up on this in his 'Soccer Sideshow' column in the Daily Mirror.

Under the heading "Give Cullis a fair deal!" he wrote: "Sitting on a porter's truck at Portsmouth station while we awaited the train home, Stanley Cullis, the Wolves centre-half, the most booed man in big soccer, talked to me about the fickleness of crowds. I had just watched him play one of his finest games. He had not been guilty of a single unfair move yet the crowd was against him almost from the start. 'A few years back,' said Stan, 'they would have been cheering, and all for me. Now away crowds seem to save up all their barracking for me. As soon as I step on to the field I know I am in for it whatever I do.' I believe that this great centre-half is justified in his complaint. Portsmouth fans should be sorry for the way they behaved."

The 1-1 draw at Fratton Park saw Wolves without the services of Billy Wright, one of their most influential players. England had arranged three international friendlies for the end of the season and the national side had first call on players, with their clubs not allowed to postpone games. So when Wolves were dropping a point at Portsmouth on Saturday, May 3, Wright was at Highbury helping England to beat France 3-0. Then came two matches on foreign soil, England losing to Switzerland 1-0 but redeeming themselves with an astonishing 10-0 defeat of Portugal in Lisbon. Wright did make a brief return when Wolves faltered again, losing 3-2 at home to Everton with Cullis's old adversary Jock Dodds a scorer. Jimmy Alderton did not let the side down as Wright's deputy in the next two games but maybe the England man would have made a difference in the home game with Blackburn which ended 3-3 and saw another vital point lost.

The Blackburn game was a real roughhouse and it proved costly as Tom Galley and Dennis Westcott were both injured and would miss the last two matches – away to Huddersfield and at home to Liverpool. "Nomad" in the Express & Star said that referee Womersley of Davenport seemed to have little or no control over the game after the interval. He went on: "There can be no excuse for players on either side adopting the tactics they did but had the referee intervened by calling both captains together or administering a general warning then there would probably have been a continuance of the tip-top football we saw in the first half." Wolves led 2-0 at the break but they found themselves 3-2 down thanks to goals from Scots Jack Weir (2) and Alec Venters, as the match boiled over. "Nomad" went on: "However as a result of over robust tackling, to say the least, trainer Jack Smith was on the field no fewer than nine times. On one occasion he had to leave the injured Westcott on the touchline to rush over to the outstretched Cullis." Galley grabbed an equaliser with a goal in the final minute but he and Westcott stayed behind for treatment when the other players left for a few days of rest and training in Blackpool.

Although there was a nine-day gap until the next game, away to Huddersfield Town, the injured pair were unable to play, but Wolves won 1-0 thanks to a Johnny Hancocks goal. Westcott had already been ruled out for the rest of the season but Galley was still having treatment for a leg injury. His battle to play in the crucial last match was doomed to failure, however. Westcott was a considerable loss – he had scored 38 goals in just 35 league games and it remains a record for the club.

That the season should reach its climax at Molineux on Saturday, May 31, 1947, reflected great credit on Liverpool. They too had their problems, with regular half-backs Phil Taylor (last three games) and Bob Paisley (last two) sidelined during the run-in. They were also deprived of the services of their star winger Billy Liddell. He was chosen to play for Great Britain against Europe in the game at Hampden Park to celebrate the British countries' return to FIFA. He pulled a muscle in that match and was not fit again until his club's crucial visit to Molineux. Without the charismatic Scotland international, Liverpool still took five points from the three games before the final showdown. Those three games were a trio of trips to London on successive Saturdays, beating Charlton 3-1, thanks to an Albert Stubbins hat-trick, drawing 1-1 at Brentford then winning 2-1 at Arsenal. So all credit to them, they had survived the loss of important players and had earned the right to be still in contention when they came to Molineux for their fourth successive away game. While Liddell was available again manager George Kay decided to keep his deputy, South African Bob Priday, in the team. Priday had scored in the vital win over Arsenal at Highbury so it was right-winger Willie Fagan who made way for Liddell.

It has been said that a draw would have been enough to give Wolves the title. This was not so, as no-one knew at the time that Stoke would fail to win their final game two weeks later. If Wolves had drawn 0-0 with Liverpool, the Potters would have needed a 3-0 win at Sheffield United to take the title. A 1-1 or 2-2 draw would have left Stoke needing to win only 2-0. So, let the record now be put straight – only a win would have guaranteed the championship coming to Molineux. If there was not enough tension surrounding the game, Cullis then added to it.

The week leading up to the vital game was spent in Blackpool so the players could relax. The team returned on the Friday and on the day of the game manager Ted Vizard took his players for a pre-match meal in Sutton Coldfield. It was there that the centre-half told them he would be calling an end to his playing days. This is how Billy Wright recalled it in his book One Hundred Caps and All That: "During the meal Stan stood up and informed us, much to our surprise, that this was going to be his last game. 'This is the end of the road for me,' he said, 'I've decided the time has come for me to retire.' His voice was choked with emotion and there were even tears in his eyes. 'This is a wonderful club,' he went on, 'and I want to thank you all from the bottom of my heart for the many ways in which you have helped me.' I think we all made up our minds there and then that nothing was going to stop us beating Liverpool that day."

It could have been that the players were too fired up for the game and – though hindsight is a wonderful thing – it might have been better if Cullis had said nothing. It was reported that half an hour before the gates were due to be opened, there were 40,000 fans jostling to get into Molineux. If Cullis's pre-match "This is my last game" announcement was not enough drama there was no shortage of it during the match itself. Jack Balmer gave Liverpool the lead after 20 minutes when Cullis and his defenders were guilty of some slack marking. Inside-left Bill Watkinson found himself in "acres" of space on the right wing and was able to cut in and give Balmer a tap-in.

Seventeen minutes later, dashing centre-forward Albert Stubbins raced away from Cullis to score the crucial second goal. The Wolves centre-half declined to stop him by foul means with a trip or shirt grab. He did not want to go down in history as a player who had helped win the title by means of a professional foul. This was how Stanley Halsey reported the crucial goal in the Daily Express: "Much of Stanley's (Cullis's) slip-stream speed was lacking but not until the 38th minute did Stubbins get the better of him. Alert Priday began it with a low swift pass to Stubbins. Albert snapped into action like a sprinter. Adroitly holding the ball, he sidestepped Stan, streaked away and at the top of his pace coolly, precisely, placed the ball clear of the advancing Williams."

With no Dennis Westcott in the side for this game and the previous one, Jesse Pye had moved to centre-forward with young Jimmy Dunn brought in at inside-right. It was Dunn who gave Wolves hope when, 25 minutes from time, he scored his first Football League goal for the club. It was not enough. This was how the great Billy Liddell recalled the match: "It was extremely hot, with the thermometer somewhere in the eighties, and I remember remarking to Albert Stubbins about the vast number of spectators in shirt sleeves. We were the first to score when Jackie Balmer steered one into the net and when Albert Stubbins got the second we thought the game was safely in the bag. Wolves, however, were never a team to give up without a struggle. Cullis was a wonderful inspiration urging his players on and making them fight as though their lives depended on it." It was ironic that one of those who did most to prevent Wolves getting back into the match was their former teammate, goalkeeper Cyril Sidlow, who still lived in Wolverhampton and was allowed to train at Molineux.

Several people found the heat too much that day. Clive Corbett told me: "My Uncle Fred passed out on the South Bank and had to be passed over the heads to the front so he could receive some treatment. Mind you, he was wearing a tie!"

There was much sympathy for Cullis, with the words of John Thompson in the Daily Mirror summing it up well: "Stanley Cullis, grocer's boy who became the greatest centre-half of his day, picked up the black and gold colours he would never wear again and stared at them for a moment. Then he placed them sadly on the bench. Instead of the triumph on which he hoped to end his colourful and often splendid career, there was only failure. And ironically the man who has led Wanderers to so many successes was responsible for Liverpool's second goal, a solo dash by youthful Albert Stubbins, in which he outpaced Cullis all the way. 'I'd no idea Stubbins was so near, and then I saw his red head flash past,' Stan said. 'He's got amazing speed.' On the championship they missed Cullis said 'We were on top too long. It was as though Sydney Wooderson had tried to win a race by leading all the way, instead of keeping handy in second or third place. It's been the hardest season I've known and it's ended in the second great disappointment of my career. This was as big a blow as our defeat by Portsmouth in the 1939 Cup Final.' From Ted Vizard, Wolves manager, came the aptest summing-up. 'We had our chances and failed to take them.' Down the corridor in Liverpool's dressing room players joyfully toasted each other in lemonade, and reminded each other that this victory made up for the thrashing Wolves had given them earlier in the season. 'They gave us only two chances to score and we grabbed them both,' said their captain Jack Balmer."

Teams at Molineux Grounds, Wolverhampton, on Saturday, May 31, 1947:

Wolves: Williams; McLean, W Crook; Alderton, Cullis, Wright; Hancocks, Dunn, Pye, Forbes, Mullen;

Liverpool: Sidlow; Harley, Lambert; Jones, Hughes, Spicer; Liddell, Balmer, Stubbins, Watkinson, Priday.

While Cullis and his teammates were left to reflect on what might have been, Liverpool were forced to wait two weeks until Stoke visited Bramall Lane to try to contrive one last sensational twist to the league season's epic last few weeks. It did not happen and another man coming to the end of his career had a big say in the matter. Inside forward Jack Pickering, a former England international who was by then 38 and had made his Blades debut 20 years earlier, was given his first game of the season. He was made captain for the day, scored the first goal and made the second for Walter Rickett as the Potters were beaten 2-1. It was 1-1 at half-time, after left-winger Alex Ormston hit the visitors' goal. News of the result reached Anfield shortly before the end of the Liverpool Cup final between Liverpool and Everton. When it was announced to the crowd the action on the pitch was forgotten.

All they wanted was the final whistle, which came after Liverpool had won 2-1, so they could invade the pitch to engulf the newly-crowned champions. Henry Rose, a football writer fated to die in the Munich Air Crash, wrote in the Daily Express: "Congratulations to Liverpool but their best friends – and despite the fruit throwers of the Spion Kop, I count myself one – wouldn't claim they are the best side this season. I asked six colleagues to name the best side they saw and none named Liverpool." Such comments mattered not, the title was at Anfield, not Molineux, after football's longest season. This is how the run-in went after Easter (Results, scorers and gates):

Saturday, April 12

Blackpool 0 Stoke 2 (Ormston pen, G Mountford) 17,260

Brentford 0 Manchester United 0 22,035

Top of table (Goal averages in brackets):

Wolves 35-48 (1.883), Manchester United 36-47 (1.600), Blackpool 40-47 (1.388), Stoke 36-46 (1.653), Liverpool 35-44 (1.532)

Saturday, April 19

Blackburn 0, Manchester United 4 (Pearson 2, Rowley, Higgins own goal) 46,390

Bolton 0 Wolves 3 (Hancocks, Mullen, Pye) 34,419

Brentford 1 (Naylor), Stoke 3 (Steele, G Mountford, Matthews) 28,966

Liverpool 1 (Stubbins) Sunderland 0 41,589

Middlesbrough 1 (Spuhler) Blackpool 2 (Eastham, Mortensen) 28,849

Top of table:

Wolves 36-50 (1.953), Manchester United 37-49 (1.680), Blackpool 41-49 (1.400), Stoke 37-48 (1.680), Liverpool 36-46 (1.553)

Saturday, April 26

Aston Villa 1 (Evans) Liverpool 2 (Watkinson, Fagan) 35,429

Blackburn 0 Stoke 2 (Ormston, Matthews) 26,323

Portsmouth 0 Manchester United 1 (Delaney) 30,623

Wolves 6 (Forbes 2, Hancocks 2, Westcott 2) Chelsea 4 (Machin, Spence, Lawton, Goulden) 44,260

Top of table:

Wolves 37-52 (1.915), Manchester United 38-51 (1.700), Stoke 38-50 (1.720), Blackpool 41-49 (1.400), Liverpool 37-48 (1.562).

Saturday, May 3

Liverpool 1 (Stubbins) Manchester United 0 48,800

Leeds 1 (Short) Stoke 2 (Steele 2) 21,714

Portsmouth 1 (Reid) Wolves 1 (Westcott) 37,711

Top of table:

Wolves 38-53 (1.897), Stoke 39-52 (1.725), Manchester United 39-51 (1.666), Liverpool 38-50 (1.583), Blackpool 41-49 (1.400).

Saturday, May 10

Charlton 1 (Robinson) Liverpool 3 (Stubbins 3) 45,608

Preston 1 (McLaren) Manchester United 1 (Pearson) 23,278

Wolves 2 (Mullen, Westcott) Everton 3 (Dodds, Fielding, McIlhatton) 40,033

Top of table:

Wolves 39-53 (1.8723), Stoke 39-52 (1.725), Manchester United 40-52 (1.654), Liverpool 39-52 (1.612), Blackpool 41-49 (1.400).

Saturday, May 17

Blackpool 0 Charlton 0 16,771

Brentford 1 (Stewart) Liverpool 1 (Priday) 18,228

Manchester United 3 (Mitten, Morris, Rowley) Portsmouth 0 37,746

Stoke 0 Sunderland 0 28,709

Wolves 3 (Galley, Pye, Westcott) Blackburn 3 (Weir 2 Venters) 42,380

Top of table:

Wolves 40-54 (1.777), Manchester United 41-54 (1.712), Stoke 40-53 (1.725), Liverpool 40-53 (1.600), Blackpool 42-50 (1.400).

Saturday, May 24

Arsenal 1 (McPherson) Liverpool 2 (Balmer, Priday) 44,265

Top of table:

Liverpool 41-55 (1.608), Wolves 40-54 (1.777), Manchester United 41-54 (1.712), Stoke 40-53 (1.725), Blackpool 42-50 (1.400).

Monday May 26

Aston Villa 0 Stoke 1 (G Mountford) 39,947

Manchester United 6 (Rowley 3, Morris 2, Pearson) Sheffield United 2 (Collindridge, Nightingale) 34,209

Wolves 1 (Hancocks) Huddersfield 0 25,401

Top of table:

Wolves 41-56 (1.796), Manchester United 42-56 (1.759), Stoke 41-55 (1.745), Liverpool 41-55 1.608), Blackpool 42-50 (1.400).

Saturday, May 31

Wolves 1 (Dunn) Liverpool 2 (Balmer, Stubbins) 50,765

Top of table:

Liverpool 42-57 (1.615), Manchester United 42-56 (1.759), Wolves 42-56 (1.750), Stoke 41-55 (1.745), Blackpool 42-50.

Saturday, June 14

Sheffield United 2 (Pickering, Rickett) Stoke 1 (Ormston) 26,890.

Top of table:

Liverpool 42-57 (1.615), Manchester United 42-56 (1.759), Wolves 42-56 (1.750), Stoke 42-55 (1.698), Blackpool 42-50 (1.400).

For a third successive First Division season Wolves had been so near and yet so far from becoming champions of England, and on each occasion they had only themselves to blame. In 1937-8 and in 1946-7 they needed only to win their final game to take the title while in 1938-9 it was at the beginning, rather than at the end, of the campaign that their title bid failed when they left themselves far too much to do in order to catch Everton.

The 1946-7 finish was the closest in the top division since the Football League began in 1888 with the fourth side in the table just two points behind the champions. There was not a closer finish until 1972 and Wolves had a say in that one as well. When they beat Leeds at Molineux to deny them the Double it meant Derby were champions with Manchester City in fourth place only a point behind them.

Chapter 11 A ban from the FA

Frank Butler in the Daily Express wrote: "I congratulate Stanley Cullis on fulfilling a promise he made to himself before the war: 'I shall keep on top of soccer,' he said, 'but when I begin to slip I shall get out.' Stan is still a great player but has never quite recovered his pre-Italy form when he was the greatest centre-half I have ever seen. Cullis is one of soccer's deepest thinkers and usually gets what he wants. That is why I believe that by next season he will be piloting one of the league clubs." Butler knew that there would be no shortage of clubs willing to give Cullis his first taste of management . . . but Wolves had their own plans for him. At this stage, though, he was not inclined to talk publicly about his future.

On the Monday after the Liverpool game, "Pilgrim" reported in the Express & Star: "It is still a secret what position Stanley Cullis will hold with Wolves next season but it is a fact that at Blackpool last Wednesday he signed a new agreement. Stan is silent about his playing retirement which came as a bombshell to the 50,000 spectators at Molineux on Saturday." The diligent reporter had been to Cullis's house and found him in his garden where Cullis said: "I have nothing further to say more than my statement on Saturday – which is wait and see." Manager Vizard would only say: "I have not heard anything of Cullis coming back to Molineux in any capacity other than that of a player."

What is not widely documented is that if Cullis had decided to play on he would first have had to serve a 14-day suspension. Cullis, the man who as a manager insisted on self-control from his players, was given a ban by the Football Association. It seems he got into trouble with the referee during Wolves' crucial match against Manchester United on Easter Saturday, April 5. Henry Rose mentioned it briefly in his Daily Express report of the game: "Cullis had his name taken when he argued for off-side instead of a goal kick." Cullis had been apt to cross swords with referees and it seems previous misdemeanours led to the suspension – a thing not dished out as readily as in today's game. The FA's letter to Wolves made it clear why Cullis had been banned:

"Manchester United v Wolverhampton Wanderers, April 5, 1947. The referee's report and subsequent correspondence relating to the action administered by the referee to the player S Cullis has been considered by the disciplinary committee who have decided that Cullis be suspended for 14 days from Monday, August 18. In arriving at the decision the committee took into account the previous record of cautions recorded against the player."

The caution against United was Cullis's third of the season, each one for dissent. One fears for any referee who got "verbals" from Cullis. He famously never swore but he could express himself in no uncertain terms. Yet, as a boss, he would not tolerate his players giving unnecessary backchat to a referee and his linesman.

Despite his retirement announcement and, despite medical advice he should not play on, there was still talk that he could be persuaded to change his mind. Cullis's name was widely linked with a move to Hull where his old Molineux mentor, Major Frank Buckley, was now manager. Buckley would surely have welcomed him on or off the field. The possibility of Cullis playing on was remote but not completely out of the question. He had, after all, again signed on as a player at Molineux.

On the day in early July, 1947, that Cullis's playing ban was announced, Wolves held their annual meeting and the Wolverhampton Express & Star reported the following day: "Since publication of Cullis's retirement there have been stories with regard to his future with the club for which he has signed terms. So far, however, the directors have refused to make any official announcement. Indeed, pressed by shareholders at last night's annual meeting of the club, Mr James S Baker, chairman, said that no decision had yet been reached in respect of Cullis."

Baker was merely stalling as two days later Wolves announced that Cullis had joined the staff at Molineux. The paper reported: "His future, however, is still shrouded in mystery inasmuch as the capacity in which he will serve was not divulged. It is understood it will be on the general indoor staff, whether as coach, scout or assistant manager."

Wolves clearly wanted to hang on to Cullis but that did not stop the rumours of a move to Hull. It was not surprising that Cullis's name should be linked to that of Buckley – they had been a fine partnership at Molineux. Speculation had been rife after the Major was spotted in Wolverhampton during the summer but he insisted he was merely visiting friends – not trying to tempt Cullis to Yorkshire. Buckley told the Hull Daily Mail: "While I was in Wolverhampton I never saw nor interviewed Cullis. There is no secret at all about the fact that I would be delighted to have him at Hull as a player, but that is impossible. Some time ago efforts were made to get him here, but Cullis has definitely retired from active participation in the game and I understand that he has signed a contract for a number of years as assistant manager of the Wolverhampton club."

Despite what Buckley said, Wolves still had not made Cullis's position known when the players reported back for training two days after the Major's comments. That had the Express & Star's Wolves man, "Pilgrim", writing "I have it on good authority that Cullis will probably start his new sphere with Wolves as a coach." In fact, Buckley was better informed than the local reporter and on August 19, 1947, four days before the start of the new season, it was officially announced that Cullis was indeed assistant manager. It was an historic appointment as the Express & Star explained: "It is the first time in the club's history that an assistant manager has been appointed. In fact, only a few clubs have such an official." Cullis was given his own office and Vizard must have been acutely aware that rather than having an assistant he had acquired a successor in waiting. It would have taken the league title or the FA Cup to keep Vizard in his job.

Eventually Cullis would take charge of the reserve team while the immediate task for manager Vizard was to find a replacement for Cullis the player. No way were they going to find someone ready made who could match the commanding figure who had made such an impact on club and country. However, Vizard, apparently with the approval of his new assistant, decided to buy 23-year-old Gordon Brice from Luton Town for £10,000. As would often happen at Molineux in future years, the new man was not the solution and, as would also happen at Molineux in future years, there was already someone on the books who was far better suited to what the team needed.

Brice played the first 11 games of the 1947-8 season. While the results were not too bad – six wins and a draw in the opening nine matches – it was clear that Brice had not bridged the gap between Second Division and First Division. He was struggling. After a 5-1 defeat at Charlton, he was dropped in favour of 25-year-old Bill Shorthouse, a hard man but skilful enough to play equally well at full-back. Shorthouse would serve Wolves well for nearly a decade, collecting an FA Cup winner's medal and league championship medal on the way. Brice played only one more game, as deputy to Shorthouse, and was sold to Reading before the season ended.

If Brice did not live up to expectations, the same could not be said of another of Vizard's close-season signings – Sammy Smyth. The Irish inside-forward settled in well during a season which was something of an anti-climax after the drama of 1946-7. There were emphatic wins, such as 8-1 against Derby in the first home game of the season but also some emphatic defeats. Manchester United came to Molineux and won 6-2, when four of their five forwards were scorers. The odd man out was Wulfrunian Jack Rowley, who made up for it next game by scoring all United's goals in a 4-4 draw with Huddersfield.

With Cullis retired and Alex Scott and Teddy Maguire transferred, Tom Galley and Dennis Westcott were the last links with Buckley's pre-war FA Cup finalists. They would not remain much longer. Galley was sold to Grimsby early in the season and Westcott to Blackburn in the final weeks. Vizard was re-building and most clubs would have been happy with the way things were going. Wolves reeled off four wins in a row leading up to the last game of the campaign, which had a familiar ring to it – a 2-1 defeat by Liverpool, though this time at Anfield. Nevertheless, Wolves had finished a respectable fifth, 12 points behind champions Arsenal. The make-up of the side was gradually changing and Wolves did well to finish so high in the table. That was still not enough to keep Ted Vizard in his job. Cullis had emphasised his managerial credentials by his work with the reserve team who moved steadily up the Central League table in the second half of the season. They finished in third place on 57 points, one behind runners-up Manchester United and four behind champions Newcastle.

The performance of the reserve team under Cullis must have impressed the Wolves board. The side had won only six of their opening 19 games and then came a quite remarkable transformation, starting just before Christmas. A 16-game unbeaten run, which included eight wins in a row, saw the team zoom up the Central League table. Among the victories was a 3-2 defeat of eventual champions Newcastle at St James' Park. The Cullis effect would not have gone unnoticed.

Moves behind the scenes must have been afoot almost as soon as the season ended to get Vizard out and Cullis in. Yet the close season began with Vizard taking the team on a trip to Europe where they played three games. They beat a Dutch Combined XI 3-2 and a Dutch national XI 1-0, before losing 3-1 to Stade Francais in Paris. Back home Vizard set about looking to the new season and to adding to his squad. He had his sights on the most exciting English player of the moment, Middlesbrough and England inside forward Wilf Mannion. It was reported in the Express & Star that Vizard had already had discussions with Middlesbrough boss David Jack, a teammate of Vizard's from his Bolton days. The paper stated: "Vizard said the club would meet Boro demands for a fee or players exchange." Mannion would have been a momentous signing but, alas, Vizard's days were numbered.

It was on Saturday, June 12, 1948, five days after Vizard's 59th birthday, that the axe fell and the club statement said a difference of opinion had arisen between the board and the secretary manager on the future policy of the club. "Mr Vizard has tendered his resignation which has been accepted with regret," it said. Chairman James Baker would not elaborate and said he preferred not to discuss the matter of a successor at that time and that any decision would be announced in due course. In the Express & Star's front page report Vizard confirmed that differences of opinion had existed for some time and in a farewell message added: "I am leaving feeling I have done well for the club in overcoming post-war difficulties and signing players, particularly promising youngsters, to keep the club in a good position in the league in years to come. There has been a real team spirit among the players on and off the field. When I came here four years ago I stated I wished to be judged by results on the field. I am sure the reputation of Wolverhampton Wanderers has not suffered during my management. I wish to thank all the players and staff for their support, particularly Mr Jack Howley. In conclusion I want to thank the many thousands of spectators for their support and wish the club and Wolverhampton every success in the future."

The Express & Star's inside page report added: "Mr Stanley Cullis, former captain and England international, is the club's assistant manager. Appointed last season he is at present on holiday. His handling of the reserve side was such that in a short space of time the Central League team rose from the lower half of the table to the leading positions and they were only just beaten for the championship". If ever there was a broad hint at what was about to happen, that was it.

Vizard left with his head held high and told Henry Rose of the Daily Express: "I am not worrying. I feel that if they don't appreciate what I have done, other clubs will. Things were never right from the beginning at Wolverhampton. We disagreed on certain points of playing policy and there were things I knew were right I was not allowed to do. I learned very early after I took over in April, 1944, my position was not as secure as I would have liked it to be." Rose also forecast that Cullis would be the new man in charge: "These moves were earmarked from the moment Cullis pulled off his jersey for the last time," he wrote. Rose, a journalist of the old school, had good contacts and the appointment was confirmed on June 23, 1948. So Cullis's stint as assistant did not last a number of years, as forecast by Buckley, but just one.

There was no front page splash in the Express & Star, but a factual report on an inside page from sports editor George Gillott which read: "Just after seven o'clock last night the Wolves directors filed into the club's boardroom to take their seats at the annual meeting. As they entered it was seen that Stanley Cullis was in the position usually occupied by the manager and the news which all Wolves followers have been awaiting and expecting was out. Applause greeted the formal announcement by Mr J S Baker that the 31-year-old former captain of the club and probably the greatest centre-half England has yet known, had been appointed to succeed Mr Ted Vizard as manager. Cullis said many tempting offers had been made to him by other clubs but he wanted to stay in Wolverhampton." Vizard's days as a football manager were virtually over and after a brief spell looking after Birmingham League side Cradley Heath, he became licensee of the Crown public house at The Wergs, Tettenhall, just a couple of miles or so from Molineux.

That the new boss differed from his predecessor was soon made clear. Cullis was determined to build on what Buckley had begun and to make Wolves the best team in the land. He was totally driven and wanted the same dedication from his players as they discovered when he called a meeting of the whole playing staff. The assembled group were told: "I want us to see eye to eye from the start. I want, and am going to get, one hundred per cent effort from you all, both on and off the field. If I get this support you can take it from me I will be one hundred per cent behind you. Nothing else is going to be enough." Billy Wright recalled: "The manner in which he made his point left us all in no doubt that Cullis meant exactly what he said. From that moment on Wolves' manager never forgave a player who didn't always try his hardest, and I do not think I am breaking any confidences when I say that this is the reason why more than a few players have since left Molineux." Wright added that Cullis kept his part of the bargain, making sure that playing, training and living conditions for the players were the best possible and attending to the welfare of all, whether it be a first-team star or a youngster in the Worcestershire Combination side. The manager also let it be known that his office door was always open – to star player or a ground-staff boy. Equally he made it clear what he wanted in return and a sign soon appeared in the home dressing room: "There is no substitute for hard work."

Chapter 12   A winner at last

Cullis had been left a group of fine players by his predecessor. Among those Vizard signed for Wolves were goalkeeper Bert Williams and forwards Johnny Hancocks, Sammy Smyth and Jesse Pye, who would make significant contributions in the coming seasons. Add to those Billy Crook, Billy Wright, Jimmy Dunn and Jimmy Mullen and there was a team which only needed fine tuning. Yet the directors must have felt that Vizard was not the man to take the side to greater heights. A similar situation would arise some 20 years later when Ronnie Allen had guided Wolves to promotion from the Second Division and had brought to the club Mike Bailey, Derek Dougan, Derek Parkin, Frank Munro and Kenny Hibbitt. The directors wanted the iron hand of Bill McGarry to take that talented squad to a higher level and they were probably proved right in their decision. The same could be said of the Wolves board in 1948.

While Cullis may have realised he had been left the nucleus of a good team, one of his first moves as manager was to recall from loan the young forward, Dennis Wilshaw. The Stoke-born player had been on the Molineux books since 1943 but had been farmed out to Walsall where a full season brought him 18 goals. Cullis had made a few wartime appearances alongside Wilshaw and must have realised that he should be part of Wolves' future even though the 22-year-old was by then carving out a teaching career. Cullis recalled him from his loan stint in early September, 1948, and he would make his mark before the season was over. In time he would be a vital cog in Cullis's great team of the early 1950s.

There was no question of the new chief immediately trying to strengthen his playing staff. Apart from the fact the squad looked pretty strong in any case, there was no pre-season transfer window in those days and signings could be made during the season. Cullis's first signing was, in fact, a low key one, a youngster from Flint by the name of Ron Hewitt. He subsequently got plenty of reserve team football but did not break into the first team. He moved on loan to Walsall, where he got his first taste of league football, before signing for Darlington. He had several seasons with Wrexham before joining Cardiff and gaining a place in the Wales squad at the 1958 World Cup in Sweden. He won five caps.

Having made the change of management, Wolves' board did not reap instant rewards. The first two games of the Cullis regime were at Molineux but a 2-2 draw with Birmingham City was followed by a 1-0 defeat by Sunderland. The first win for the new boss was 5-0 against Bolton at Burnden Park, where wingers Johnny Hancocks and Jimmy Mullen each score twice. League form could be erratic and a 7-1 home win over Huddersfield, when Bert Williams saved a first-minute penalty, was followed a week later by a 3-0 home defeat by Middlesbrough.

Christmas proved painful in more ways than one, thanks in no small way to rugged Welsh centre-forward Trevor Ford, who thrived in an era when challenges on goalkeepers were accepted as just part of the game. A collision with the Welshman on Christmas Day saw Bert Williams carried off with concussion and a stint in goal for Sammy Smyth. In the return match, at Villa Park, the next day Ford rubbed salt into the wounds by hitting four goals past deputy keeper Dennis Parsons – three of them came in the last 15 minutes – as Villa won 5-1. Not a good end to the year but things were about to get better, very much better.

A league title challenge had not materialised but by the end of January Wolves were in the last 16 of the FA Cup, thanks first to a 6-0 home win over Chesterfield. Then three second-half goals brought a 3-0 win over Sheffield United before a Bramall Lane gate of just under 50,000. Interest among the fans was high and it would get even higher when Wolves were paired with Liverpool, the club who had ruined Cullis's grand finale two years earlier. For the first time at Molineux a game was made all-ticket and the fifth-round tie saw 54,983 witness the visit of a side still boasting six of the men, including Albert Stubbins, who had won so dramatically in May, 1947. Jimmy Dunn, a survivor of that game, gave Wolves the lead just before half-time and though Cyril Done cancelled it out, two goals in the space of seven minutes, from Sammy Smyth and Jimmy Mullen, saw Wolves into the last eight and yet another high profile tie.

West Bromwich Albion were making what would prove a successful Second Division promotion bid. Last time the clubs had met in the Cup was in 1931 when Albion won the trophy and gained promotion to the First Division – a unique double. Five Cup meetings of the Black Country rivals over the years had brought five Albion wins. So history was against Wolves but, more practically, an injury to right-winger Johnny Hancocks was what concerned Cullis. The potential match-winner was not fully fit and it was not until half an hour before kick-off that the manager decided to play him. It was a gamble but it paid off as the Baggies had to focus on a major threat from both wings. The man on the other flank, Jimmy Mullen, scored the game's only goal on 59 minutes and Wolves were in the semi-final.

Cullis may not have allowed himself to dream of making up for the massive disappointment of 1939 as he knew he first he had to get past Manchester United, a team managed by one of his best friends in football – Matt Busby. Cullis always said that Busby was the player on whom he tried to model himself. They had been comrades during the war and had played against each other and in the same teams. Now both were engaged in building two great football dynasties. The Scot had acquired his first trophy in 1948 when United won the FA Cup, beating Blackpool 4-2 at Wembley in a classic final, high on skill and drama. For Wolves to beat the holders would be no easy task. United were chasing the league and Cup double and were destined to finish First Division runners-up for a third successive season. In the fifth round they had summarily dismissed giantkillers Yeovil Town 8-0 before 81,000 fans at Maine Road, with Jack Rowley scoring five times.

Getting past United would produce two epic games which have gone down in Wolves folklore. Like Wolves, United carried a danger down either wing in the shape of Jimmy Delaney and Charlie Mitten and the last thing Cullis needed was for his full-backs to get crocked. However, that was what happened at Hillsborough, Sheffield. Left-back Roy Pritchard was injured after six minutes and right-back Lawrie Kelly was carried off 23 minutes from time. By then the score was 1-1, Mitten having quickly cancelled out Sammy Smyth's early goal for Wolves. With 30 minutes' extra time to negotiate as well, the ten men defended superbly to earn themselves a replay a week later at Goodison Park, home of Everton.

Billy Wright recalled many years later that Cullis had struck just the right note in the white hot atmosphere of Sheffield: "The tension was unworldly and at half-time a wrong word or a wrong action would have sent us to pieces. Stan sensed that nothing but encouragement was needed, and he said exactly the right things. He again struck exactly the note we needed after ninety minutes when extra time was necessary – and during the last desperate half hour he came right down to the touchline to encourage us as we battled, successfully, for a draw. He showed us that day what a great manager he was."

Cullis had already been denied the services at full-back of the experienced Angus McLean through a long-term injury and now knew Kelly and Pritchard were highly unlikely to recover for the replay. He drew a veil of secrecy over his line-up until just before kick-off. Then it was announced that Alf Crook, elder brother of Billy, would make his first-team debut at right-back, with Terry Springthorpe, who had lost his place to Pritchard earlier in the season, recalled at left-back. The hefty Springthorpe was a hard-tackling defender and he soon let Jimmy Delaney know he was around while Crook dealt well with Charlie Mitten. The match was again a close-run thing until Smyth scored the only goal four minutes from time. United keeper Jack Crompton blocked a fierce shot from Jesse Pye but, despite Johnny Carey being on the line, Sammy Smyth got to the ball first to put it home. Cullis had guided Wolves back to the FA Cup final, ten years after the nightmare of 1939.

It might so easily have been the same 1939 participants as Double-chasing Portsmouth were in the other semi-final and faced Second Division strugglers Leicester City. It was quite an upset when Don Revie scored twice at Highbury as First Division leaders Pompey were beaten 3-1. The opposition might not be the same as 1939, but there were similarities as again Wolves would be hot favourites, their opponents' major concern being to avoid a drop into the Third Division. City had no easy path to the final, needing three games to get past Birmingham City in the third round, then beating Preston 2-0 at home in the fourth before the fifth-round clash with Luton Town saw two games produce 18 goals. After a 5-5 draw at Kenilworth Road, City won the replay 5-3 at Filbert Street to earn a sixth-round clash with fellow strugglers Brentford whom they beat 2-0.

Nine days after the semi-final replay win came evidence of Cullis's standing in the town of Wolverhampton. He and Billy Wright were jointly honoured by a civic banquet. The lavish affair at the Civic Hall was the idea of the mayor, Alderman Ted Lane, and recognised the town's pride in seeing its football club provide two captains of England. A sizeable organising committee ensured the gala evening was graced by football luminaries such as Football Association chairman Amos Brook Hirst, FA secretary Sir Stanley Rous, Football League secretary Fred Howarth and Major Buckley. A note in the banquet brochure said: "It is the fervent hope of all Wolves fans that Mr Cullis will continue to adorn the game as manager, as he did in a playing capacity." Among an attendance of nearly 500 were Cullis's wartime England colleagues Cliff Britton and Joe Mercer and his old adversary Matt Busby.

It was a pleasant diversion but Cullis had quickly to turn his attention to pressing problems as the trip to Wembley approached. The full-back situation was his main worry and it had become worse when Alf Crook was given his First Division debut at Liverpool four days after the semi-final replay. He sustained a second-half injury and was finished for the remainder of the season. Fortunately, Pritchard was fit again and able to take over. However, when Lawrie Kelly recovered in time for the final it left Cullis with a selection dilemma that he did not handle very well. He decided that Springthorpe would keep his place as he had impressed in the games that followed the semi-final replay. The manager also reasoned that Lawrie Kelly might be physically fit but would be lacking that extra edge that is known as "match fit". The manager ought really to have taken Kelly on one side and told him of his decision. This would have allowed him to come to terms with his disappointment. Instead, Kelly learned of his omission on the coach journey to Wolves' pre-Wembley retreat.

Let Billy Wright take up the story: "On the Thursday before the Cup Final our party of first-team men left by coach for Weybridge where we planned to stay until Saturday morning. The team had not been announced because then, as now, Stan liked to leave such announcements until as late as possible. But about four miles outside Wolverhampton Stan came up to me and said: 'Have you told the lads the team yet, Bill?' 'No,' I said, 'I thought you were going to do that.' 'Well you can do it, go on,' came the reply. I read out the names of the lucky eleven slowly and distinctly and I know that, without disagreeing with Terry's selection, we all sympathised with Lol Kelly, who was a very fine player and clubman. Lol was bitterly disappointed. He was convinced he was fit and so strongly did he feel that at Oxford he disobeyed almost every rule in the book and left the coach to return to Wolverhampton. Cullis, the disciplinarian, was furious. 'You'll suffer the consequences if you don't come back,' he roared after the retreating figure of Kelly. I've never seen him so angry or determined. Yet the matter was never mentioned again – because I think Stan realised Lol should have been told before. He put himself in the player's place, understood his feelings and decided to forget about the whole matter."

Another who could have felt disappointed was Dennis Wilshaw. He had made his league debut as deputy for Jimmy Mullen and hit the headlines by scoring a hat-trick as Wolves beat Newcastle 3-0 at Molineux. He had then deputised for Jesse Pye and in six games at centre-forward, he scored seven goals to put himself in contention for a Wembley place. Cullis did not use the criterion for Pye that he had used for Kelly and decided that his proven match-winning ability made playing Pye a risk worth taking. So it would turn out.

Leicester boss Johnny Duncan had selection problems of a different kind as, on the Saturday before the final, star forward Don Revie received a blow in the face in the 1-1 draw at Plymouth and burst a blood vessel so badly he needed a transfusion. He would miss the final and was still in hospital on the big day, having to follow the Wembley events via the radio commentary. Goalkeeper Ian McGraw was also ruled out after breaking a finger in an accident at home. It all added up to the Wembley game being a foregone conclusion but Cullis knew all about what can happen to red-hot FA Cup final favourites.

If Cullis did not get it right in telling Kelly of his fate, he certainly had learned a lesson from 1939 and knew that travelling to Wembley on the morning of the Cup Final was no way to build up to a game of such importance. The team were based at the Oatlands Park Hotel, Weybridge, a quiet retreat with a nine-hole golf course. On Thursday evening the team went to watch local amateur side Walton and Hersham play Dutch touring side Nijmegen, Billy Wright being introduced to the teams before kick-off. On Friday morning the Wolves players received a good luck telegram from Charlie Stowe, Wolverhampton's popular amateur golfer from Penn, who also had a final date – in the Amateur Golf Championship. It read: "Sorry I cannot be with you today. Will do my best to make it a Wolverhampton double. Good luck to the boys." Cullis sent a message back wishing Stowe good luck from himself, the players and directors. Alas, Stowe was beaten 5 and 4 by Ronnie White in the final at Formby.

Another Cullis touch was to take the players on Friday afternoon to Wembley so they could get a feel of the arena and look at the playing surface. Only Bert Williams, Billy Wright, Jesse Pye and Jimmy Mullen had played there before. On Friday evening Cullis had a team meeting when he analysed the opposition, going through each member of the Leicester City team, detailing their strengths and weaknesses. It was the sort of thing that is routine today but there were no recordings to play to the squad in 1949 and the players had to listen to what the manager had learned about their opponents.

So it was a relaxed atmosphere for the Wolves team before an early night was ordered for all. The following day Cullis ensured his team were at Wembley Stadium by 1.30 as he always liked to arrive at a ground well before kick-off. The preparations had gone smoothly and it all added up to a group of players far better placed to play a cup final than Buckley's team had been in 1939. Certainly, the Wolves captain ten years later did not bear a worried look and was not nervously bouncing the brand new football as the teams made the long walk on to the pitch.

If Billy Wright and the players were calm, there was no calmness on the touchline bench once the match began as Cullis lived every moment, hardly ever still, making, metaphorically, every tackle, pass and shot. Yet if he had any nerves they should have been settled after only twelve minutes when the man he opted for, Jesse Pye, timed his run perfectly to head home a pinpoint right-wing centre from Johnny Hancocks. It was Pye again, in the right place after a shot had been blocked, who doubled Wolves' lead a few minutes before half-time. Welsh winger Mal Griffiths scored two minutes into the second half and Leicester had Wolves rattled for a time. The turning point came when Ken Chisholm netted, only to be ruled off-side by Huddersfield referee Reg Mortimer. It was a marginal decision but a correct one by the official who had been in charge of the Wolves-Albion quarter-final. Within two minutes, Sammy Smyth weaved his way imperiously through the Leicester defence to score one of Wembley's great goals. It was his sixth in seven Cup games that season. Even Cullis must have relaxed slightly as the balance of power tipped again towards Wolves who were rarely troubled after that.

Teams at Wembley Stadium, London, on Saturday, April 30, 1949:

Wolves: Williams; Pritchard, Springthorpe; W Crook, Shorthouse, Wright; Hancocks, Smyth, Pye, Dunn, Mullen.

Leicester City: Bradley; Jelly, Scott; W Harrison, Plummer, King; Griffiths, Lee, J Harrison, Chisholm, Adam.

It had been 41 years since Wolves had won the Cup and at last Cullis had the major trophy that eluded him as a player. At 32 he was – and remains – the youngest ever manager of a Wembley FA Cup side. He could even afford a smile at a Royal gaffe as Princess Elizabeth, our future Queen, was wearing a hat and coat of blue – Leicester City colours – when she presented the trophy to Billy Wright. The greatest period in the history of Wolverhampton Wanderers had begun and would stretch across more than a decade.

If Cullis had been on tenterhooks during the game, he could relax at the club's post-final banquet at the Café Royal before a trip to the London Palladium to see the American entertainer Danny Kaye. It was back to the Weybridge hotel afterwards and the following morning the party travelled by train back to Wolverhampton where a coach took them from the Low Level station to the Town Hall with huge crowds bringing the town to a standstill.

Happily, Lawrie Kelly was with the party in the open-top coach to share in a triumph which he had helped bring about by playing five times in the competition that season. Cullis emerged from the civic reception on to the Town Hall balcony and told the throng: "The players have asked me to express their gratitude for the wonderful support you have given us throughout the season. I can assure you it has been a great contribution on the road to Wembley." With a fine sense of drama, he kept the fans waiting briefly before announcing: "I want to introduce to you probably the most popular man in Wolverhampton today." With that, Billy Wright emerged brandishing the gleaming Cup and the other players would eventually join him to salute the crowd.

The following day, Wolves had a home game with Preston and, apart from Dennis Wilshaw deputising for Jimmy Dunn, fielded the Cup-winning side and such was the continuing euphoria that there was a gate of 54,425 to welcome the Wembley victors back to Molineux. The game kicked off at 6.30 after the trophy had been paraded around the ground. It looked as though the happy fans might see a big win when wingers Hancocks and Mullen put them two up after 22 minutes but the only other goal was a penalty by Bobby Langton for the visitors three minutes from time.

Beaten finalists Leicester were required to play three games in four days after the final and their last game of the season found them needing a point at Cardiff to avoid relegation. They got it but only thanks to an equaliser from Jack Lee in the 77th minute. The result meant that Nottingham Forest dropped out of the Second Division along with Lincoln City.

As a reward for their success, the Wolves players were taken on a holiday to Ireland expecting a relaxing time. They knew there would be some football but hoped no-one would take it too seriously. They were forgetting that Cullis was over there with them and soon got a rude awakening as inside-forward Jimmy Dunn recalled: "We thought it was a holiday and we were there to enjoy ourselves but Stan wanted to win every match. In one, we were 2-1 down at half-time and when we went into the dressing room Stan made straight for me. If he did that you knew you were in trouble. He said: 'You're letting that wing-half walk all over you. If you don't get your finger out you'll be on the next boat home.' So I really got wound up and the first time in the second half I challenged this wing-half, a big fella, we went up for a header and I went in so hard I cut his eye open. We were in Cork and they gave us a banquet afterwards at the town hall and you might know I'd be sitting next to this fella with a great bandage on his eye. He was all right about it – but we'd won the game 3-2 and I didn't have to go home. That was the effect Stan had on you."

Chapter 13 Pompey chime in again

All in all, it had been a season to savour and a way for Cullis to banish the memory of the shambles that was Wembley 1939. Having exorcised one of his demons he now had to try to do the same with another – the First Division title.

Boosted by their FA Cup triumph, Wolves made a wonder start to the 1949-50 season which gave rise to speculation that Cullis could guide Wolves to the championship that had eluded him three times as a player. Apart from Lawrie Kelly bring reinstated at right-back, the team who had triumphed at Wembley began the season and reeled off six successive wins. Fans responded, too, and three of the first four Saturday home games saw crowds exceed 50,000. Molineux's average attendance for league games was eventually 45,347, a seasonal figure that remains the highest in the club's history. Wolves were top of the table and looking good . . . then came the slump. The first home point dropped came in the clash with Staffordshire rivals West Bromwich Albion at Molineux when selections by England for their game against Wales meant Wolves were without Bert Williams, Billy Wright and Johnny Hancocks. In the circumstances, Wolves did well to draw 1-1.

England's 4-1 win in Cardiff saw Billy Wright injured early on and spend the rest of the match hobbling on the left wing and Williams, too, was limping by the finish, able only to throw the ball out to his teammates rather than kick it. It was after the Albion game that Cullis took his team to Highbury to face Portsmouth in the FA Charity Shield, a traditional fixture usually featuring the Football League champions against the FA Cup winners. Of the three men who had been on international duty in Cardiff, only Hancocks was fit and his goal from the penalty spot earned Wolves a 1-1 draw, Duggie Reid scoring for Pompey. There were no penalty shoot-outs in those days and the FA decided that for the first time in the match's history the trophy would be shared.

Three days after the Charity Shield match came the first league defeat – in the 13th game – at the hands of Manchester United, 3-0 at Old Trafford, where they had been reinstated at the beginning of the season. The next ten games would yield just four points for Wolves. Bert Williams and Billy Wright missed a few games through injury but there was no real explanation for the slump as the one-time leaders were down to sixth after being beaten 2-0 at Newcastle on Christmas Eve.

Cullis did not make wholesale changes, though Lawrie Kelly made way for Angus McLean, Eddie Russell was given a few games at half-back and there was a debut at inside-right for Roy Swinbourne. The Yorkshireman would later switch to centre-forward and it was clear the manager had unearthed a rare talent. Swinbourne hit two goals when at last the rot was stopped with a 4-1 win at Villa Park, two days after Christmas. Villa had won 3-2 at Molineux on Boxing Day.

It was around this time that Cullis was confronted by Johnny Hancocks. The little right winger had been capped for England at outside-left against Wales in October and told the manager that the left wing was where he wished to play in order to further his international career. Hancocks seemed not to have taken into account that Wolves already had one of the country's best outside-lefts in Jimmy Mullen. Hancocks had also forgotten that a major barrier to an England career was his aversion to flying. Cullis showed his steel by saying "Nothing doing" and for a couple of games played Hancocks in the reserves. Hancocks then took his request to chairman James Baker who backed up the manager by saying he could not have a transfer. Hancocks eventually accepted the situation and resumed his inimitable contribution on the right wing. However, it was an unwanted distraction as Cullis tried to revitalise the title bid.

A corner had not been entirely turned and a 2-0 defeat at Middlesbrough saw the one-time leaders again down in sixth place. Maybe Cullis could find some encouragement when the defence of the FA Cup began. Instead it brought three replays, Wolves beating Plymouth 3-0 at home after a 1-1 draw, then winning 4-3 at Sheffield United after being held 1-1 at Molineux. They finally went out to Blackpool 1-0 in a bad-tempered Bloomfield Road replay after a goalless meeting at Molineux. So it was back to the league for Cullis and three days after the Cup exit champions Portsmouth came to Molineux and the manager decided to gamble. With Jesse Pye injured, he opted to move full-back Angus McLean to centre-forward and he rose to the occasion – literally – leaping to head home a Jimmy Mullen corner after just six minutes for what proved the game's only goal on a day Scottish inside forward Johnny Walker was given his debut.

While McLean reverted to full-back, Cullis kept Walker in the team and appeared to have Wolves back on track for a title challenge. Yet he could have been excused for thinking it was all a question of who would finish second to Manchester United. Matt Busby's side, runners-up the previous three seasons, led Cup-preoccupied Blackpool by two points with ten games to play. United had just beaten Middlesbrough 3-2 away to follow up a 7-1 home win over Villa when left-winger Charlie Mitten achieved the remarkable feat of a hat-trick of penalties. Wolves were seven points behind United and five adrift of Blackpool but would finish ahead of both teams. United would not win again until the final day of the season and Blackpool managed only one win in their last ten matches. Sunderland put themselves into contention with three successive wins only to promptly follow it with three successive defeats.

Easter yet again proved decisive and Wolves were held 1-1 at home by Manchester United on the Saturday and then were unexpectedly off key at Maine Road where Manchester City won 2-1. For the return game the next day, Cullis made bold changes, dropping Lawrie Kelly, moving Bill Shorthouse to left-back and bringing in Ray Chatham at centre-half .The rejigged defence looked much more assured in a 3-0 victory. That put Wolves on 46 points, behind Portsmouth (47) and Manchester United and Sunderland (48). Not for the last time the crucial run-in to the championship was affected by the rule that fixtures had to be played on the same Saturday as England games. Cullis, always so proud to represent his country over the years, must have found it inconvenient having to release key men Bert Williams and Billy Wright for the game at Hampden Park on the same day Wolves were visiting Chelsea.

Nigel Sims, successfully blooded by Cullis as a 17-year-old the previous season, did not let the side down but Wright was missed both as player and skipper as the game at Stamford Bridge ended goalless. That point dropped would prove decisive because Portsmouth could lose 2-0 at Arsenal in their penultimate game and still have their fate in their own hands. They and Wolves came to the final day both on 51 points but with Pompey having a vastly superior goal average. Wolves, who had kept up the pressure after the Chelsea draw by beating Arsenal 3-0 at home and Bolton 4-2 away, would need a double-figure final-day victory over Birmingham City unless Portsmouth lost or drew their game at home to Aston Villa. Pompey never looked like losing and were 2-0 up at half-time, running out 5-1 winners. Wolves did their best, being 5-0 up at the break against relegated Blues but their ultimate 6-1 victory made no difference. That dropped point at Stamford Bridge had been critical. For a fourth time Cullis had come close to bringing the title to Molineux and for a third time he had missed out on the last day of his team's season. Goal average was arrived at by dividing goals scored by goals conceded. Portsmouth and Wolves were level on 53 points but the goal average was an emphatic 1.947 to 1.551 in Pompey's favour. So near yet again so far. That dreadful spell in mid season when 12 games brought only seven points out of a possible 24 was what really scuppered Wolves' chances.

Only previous occasion the championship had been decided on goal average was in 1924 when Huddersfield edged out Cardiff City as they began their historic hat-trick of First Division titles. Cullis believed it was not the way to settle the issue if teams finished level on points at the top of the table – and that would have been his view even if the goal average had been in Wolves' favour. He favoured a play-off and said: "Portsmouth were worthy champions and no-one begrudges them the title, but I can't help feeling that it is unsatisfactory for such an important title to be won and lost on goal average."

Cullis was a lone voice and even now there is no suggestion of a play-off should teams finish level on points. Goal difference replaced goal average in 1976-7 and it enabled Manchester City to pip Manchester United for the Premier League title in 2012 while Arsenal won the First Division title in 1989 by virtue of goals scored when level with Liverpool on both points and goal difference.

While Cullis would spend the 1950 summer at home, some of his players were occupied elsewhere. Jimmy Mullen wrote his name into the record books when he became England's first ever substitute in a full international, not only replacing Jackie Milburn in a 4-1 defeat of Belgium in Brussels but scoring as well. He, Billy Wright and Bert Williams were named in the squad for Brazil, the setting for England's first ever appearance in the World Cup finals. It seems amazing now that despite such an important tournament, the FA still arranged a tour of Canada and the United States at the same time. As the tourists were going to North America by sea, reluctant flyer Johnny Hancocks was able to accept the FA's invitation to join the squad. The little winger went on to be top scorer on the tour with 16 goals and hit the only goal when the tourists beat the USA national team. That result came just two weeks before the same USA side, apart from one player, sensationally beat England in the World Cup.

Williams, Wright and Mullen wanted to forget their World Cup exploits, but Johnny Hancocks should have been buoyant after his summer exertions. Instead, the little winger returned to Molineux in a disgruntled mood, still nursing dreams of playing on the left wing, and again presented Cullis with a problem he could do without by refusing to re-sign on August 1, as did Roy Pritchard. While the full-back relented within a week, Hancocks held out until the end of the month. Hancocks was the team's penalty-taker and during his absence two kicks awarded to Wolves went begging, Pye missing in the 2-1 defeat at Fulham and Mullen in a 3-2 home loss to Derby. It was a relieved Cullis when Hancocks finally came to his senses and re-signed.

When Hancocks at last made his 1950-1 seasonal debut it was in sensational style, scoring twice in the first ten minutes against Bolton at Molineux as Wolves roared to a 7-1 win, Roy Swinbourne hitting a hat-trick. Towards the end of the previous season Cullis had decided the time was right to give Swinbourne his chance at centre-forward, moving Pye to inside left to the exclusion of FA Cup hero Sammy Smyth. It was a decision that bore substantial fruit for Swinbourne and for Wolves. There was also evidence for Cullis that there were reserves of quality pressing for first team places, namely Dennis Wilshaw and winger Leslie Smith. In defence, Jack Short, one of the products of Wath Wanderers, the nursery club in Yorkshire, would be given his chance by the manager and would take it well. Short vied with Angus McLean for the right-back spot and Lawrie Kelly took the hint he was not wanted and Huddersfield Town were happy to sign him in October, 1950.

After the previous season's near miss, Cullis must have hoped again to make a challenge in 1950-1 even though Spurs, with their "push and run" brand of football were taking the First Division by storm as they had the Second the previous season. At Christmas, Wolves trailed the Londoners by only three points and to get the fans excited in the new year along came another FA Cup run. Cullis had to make one of those tough decisions that every manager faces and drop a player who had served him well. Out went another of the Wembley heroes, Jesse Pye. Johnny Walker was given his chance and would figure prominently in the Cup adventure, scoring the winner 20 minutes from time when Wolves negotiated a tricky third-round hurdle 2-1 against Plymouth in stormy conditions at Home Park. A week later Blackpool earned a 1-1 draw at Molineux but Wolves had still stretched their unbeaten league run to nine matches and were four points behind joint leaders Tottenham and Middlesbrough, who had 36 points from 26 games. Wolves had a game in hand so were still in contention, only to lose 2-1 at Tottenham before a gate of 66,796 the following Saturday. The sixteen league games after that brought only two wins.

Next up in the Cup were arch rivals Aston Villa, whose left-back was Dickie Dorsett, teammate of Cullis's on that ill-fated trip to Wembley 12 years earlier. A crowd of 53,148 were at Molineux for the visit of Villa on one of those magical FA Cup days full of incident. Walker and Swinbourne scored goals in the space of four minutes around the half-hour mark and then goalkeeper Bert Williams saved a Con Martin penalty. Cullis must have been a worried man when Johnny Dixon narrowed the deficit two minutes into the second half but could finally relax – if it could ever be said that Cullis relaxed during a game – seven minutes from time when Jimmy Mullen made it 3-1.

Favoured with a home draw, Wolves, without greatly impressing, did enough to negotiate the fifth round with a 2-0 win over Huddersfield Town, Lawrie Kelly and all. Jimmy Dunn proved a gutsy match-winner, scoring both goals. He flicked home a Jimmy Mullen centre on 24 minutes but later sustained a kick to the right leg which meant he had to limp along the left wing for the rest of the game. This did not prevent him using his injured leg to fire home a vicious volley six minutes from time. Wolves were in the last eight of the FA Cup for the second time in three seasons. Could Cullis be on course for a second trophy? Before the answer came to that question, the manager did some business which would benefit the club beyond all expectation. He signed Peter Broadbent.

It was a good day's work when Cullis decided to employ George Poyser as a coach at Molineux because it would not be long before Poyser would be telling Cullis about a forward at his old club Brentford. He was 17-year-old Broadbent and Poyser believed he had the potential for football greatness. Poyser had first come across him while with Dover FC and when Poyser joined Brentford he quickly ensured that Broadbent followed.

The Express & Star reported Broadbent's Wolves signing on February 22, 1951, and said: "Mr Stanley Cullis regards the investment on the youngster as long term and is convinced he will develop into a first-class player." So convinced was the manager that he persuaded Wolves to pay out £10,000, at the time a record fee for a teenager. The deal would turn out to be a bargain as Broadbent became the brains behind the team in the late 1950s when, like all great players, he made the game look easy. Broadbent has a special place in the affections of fans who watched him in his pomp. He was arguably the most naturally-gifted player to don the gold jersey.

While Broadbent was turning out for Wolves reserves two days after his transfer in a Central League match against Stoke, his new club were keeping their Wembley hopes alive by drawing 1-1 against Sunderland before 62,373 fans at Roker Park. Dickie Davis's 11th-minute goal for the home side was cancelled out within two minutes by Johnny Walker. There may have been no more goals but there were plenty of thrills in a typical FA Cup tie. The replay four days later brought a Molineux gate of 54,243 as Wolves belied their league form – they had lost three successive matches – to breeze into the semi-final with a 3-1 win. Jimmy Dunn and Roy Swinbourne scored either side of half-time and Johnny Walker hit a third on the hour. Trevor Ford's reply for Sunderland did not arrive until the last minute. Wolves had thus spoiled the prospect of a North East semi-final as the winners had been drawn against the winners of the Bristol Rovers-Newcastle tie which the Geordies won after a replay on the same night as the Molineux game.

For the second time in three seasons Wolves were engaged in a semi-final replay but this time they failed to win at the second attempt. Cullis had the build-up right for both games against Newcastle. The team stayed overnight at Mapleton in Derbyshire before journeying on Saturday morning to Sheffield where the game at Hillsborough produced a goalless draw. It was back to Sheffield three days later for a stay at the Grand Hotel before next day travelling to Huddersfield where hopes of another trip to Wembley were dashed at Leeds Road as Newcastle, destined to win the trophy, scraped home 2-1. The scoring was done in the first half when Johnny Walker gave Wolves the lead after 16 minutes only for Jackie Milburn and Bobby Mitchell to score within the space of four minutes around the half-hour.

Cullis, for the first time in his managerial career, then faced a crisis as the Cup exploits were merely a diversion from a league season which had fallen apart. Eighteen league games from the turn of the year produced just two wins as Wolves' title bid became a distant memory. Amazingly, only one of Wolves' 19 league defeats that season was by more than one goal – 2-0 at Burnley. Even Cullis's trusted lieutenant, Billy Wright, had lost his form and was eventually dropped by England. Three days after the semi-final defeat, Cullis gave young Broadbent his league debut in a 3-2 home defeat at the hands of Portsmouth on a mud heap of a pitch at Molineux. In eight more games before the end of the season Broadbent gave more evidence that he might make it in the top flight. Before then there would be some worrying times for Wolves' young manager.

Chapter 14 Job on the line

There was no time to ponder too long on what had gone wrong in a season which had started promisingly but had ended with Wolves in 14th place in the First Division. A few days after the final league match of 1950-1, Wolves set off for South Africa, where a demanding 12-match tour had been arranged. The team travelled in two separate parties, the first via Tripoli, Kano and Brazzaville to Johannesburg and the second, which included Cullis, by way of Rome and Lydda before also arriving at Johannesburg where the opening match was played. A 4-1 victory over Southern Transvaal at the Rand Stadium was the first of five successive wins before Cullis made an interesting team selection. He named himself at right-half.

Yes, for the game against South Western Districts at Mossel Bay, Cullis came out of retirement. Not only that, he did something he had never managed before in his time with Wolves and England – he scored a goal. It was no tap-in either but a long-range effort, the eighth goal in a win every bit as comfortable as the 11-0 scoreline would suggest. Jimmy Mullen returned to England soon afterwards as his wife was expecting their second child and the winger told the Express & Star about Cullis's comeback. Mullen said Cullis still looked a master half-back with all the old touches which made him England's automatic captain. Unfortunately, Mullen had not witnessed a subsequent game against Border in East London when Cullis decided he would give himself another run-out. Border were a vastly different proposition from South Western Districts and it soon became clear that Cullis faced a demanding afternoon. It took 64 minutes for the deadlock to be broken when Bill Baxter scored, and soon afterwards Cullis provided the through ball from which Johnny Walker made it 2-0. Then the pace began to catch up with the manager and it was clear he was struggling. Stubbornly the boss refused to come off and, in any case, Wolves had already used two substitutes, Eddie Russell replacing full-back Jack Short after 28 minutes and Billy Wright coming on for Sammy Smyth on 55 minutes after the inside-right had sustained a cut eye. It was fortunate Cullis had players like Baxter, Wright and Bill Shorthouse to cover for him as he tired in the final half-hour. It is reasonable to suppose that there and then he decided his playing days were definitely a thing of the past. He would have had an easier time if he had played in the game that followed the one against Border. East Transvaal were beaten 13-0 in Benoni, with Roy Swinbourne scoring six goals.

On returning home after Wolves had won all 12 matches, Cullis praised the organisation and the hospitality of the South Africans and spoke highly of the way his players had conducted themselves both on and off the field. He explained his reappearance as a player as being merely to give a couple of his touring squad a rest.

Cullis also related a rather scary moment during a two-day visit to a game reserve. A truck in which he and some of the tour party were travelling was in danger of being charged by a rhinoceros. The intrepid would-be explorer was not fazed. "I kept my cine camera trained on it and I hope to have some good pictures to show a thrilling experience," he said. In the coming season, Cullis would need all that sang-froid to cope with his fourth season as a manager.

After a defeat and a draw in their first two games, Wolves made a useful start to 1951-2 with the first 11 games bringing seven wins. First of those was 2-1 at home to Arsenal when half-back Norman Deeley, a pint-sized former England schoolboy international, was given his debut. It was after this match that centre-forward Roy Swinbourne asked Cullis if he could be dropped even though he had scored the winning goal three minutes from time. He was unhappy with his game and felt a run in the reserve team would help him regain his confidence. Cullis admired the player's honesty and agreed to the request which ultimately helped Swinbourne back to his best form. The manager was fortunate to have England B international Dennis Wilshaw to bring into the attack in Swinbourne's place. The 11th game of the season saw second-placed Bolton come to Molineux, giving a debut to 15-year-old future England inside-forward Ray Parry. With Jesse Pye grabbing a hat-trick, Wolves blew the northern Wanderers away, scoring four goals in the space of 20 minutes, starting in the 20th minute. The 5-1 win meant Wolves were then on 15 points, only three fewer than leaders Manchester United. Wolves had by then totalled 31 goals, having two games earlier set a club away win record when they brushed aside relegation-destined Huddersfield 7-1 at Leeds Road. The outlook seemed bright. Then came four successive defeats followed by three draws. Wolves were on the slide.

One of those drawn games was on an overcast winter's day at home to Charlton and Cullis, with the aid of club secretary Jack Howley, came up with an innovation to defy the gloom. Wolves' old gold was hardly a bright colour and so a set of fluorescent shirts had been commissioned by the manager and club secretary, the theory being the kit would be more visible on dark afternoons in mid-season. There were no floodlights allowed in league games at that time so clubs were at the mercy of the weather and against Charlton Cullis ordered his team to change into the new shirts at half-time. "Commentator" reported in the Express & Star: "In their new luminous yellow shirts, Wolves shone through the gloom of Molineux on Saturday but did not dispel it. They made history but did not make a good impression." Leading 2-1, Wolves were pegged back to 2-2 through a late goal by Chris Duffy. Cullis said: "We bought the shirts six weeks ago. They are tougher than ordinary shirts but we intend to use them when conditions are gloomy."

On their visit to Fulham a week later, a note in the home programme said: "In their match against Charlton last week, Wolverhampton started something new by appearing in the second half in shirts of yellow made of material that glows in the semi-darkness. New ideas are always welcome, especially when they are to the benefit of the spectators, as this one is." The shirts were used again in the second half of the next home game and brought better luck, Wolves scoring three times to clinch a 4-0 win over Middlesbrough. After that, there is no record of the shirts being used again in league matches; one suspects the Football League did not share the enthusiasm of the author of the Fulham programme and told Wolves they were not allowed. However, fluorescent shirts were worn by Wolves in friendlies once floodlights had been installed at Molineux.

Another rare highlight before the turn of the year was a 3-0 home win over Blackpool when centre-forward Ken Whitfield scored a hat-trick on his home debut. That proved a false omen and when Whitfield lost his place it was to a full-back. Such was the striker crisis that Cullis played Jack Short in the number-nine shirt. Ironically, Short had been rejected by Wolves as a centre-forward in a trial match but went away and turned up again at Molineux, this time as a defender. Short scored twice as Wolves beat Manchester City 4-1 in a third-round FA Cup replay but a brief run in the league side showed that as a centre-forward Short was a good full-back! He would not be the last defender played at centre-forward by Cullis, however.

Liverpool put a quick end to any hopes of a Cup run, winning 2-1 before what remains an Anfield attendance record of 61,905. By coincidence, the FA Cup meeting of the teams in 1939 had set Molineux's best gate. The Reds were now managed by Don Welsh who had played alongside Cullis eight times for England in wartime internationals. Bob Paisley, who would years later become Liverpool's most successful manager, scored after just five minutes and Cyril Done struck again four minutes later. Jimmy Mullen's reply came late in the game. Both Paisley and Done had won championship medals with Liverpool in 1947 but were sidelined by injury for the vital win at Molineux in Cullis's dramatic career finale.

On the league front, Matt Busby, at Old Trafford, had stolen a march on his wartime pal, and his team of old campaigners like Johnny Carey, Henry Cockburn, Allenby Chilton, Jack Rowley and Stan Pearson were on their way to a deserved title win, having been runners-up in four of the previous five seasons. Brian Birch, a former England youth international, was in the United side who won 2-0 at Molineux but could not command a regular first team place. So Cullis moved in to sign him late in the season in the hope his early promise might be realised at Molineux. It was not and he was soon sold to Lincoln City, an early example of an unsuccessful Cullis venture into the transfer market.

While Billy Wright had recaptured his form to such an extent that he would be named Footballer of the Year, his was a lone individual success and the Wolves side were in a transitional stage. They finished 16th in the table, their lowest position since their first season back in the top flight – 1932-3. Trouble was that the appetite had been whetted with Wolves in recent seasons going close to becoming champions of England. The Molineux board wanted that title and, for some, 16th place was not good enough. For the first time, questions were being asked about Cullis's management.

Veteran football correspondent for the Times, Geoffrey Green, reckoned in his book, Soccer in the Fifties, that there were, indeed, strong voices on the board calling for a change. Wrote Green: "Here was a deep backstage crisis. Cullis, however, was saved by the energetic advocacy of one of his directors, the bluff, burly Mr Jim Marshall, a powerful figure on the board, who owned a majority of shares in the club. Cullis stayed and just as dramatically from that moment Wolves found a new tide that took them to success after success." Marshall, who would later be chairman of the club, did Wolves a great service by championing Cullis's cause. It would have been easy to send him on his way and that is what would probably happen in today's football world with its demand for instant success. Thankfully, attitudes were different in the early 1950s and Cullis survived this crisis.

Times were changing at Molineux and Jesse Pye, a two-goal star of the 1949 FA Cup final, was sold to Luton Town before the 1952-3 season began and teammate Jimmy Dunn would soon move on to Derby County. While Pye moved to Luton, in the other direction came John Taylor, an England B international forward, and sadly it was another Cullis transfer move that failed to pay dividends. Taylor made just ten appearances, scoring only once. However, Cullis got lucky just before the new season began when he received a letter from a personable young man who had just been appointed to a post at Birmingham University and wondered if there might be the chance of a game with Wolverhampton Wanderers. Author of the letter was W J Slater, an amateur international who had played in the Olympics earlier in the year and was in the Blackpool side beaten at Wembley the previous year by Wolves' semi-final conquerors Newcastle United. He remains the last amateur to appear in an FA Cup final.

W J Slater – Bill Slater – would often recall how he was taken to task by Cullis for expressing merely the desire to get a game of football with the club. Cullis made it abundantly clear that he wanted players with ambition to get in the first team. For Slater it was a no-win situation. If he had written demanding first-team football, Cullis would have quickly put him in his place. So it was that Slater arrived and his debut came just a couple of games after that of Ron Flowers, yet another product of the Wath Wanderers nursery. Here were two men who would soon make Wolves' half-back strength the best in the land while waiting in the wings was another, young Edwin Clamp, from Coalville, Leicestershire, a member of the celebrated 1950 England schoolboys side that also featured Johnny Haynes.

Wing-half Flowers made his debut nominally at centre-half and scored from a corner in a 5-2 home defeat by Blackpool. Two games later, the 18-year-old was played at right-half in place of Billy Crook while Slater was given his debut at left-half in place of Billy Wright, who was playing for England against Northern Ireland in Belfast. Visitors to Molineux that day were champions Manchester United, who raced into a two-goal lead only to be sent packing 6-2. Here was a glorious glimpse of Wolves' future with Swinbourne, a born-again first teamer, collecting a hat-trick.

Other young men were starting to repay the faith Cullis had shown in them. Peter Broadbent played 25 games that season though he later lost his place to Ron Stockin, a player signed from Walsall in February, 1952. Broadbent's progress owed something to Cullis's attention to detail the previous season. The manager had photographs taken of the player in action and they confirmed what he had suspected – Broadbent was playing with his mouth open! So Cullis arranged for him to see a top specialist in London and his examination showed that Broadbent was not breathing from his diaphragm. Graduated exercises and medical attention produced a rapid improvement in Broadbent's performances.

Dennis Wilshaw established himself as a fine striker with 17 goals in 29 league games and with old faithfuls Johnny Hancocks and Jimmy Mullen on the wings, a team of some force were taking shape. Not that Cullis was afraid to drop a star player if he felt it was for the benefit of the team and internationals Hancocks and Bert Williams were both omitted when the boss felt it necessary. It was with Nigel Sims in goal and Les Smith in Hancocks's right-wing spot that Wolves beat Manchester City 7-3 in November. It was the first time in his Wolves career that Williams had been dropped yet just over a year earlier he had been England's first choice, only losing his international place through injury. After three weeks in the reserves, Cullis restored him to the first team.

Injury to Williams would give Sims his chance again later in the season and Cullis kept him in the team for nine games. With Williams out of favour who should come calling on Cullis but his old mentor Major Buckley who was by then having a final managerial fling as boss of Walsall. Buckley wanted Williams to return to Fellows Park where his career had begun. Reports said terms had been agreed but Williams won back his Wolves place and decided to stay put, which proved a welcome decision for player, club and country.

The win over City took Wolves to the top of the table and once again that elusive First Division title was in Cullis's sights. A 2-1 win a week later at Stoke, where Sims saved a Frank Mountford penalty late in the match, kept the side top. Cullis was a happy man as he journeyed home from the Potteries and was able to lend a helping hand to some Wolves fans on their way back to Kingswinford, near Dudley. Their coach had been in collision with a lorry and Cullis stopped to offer a lift with the players on the team coach. Sadly, Wolves title aspirations did not reach their destination. There followed a slump to bring Cullis back down to earth. It began with a 2-0 home defeat by Preston, Dennis Wilshaw being a passenger for much of the game.

His injury was untimely as he had been named as a reserve for England's game against Belgium four days later. A run of nine games brought Wolves just one win and four defeats, five goals being conceded at both Sunderland and Arsenal. Wolves also conceded five at Deepdale as Preston ushered them out of the FA Cup 5-2, centre-forward Charlie Wayman grabbing a hat-trick.

Hancocks had won back his place by the time Wolves beat Stoke 3-0 on Easter Saturday and headed the First Division once again. Their pursuers, however, had games in hand and Arsenal would emerge as champions on goal average ahead of newly-promoted Preston with Wolves third. They were only three points adrift of the top two emphasising just how costly that nine-game mid-season slump had been when only six points were gained from a possible 18. Nevertheless, it had been a good season and the faith shown in Cullis had been justified.

Not that the campaign had run completely smoothly for Cullis. He could not contain his anger when former England inside forward Wilf Mannion denied Wolves a win at Middlesbrough by clearly using his hand to knock the ball out of Nigel Sims's grasp. The match ended 1-1 and later Cullis made his feelings known when he wrote to the match referee Tom Seymour of Wakefield. It landed the manager in hot water as the FA disciplinary committee considered it an action likely to bring the game into disrepute. Cullis had to give them an assurance it would not happen again.

A happier aspect of the season was the progress of the youth team. With his chief scout George Noakes running a fine talent-spotting network, Cullis had encouraged the recruitment of young players. At the end of the 1952-3 season, Wolves reached the final of the inaugural FA Youth Cup competition though in the final they met a Manchester United side boasting Eddie Colman, Duncan Edwards, Liam Whelan, David Pegg and Albert Scanlon and were beaten 9-3 on aggregate. Cullis had carried on the policy of Major Buckley in finding and nurturing young players and, at Old Trafford, Matt Busby had the same belief in youth. Though most youth team players failed to progress to Football League level, a significant number of this group did make it.

Teams at Old Trafford on Monday May 4, 1953, in the first leg of the first ever FA Youth Cup final:

Manchester United: Clayton; Fulton, Kennedy; Colman, Cope, Edwards; McFarlane, Whelan, Lewis, Pegg, Scanlon.

Wolves: Owen; Hodgkiss, Clamp; Timmins, Peter Russell, Bolton; Punter, Walker, Smith, Booth, Cooper.

There were three goals in the first six minutes at Old Trafford, Noel McFarlane giving United the lead, Wolves centre-forward Harry Smith cancelling it out and then Eddie Lewis making it 2-1. David Pegg added another before half-time and in the second half there were goals from McFarlane, Lewis, Albert Scanlon and Liam Whelan. It was a hopeless task for Wolves in the second leg five days later though Smith gave them a flying start with a goal on six minutes. Lewis and Whelan put United ahead by the break, however, before Smith made the result 2-2. Despite the 7-1 defeat in the first game, there was still a gate of 14,290 for the Molineux leg. Of the United side, Colman, Ronnie Cope, Edwards, Whelan, Pegg and Scanlon all established themselves in the United first team. Gordon Clayton and Eddie Lewis also had a few appearances. Of the Wolves side, the only real graduates were Eddie Clamp and Colin Booth, though Peter Russell did have three first team games.

Edwards, of course, was by common consent the outstanding English footballer of his generation and though he was born and bred in Dudley, Wolves were fighting a losing battle in trying to sign him. His father, Gladstone, was a Wolves fan and would have loved Duncan to sign for the club. His mother, Sarah Anne, whom everyone called Annie, would have liked him to join a local team so he would continue to live at home. However, both parents were happy to leave the decision to Duncan and he was always a United fan. It was a dream come true when he went to Old Trafford. Not that Cullis did not try to get him to Molineux. He and chief scout George Noakes would sit in a parked car outside the Edwards home, awaiting the gifted youngster's return from school. Despite talks with the lad and his parents, there was no getting him to sign for Wolves, even though it had the added incentive of being a club "on his doorstep". Perhaps any slight reluctance by his parents to back a move to United subsided when Busby presented them with a washing machine and fridge, luxury items in the 1950s. Many years later, Annie Edwards told sportswriter David Harrison: "Mr Cullis was a lovely man, a proper gentleman who tried all he could to get Duncan to Wolves. But Duncan always had it in his head he wanted to play for Manchester United and nothing was going to stand in his way." Harrison readily confirms that for Cullis, Edwards would always remain the one that got away.

Despite this, Noakes and his scouts, plus the nursery club at Wath run by Mark Crook, would find other young talent, several of whom made the grade, Another testimony to Wolves' growing strength was to be found in the reserve team who brought the Central League title to Molineux for a third season running. All the ingredients were there for a squad able to compete with the best in the land. After surviving two disappointing seasons, Cullis had seen his team make considerable progress in 1952-3. Everything was in place to land Wolves' Holy Grail – the championship of the First Division.

Chapter 15   Champions of England

Hopes Cullis might have had for an immediate impact on proceedings in the 1953-4 championship race were quickly dented when his side lost two of their first three games. All three were away from home, brought about by a decision to ensure the televised FA Cup final would be a lone fixture with no league games the same day. So the league games scheduled for May 1, the day of the Cup Final, were brought forward to the beginning of the season as the Football League created history by kicking off in midweek. That meant Wolves began with a trip to Burnley on Wednesday, August 19, 1953, and were off to a flying start, Roy Swinbourne scoring the opening day's quickest goal when he struck after only one minute and fifty seconds. It all looked good for an hour but chances wasted would prove costly as Burnley scored four goals in the last half-hour to win 4-1. Three days later it was a different story as Wolves did not let up after a good start and won 4-0 at Manchester City. Wolves then lost 3-2 at Sunderland despite a gutsy fightback after going three goals down. Cullis decided a change was called for.

After 18 successive games in the number-eight shirt, Ron Stockin was dropped. Cullis decided the time had again come to give an opportunity to naturally-gifted Peter Broadbent. This time the talent did not flicker only to fade but began to flower as he thrived alongside the more experienced forwards. Such was the success of the combination that in the days of five-men forward lines that of Wolves would in future be repeated by fans like a mantra – Hancocks, Broadbent, Swinbourne, Wilshaw and Mullen. Cullis had also found a settled defensive formation with which to start the season. Jack Short and Roy Pritchard had made the full-back positions their own and the half-back line looked formidable with Billy Wright and Bill Slater alongside the ever-reliable Bill Shorthouse.

A notable absentee from the first five games was goalkeeper Bert Williams but he returned to the side after injury in time to help them to a memorable win – 3-2 at Highbury where they had not beaten Arsenal for 21 years. It was 2-2 at the break and the winning goal did not come until two minutes from time. That Johnny Hancocks should score was not wholly unexpected but the manner of his goal was something unlikely from a player little over 5ft 4ins. It was a flying header which would have done justice to a Tommy Lawton or a Nat Lofthouse.

Cullis's team looked full of goals so it was a surprise when they were held to a goalless draw at Blackpool. They did have Billy Wright playing at right-back for the injured Short and were without Bill Slater who was required to play for England in the amateur international against South Africa. In stark contrast, there were goals galore next game with Wright and Slater back in the half-back line. Chelsea were only two down at half-time but left Molineux beaten 8-1 on a day with no fewer than four England captains on view. The visitors had former England amateur skipper Derek Saunders at left-half, while his opposite number, Slater, was the current amateur captain, with Billy Wright, of course, the national side's leader. Watching the proceedings, living every kick, header and tackle was a predecessor of Wright's – Stanley Cullis. After this goal feast, in which all five forwards found the net, there would be some light relief for Cullis.

The manager, always forward thinking, had long felt that football under floodlights would soon be a matter of course. However, his was a cautious approach. Other clubs had already erected floodlight systems, but Cullis, the Molineux board and secretary Jack Howley were not going to be rushed and took a good look around at what was on offer. Eventually, four pylons – one at each corner – were erected and equipped with the best lighting system available. The big switch-on was on Wednesday, September 30, 1953, when the South Africa national XI, on tour to Britain, were beaten 3-1. Cullis told the Express & Star afterwards that he was "greatly impressed" with the lighting system and emphasised it had been well worth taking their time to ensure the lights were top class. Cullis made a generous gesture to Wolves' own South African, Eddie Stuart. With the compliance of Billy Wright and Bill Shorthouse, the latter agreeing to stand down, he named Stuart at centre-half and allowed him to captain Wolves against his compatriots. It was a gesture always treasured by Stuart who had good reason to be eternally grateful to the club. He had contracted a mystery illness a year earlier and things looked so bad that his mother was flown in from South Africa to be at his bedside. Stuart slowly recovered full health and would in future years prove a player on whom Cullis could rely.

More floodlit friendlies would follow during the season but the main attention focused on league action as the title race developed into a two-horse affair with Cullis's men hard on the heels of a West Bromwich Albion side managed by Cullis's wartime international colleague Vic Buckingham. After 17 games Albion had 28 points with Wolves three adrift. All was set for a crunch meeting of the two at Molineux before 56,590 fans but Cullis was deprived of the services of two vital cogs in his smooth-running football machine. Peter Broadbent was injured and Bill Slater was required by England to skipper them in the amateur international against France at Luton.

The atmosphere at Kenilworth Road would have been a big contrast to the cauldron that was Molineux where, after four minutes, Jimmy Mullen scored what proved to be the only goal. It was the first time that season that Albion had failed to score and it meant their twin strike force of Ronnie Allen and Johnny Nicholls, with a total of 29 goals between them, had been held in check. Credit for that had to go to the half-back line of Billy Wright, Bill Shorthouse and Slater's deputy, Bill Baxter. Into Broadbent's place came Ron Stockin for what proved his final first-team game. In the summer, Cullis would feel he was surplus to requirements and would sell him to Cardiff City. Although Stockin had done a bit better than previous inside-forward signing, John Taylor, he again represented a failed venture into the transfer market.

A week after the Molineux meeting, Albion's frustrated goal duo were back in business with a bang as Cardiff City went down 6-1 at The Hawthorns, Allen scoring four times and Nicholls twice. On the same day, with Slater and Broadbent available once more, Wolves won 2-0 at Charlton. So it was still a Black Country battle at the top of the table but domestic affairs would soon be forgotten. About to arrive was a shock that would rock English football but would not be entirely a surprise to Cullis. On Wednesday, November 25, 1953, at a misty Wembley Stadium, England were given a football lesson as they lost 6-3 to Hungary.

Bill Slater had watched the Hungarian maestros, Bozsik, Hidegkuti, Kocsis, Puskas and co, win the Olympic tournament in Finland and had told the men at the FA about them and had talked to Cullis about their skill level. That, plus playing together regularly, unlike the England national side, made them a special combination. So Cullis knew in advance that England would be in for a testing afternoon, though no-one could have predicted the scoreline would have been so emphatic. However, the Wolves manager always maintained that a myth had arisen around the Magical Magyars' style of football and much of their effectiveness was achieved by the kind of direct play which he advocated. Be that as it may, the vast majority of English football's managers and players would indulge in a period of self-examination as it was realised the game had been taken by the Hungarians to a higher level. Confirmation of that came in the summer when the return match in Budapest brought England's heaviest ever defeat – 7-1. English football was at its lowest ebb and it would eventually be left to Cullis and his men famously to restore some national pride. Much was written after the game at Wembley where Cullis and his number two, Joe Gardiner, were among the spectators watching England being made to look a team of plodders.

While the pundits talked of the Magical Magyars' short-passing game, Cullis took a different view. "I was far more impressed with the number and quality of longer passes – many in the air – which the Hungarians employed," he wrote in All For The Wolves. "But at once there came a call both from the critics and the public that England should return to 'on the ground' football, and some clubs, in my opinion, were to lose precious time as they followed this advice. The critics and the public, I think, were misled by the particular brand of play employed by Hungary at Wembley at a time when they had the match well in hand. Then they used the 'free wheel' style of football in which the defenders, including the goalkeeper, and the midfield players used an innumerable total of short passes for a specific purpose. At this stage, Hungary's players were merely denying possession of the ball to England without making any great efforts to score themselves."

A legend had grown up that Hungary played most of their football "on the carpet" but the facts did not bear this out. Cullis pointed out that Puskas and his team had hit a high number of long passes and many of them in the air. They used 94 long passes at Wembley, most of them in the first hour, and more than 60 were in the air. Three of the six goals were scored after moves involving only one pass. Cullis was able to cite these facts thanks to an RAF man, Wing-Commander Charles Reep. Stationed at RAF Bridgnorth, Reep had devised a method of recording matches and it bore out the theories to which Cullis had always adhered. "Reep was able to establish, in black and white, the facts for which I was forced to trust my memory where, inevitably, some would become lost or confused," wrote Cullis, who was happy to agree to Reep's request to record future Wolves games.

Not that Cullis was dismissive of Hungary. Far from it and within weeks of the Wembley epic there were reports that the Wolves boss wanted to go to Budapest at the end of the season to see just how the Magical Magyars achieved their spectacular success. "I am hoping to go to Budapest to study Hungarian training and coaching methods, tactics and practice routines," he told the Daily Mirror. "I want to make sure that I would get full facilities for looking around and seeing things I want to see in Hungary. If the Hungarians have better ideas than we have, I feel we should see them and put them into practice." Mirror man Bob Ferrier commented: "Cullis, a great centre-half and England captain in his time, is a tough, intense, restless type. He runs his team with a ruthless discipline. He spares no effort in improving even the smallest facet of his work." The planned visit never happened – it may have been that the Hungarians were not co-operative – but it is evidence that Cullis did not dismiss what had happened to England as just one of those things. He did not have a closed mind and was willing to embrace new thinking.

Meanwhile, back on the domestic front, Wolves took their unbeaten run to 18 games when they won 3-2 at Tottenham. This meant that at exactly halfway through the season they were at last ahead of Albion, who on the same day had been beaten 3-2 at home by Portsmouth. Wolves led the table on 33 points, one more than their Black Country rivals. Having reached the top, there followed a wobble. Of the next nine games, five were lost and four were won. The low point came in mid February with a 4-2 defeat at Chelsea on the same day Albion defeated Sheffield Wednesday by a similar score at The Hawthorns. Thus their rivals were three points ahead with twelve games to play.

Cullis had to make changes after the Stamford Bridge game. Bill Shorthouse was injured in the seventh minute and, after nearly 20 minutes off the field having treatment, came back to operate first at outside right and then at centre-forward. So the manager moved Billy Wright to centre-half and kept him there for six games, starting with a 6-1 home win over Sheffield United. Shorthouse recovered in time for the next game but returned at left-back. In due course the pair would switch positions but Wright's potential as a central defender was clear. The Sheffield United visit was the first game as a professional for Bill Slater, his decision to become a part-time pro being warmly welcomed by Cullis. Slater's teaching duties still came first but no more would the England amateur selectors be able to call upon the wing-half's services. However, more international recognition would eventually come Slater's way.

Suddenly it seemed it was advantage Albion in the race for the title, but for one thing – they had embarked on an FA Cup run. They were making a bold bid to do the Double, a prize that had so far proved elusive to English clubs in the 20th Century. Cullis knew all about trying to win both League and Cup in the same season with lasting memories of Wolves' runners-up "double" in 1939. So it would not surprise him when Albion's league form faltered as the Cup run gained momentum. The Baggies' sixth-round win over Tottenham was followed by a 5-0 reverse at Chelsea in midweek; the semi-final victory over Port Vale was followed by a 2-1 defeat at Sunderland. That was a let-off for Wolves as they had slumped to a 4-2 home defeat at the hands of Middlesbrough on the day Albion were clinching their Wembley appearance. If Albion had then beaten Sunderland, they would have been four points clear at the top of table. Instead they led by just two with six games to play – and the first of those was the season's second meeting of the title contenders, this time at The Hawthorns. Alas, the drama was robbed of its principal characters.

The ridiculous situation of England calls taking precedence over league matches meant the meeting of Albion and Wolves on Saturday, April 3, 1954, was played without Ronnie Allen and Johnny Nicholls of the hosts and Billy Wright and Jimmy Mullen of the visitors. The loss of their twin strikeforce was probably a greater blow to Albion and added to an untimely accumulation of injuries that saw them without England international full-back Stan Rickaby and wingers Frank Griffin and George Lee. They were forced to play half-back Ray Barlow at centre-forward. Cullis was able to switch Shorthouse back to centre-half and bring in the experienced Roy Pritchard at left-back while Les Smith was an able deputy for Mullen, playing on the right wing with Hancocks switched to the left.

As at Molineux, one goal was enough to decide a game watched by 55,000. This time it took a while coming, Roy Swinbourne scoring in the 58th minute. Peter Broadbent, the youngster on whom Cullis had gambled three years earlier, was the outstanding player with born-again centre-half Bill Shorthouse ensuring Barlow had little scope, the Albion man handicapped by sustaining an ankle injury early in the game. In the Express & Star "Commentator" wrote that Shorthouse looked "happier and much more like his old self in the position he likes best of all." At Hampden Park, all four of the absentees made their mark, Allen, Nicholls and Mullen being scorers in a 4-2 England victory.

Wolves' first win at The Hawthorns since 1928 brought the teams level on 50 points with Wolves ahead on goal average with five games to play. Cullis now had a selection problem. Shorthouse, at this stage of his career, preferred to be in central defence while the blossoming talent of young half-back Ron Flowers had seen him earn a place in the team. Fortunately for Cullis, Billy Wright agreed to play at left-back for the remaining games. It was the second full-back change made by Cullis who had given Eddie Stuart his chance at right-back after that defeat at Chelsea. The South African had more than justified the confidence placed in him by the manager.

A slender lead at the top of the table became a significant one immediately after the Hawthorns meeting. Wolves beat Charlton 5-0 at Molineux, Johnny Hancocks missing the chance to make it six and to grab a hat-trick when he sent a penalty kick wide. On the same day, Albion lost 2-0 at Cardiff. Four games to go and two points clear . . . Cullis had the scent of victory in his nostrils but he knew better than anybody how cruelly title hopes could be dashed.

The gap at the top was narrowed on Easter Saturday when Wolves were held 0-0 by Sheffield Wednesday at Hillsborough and a Ronnie Allen penalty gave Albion a 1-0 win over Manchester City at The Hawthorns. Three games to go and one point clear . . . was there to be a twist in the tale? No! It proved to be a last league win for Vic Buckingham's side as their championship hopes were as good as ended by their two Easter holiday meetings with their closest neighbours Aston Villa.

While Wolves were beating Huddersfield 4-0 at Molineux on Easter Monday, Johnny Hancocks missing another penalty, Albion were being held 1-1 at The Hawthorns by Villa. Two games to go and two points clear . . . Wolves could clinch the title next day if they won the return game with Huddersfield. However, they were beaten 2-1 at Leeds Road where a certain Lawrie Kelly kicked one Wolves shot off the line and headed another against a post before Bill McGarry thumped home the winner. It mattered not. There was sensational news from Villa Park. Albion had crashed 6-1. With one game to play Wolves led by two points with a goal average advantage too great to be affected, except if they lost heavily and Albion won by a double-figure margin. Nothing could now stop Cullis achieving his ambition of making Wolves champions of England.

A calmness might have descended upon most managers but Cullis was a one-off. He did not do calm – not while watching a football match. The Daily Express's acclaimed sportswriter Desmond Hackett felt obliged to comment: "Stanley Cullis, Mr Wolves himself, the man who will on Saturday see his club go past the Championship post for the first time ever, should this day be a calm, contented character. Almost any other manager would be dislocating his arm patting himself on the back. The only damage soccer boss Stanley Cullis is likely to do himself is to break a toe kicking out the front of the directors' box at Wolverhampton when his wonder Wolves wind up their glorious season against Spurs. That is restless, relentless Stan Cullis. The man who in the tempestuous years from March 1934 to April 1954 has gone from timid office boy to demanding captain to sergeant-major manager of the champions of England football. That is the same exacting Cullis who told his team this week 'Don't take this thing for granted. We have been near before. I want your best on Saturday.' And on Saturday he will be twitching, kicking and going with every move of the match. He confesses 'I have been told I was doing myself no good, but the only alternative is stay away, and I will never quit.' This is the same spirit that drives manager Cullis storming into his team's dressing room at half-time and putting the fear of football into any erring players. And the same Cullis will give hours of his time to train and encourage the newest recruit on his playing staff. His players will cuss him and swear they would rather quit football than play under his management. Then they will go on to the field and play their hearts out. Why? Because they are compelled to appreciate that this young man with the shining restless eyes puts everything into his job. The best or bust is the Cullis motto."

Cullis at last made Wolves champions of England when they beat Tottenham 2-0 on the final day of the season to take their points total to 57. Albion's 3-0 defeat at Portsmouth meant the margin at the top was four points, which did not reflect the closeness of a contest that had been restricted to two participants virtually all season.

When the final whistle sounded after the win over Spurs at Molineux, fans invaded the pitch, crowded in front of the directors' box and called for their heroes, Billy Wright and his team duly obliging. The captain addressed the happy throng, whose additional calls for Cullis to make an appearance were not answered. In his moment of triumph the manager was nowhere to be found. It was no surprise that a man of such intensity, so driven to do the best for his players and the fans, should be overcome by emotion. In the Express & Star, "Commentator" said: "He was, I would say, rather too full for words."

Teams in the title-clinching match at Molineux Grounds, Wolverhampton, on Saturday, April 24, 1954:

Wolves: Williams; Stuart, Wright; Slater, Shorthouse, Flowers; Hancocks, Broadbent, Swinbourne, Wilshaw, Mullen.

Goals: Swinbourne, 18, 68.

Tottenham: Ditchburn; Baker, Willis; Nicholson, Clarke, Wetton; Walters, Bennett, Dunmore, Baily, McClellan.

Attendance: 44,055

Two days later Cullis did address the fans after the second leg of the FA Youth Cup final when the Football League championship trophy was presented to Billy Wright and his team. Among the players were Roy Pritchard and Jack Short who had been the full-back pairing for much of the season with 27 and 26 appearances respectively. Football League president Arthur Drewry handed over the trophy to Wright who told the fans who had invaded the pitch: "It is going to take a darned good team to take this trophy from us." He was wide of the mark, though, as a fairly ordinary side playing above themselves would take the title from them. The crowd then called for Cullis, who duly stepped up to acknowledge their cheers and then thanked them for their support "so loyally given during a difficult but successful season." One-time Cullis teammate Bill Crook received the Birmingham League trophy which he said a lot of the youth team players had helped to win for the club. A crowd of 28,651 were at Molineux hoping to see the youths prevent Manchester United retaining the trophy. Despite gaining a 4-4 draw in the first leg at Old Trafford, after leading 3-1, Wolves' youngsters could not make home advantage tell against a United team who included Eddie Colman, Wilf McGuinness, Duncan Edwards, Bobby Charlton and David Pegg. Only goal of the game was a Pegg penalty after 34 minutes to give United a 5-4 aggregate victory.

Teams at Molineux on Monday, April 26, 1954, in the FA Youth Cup final second leg:

Wolves: Sidebottom; Griffiths, John Harris; Bolton, Timmins, Fallon; Round, Mason, Bonson, Murray, Cooper.

United: Hawksworth; Beswick, Rhodes; Colman, Harrop, McGuinness; Littler, Edwards, Charlton, Pegg, Scanlon.

When Wolverhampton Council honoured Wolves with a civic banquet, Cullis told the large gathering at the Civic Hall that the team could be compared to any side that had represented the club in his time, including that of 1938. He felt Billy Wright had set a fine example by being willing to play in any position and added a word for trainer Joe Gardiner, who was assistant manager in all but name: "Joe has had it hard for a long time," said Cullis. "First he had to suffer me as a player and now he has to suffer me alongside him on the trainer's bench." There was laughter all around at that on a night that helped eclipse memories of 1938, 1939, 1947 and 1950. Cullis had made Wolves champions of England at last.

Chapter 16 Champions of the World

One of the first things Wolves did on becoming champions of England was to change their colours. Instead of "old gold" they would now wear "gold" and there was quite a difference between the two shades. The former was nearer to brown in colour while the new gold was closer to a daffodil shade. Out of darkness cometh light, as we say in Wolverhampton. The main concern among the Press, however, was whether Cullis would decide the new shirt with the number five on it would be worn by Billy Wright or Bill Shorthouse.

Speculation had arisen as a result of what happened during England's World Cup campaign in Switzerland in the summer of 1954. During the finals, England's centre-half, Syd Owen, had been injured and Billy Wright took over the role. Although England were beaten by Uruguay in the quarter-finals, one of the few positives to emerge from the tournament was that at last they had a central defender to replace the great Neil Franklin. The Stoke City man had lost his place following his decision, just before the 1950 finals, to move to Bogota in Colombia, a country at the time not a member of FIFA. Since then England had tried no fewer than eleven players at centre-half with only Jack Froggatt having an extended run. Now, however, Wright looked the answer and it would help the national side if Wolves also played him as a centre-half. Unfortunately for the England selectors and boss Walter Winterbottom, there was no way Cullis would put the needs of the national side ahead of those of Wolverhampton Wanderers. Two days before the new season began, he was interviewed by Daily Mirror man Bob Ferrier who asked him: "What about Billy Wright, the England centre-half and the Wolves team?" The reply was short and to the point: "Billy Wright plays left-half for Wolves." Despite what seemed an unequivocal statement, Cullis would have cause to change his views in the not-too-distant future.

Ferrier's report helps paint a portrait of Cullis and his style: "He is one of the few types in football who will give you a fast forthright opinion on any football affair you care to mention," wrote Ferrier. When he asked Cullis what would be the biggest danger to the champion Wolves in the coming season he was told: "Relegation. I don't make forecasts in football." Cullis's only pre-season venture into the transfer market saw him sign winger Tommy McDonald from Hibernian and the Scot was in the squad taken to Austria to face First Vienna six days before the start of the 1954-5 season. The new man played the first half of a 2-2 draw before giving way to Les Smith for the second half.

Wolves began the league season by parading their new shirts in a 4-2 opening day win over Sheffield Wednesday at Molineux and "Commentator" waxed lyrical in the Express & Star: "With their merry marigold shirts reflecting something surprisingly like summer sunshine, Wolves made everything lovely in the Molineux garden on Saturday." He noted that as well as the gold strip there was fluttering from the Molineux flagpole a gold flag inscribed "WWFC, First Division champions 1953-4."

While Cullis had backed Bill Shorthouse to be his first-choice centre-half, events would conspire to make him soon alter his decision. In only the third game of the season, Shorthouse was injured. He and Eddie Stuart collided during the goalless draw at Portsmouth, leaving the centre-half needing several stitches in a gaping head wound. Shorthouse was sidelined and the obvious solution to the selection problem thus caused was to play Wright in his England role and recall young Flowers to the side at left-half. Wright looked immediately at home in the centre of defence and his curbing of Sunderland's rugged South African centre-forward Ted Purdon in a 2-0 home win had "Commentator" purring in the Express & Star: "Man of the match was not a forward but Billy Wright. His polished accomplished and masterful display at centre-half was the epitome of the positional requirements." In other words – he looked a natural. Cullis could see it, too, and realised that moving Wright to the centre of defence made sense in other ways. The England skipper was then 30 and his days as a rampaging wing-half were numbered. A switch to centre-half would extend his career. So when Shorthouse returned it was at left-back to the exclusion of Roy Pritchard, who the following February was transferred to Aston Villa.

Even when England duty meant Wright could not play in the Charity Shield game against Albion at Molineux, Shorthouse stayed at full-back with youngster Peter Russell at centre-half in an epic floodlit encounter which ended 4-4 to give the clubs a share of the trophy. On the day of the international against Northern Ireland, three days later, Russell was given his league debut in the 4-2 home win over Manchester United, who had lost goalkeeper Ray Wood and full-backs, Bill Foulkes and Roger Byrne, to the England side. Wolves were not only without Billy Wright for this match but also Bill Slater, in Belfast as an England reserve. A week later, Manchester's other team would visit Molineux and met a Wolves side mysteriously minus Dennis Wilshaw, the man who had top-scored during the title-winning campaign with 26 goals.

For the game against second-placed City, which ended 2-2, Wolves played Norman Deeley at inside-left in place of Wilshaw, a man who had been capped by England a year earlier, scoring two goals on his international debut against Wales in Cardiff. Four days after the City game there was no return for Wilshaw in the floodlit friendly against First Vienna, even when an injury in training ruled out Roy Swinbourne. Instead Cullis played Bill Slater at centre-forward against the Austrians and the wing-half did not do too badly despite the game ending goalless.

Clearly something had gone on and a club statement two days after the friendly announced that Wolves had suspended Wilshaw for 14 days because of a breach of club discipline. What exactly he had done was not made clear. No doubt today's intrusive press coverage would have got to the bottom of things, especially with it involving the top striker of England's champion club. However, the reason behind the suspension has to remain pure speculation. It may well have been that Wilshaw's duties as a schoolmaster in Hanley, Stoke, had cut across the needs of the football club. Bear in mind that top flight footballers were not then millionaires. These were the days of the maximum wage and Wilshaw always reasoned that a career in teaching was far more secure than one in football. Wilshaw revealed many years later that Cullis could never quite come to terms with him being a part-time professional who made school duties his priority.

Cullis had the previous month created some club history in order to fit in with Wilshaw's teaching duties. Wolves had an evening game against Sunderland at Roker Park, but Wilshaw was teaching at Hanley High School until lunchtime. So Cullis had a car drive the player to Manchester airport where a private plane was waiting to fly him to Sunderland. It was the first time Wolves had flown a player to a league game at a time when the Football League had a flying ban on teams.

After the First Vienna game, Cullis made another change at inside-forward, dropping out-of-form Peter Broadbent for the visit of Cardiff. His replacement, Bill Slater, scored in a 1-1 draw as Wolves dropped a second successive home point. Having been a reserve for England's opening game, Slater won his first full cap when he was named left-half for the game against Wales and kept his place against World Cup holders West Germany. Both matches were won 3-1 at Wembley. Broadbent and Wilshaw were back when Wolves played a fourth successive home game, with Albion the latest visitors. Wilshaw's suspension had been withdrawn, a brief club statement merely saying: "The misunderstanding between the Wolves and Wilshaw has now been cleared up." Slater moved back to his more accustomed right-half position and Broadbent and Wilshaw sparkled as the Baggies were beaten 4-0 to put Wolves second in the table, behind Manchester United. Broadbent and Wilshaw then played in the floodlit friendly against Maccabi Tel Aviv, who were beaten 10-0.

Prestigious friendlies were in the offing and Cullis knew Wilshaw and Broadbent were likely to be key figures in games that would put the world football spotlight on Wolverhampton. As champions of England, Wolves were playing not just for themselves but for the nation when they took on two giants of club football from behind the Iron Curtain – the Russians, Spartak, and the Hungarians, Honved. There was no European-wide club competition in those days and these encounters, though dubbed "friendlies", made a huge impact. After the double hammering England had suffered at the hands of Hungary, the country's football pride could hardly have been at a lower ebb.

The eyes of the nation were on Wolverhampton – and not just figuratively. BBC decided to cover the second half of both these prestige games and, as luck would have it, decided to position their main camera at the South Bank end of the ground. It was there that Wolves scored all seven goals that propelled them on to the world stage.

TV cameras were also at Highbury for the second half of the Spartak match against Arsenal, a game the Moscow club won 2-1. Anderlecht had earlier lost 7-0 to the Soviet side so Wolves knew they were in for a testing evening. Before the big game, Cullis had told his players that under no circumstances must they dispute decisions, an instruction with a touch of irony bearing in mind Cullis's own inclination to give referees a hard time during his playing days. The man who would have been suspended if he had carried on playing, told the Daily Mirror: "Our players will be absolutely forbidden to make complaints or approach to the referee. They will accept every decision unquestioningly. If Spartak are awarded a penalty kick, it will be a penalty kick, with no recriminations, no excuses. Our players will be instructed to play this one hard but also to play this one, above all, fair."

For over an hour Wolves and the Russians battled it out with little to choose between them. It took until the 63rd minute before the deadlock was broken. The ever alert Dennis Wilshaw forced the ball home through a crowded goalmouth when goalkeeper Mikhail Piraev tried to punch the ball clear from a Bill Shorthouse free kick into the penalty area. It stayed that way until the last five minutes when Johnny Hancocks (two) and Roy Swinbourne had the crowd going wild with goals that made it a 4-0 win. Television broadcast the second half, newspapers were glowing in praise. Wolves were suddenly heroes of the land. "Commentator" noted in the Express and Star: "All 55,184 of us, and of course Mr Stan Cullis, played every minute of the game with Wolves, took every kick and every knock, and suffered every apprehension, besides sharing their unbounded goal-mounting joy."

An indication of the impact of the win came in the Daily Mirror under the headline "Wonderful Wolves – Spartak slammed in our greatest post-war Soccer victory". "Wolves spoke for England under the lights and through the mists at Molineux last night," wrote Bob Ferrier in his report: "Make no mistake, they gave us a result that will reverberate around the soccer world, a result that should give heart to the England players who saw this from the stand to the grubbiest kid kicking a ball against any brick wall, and to every man who cares to watch, and who feels for this great game of ours. For Wolves it was a triumph of sheer moral courage. Their guts eventually brought about one of the most astonishing collapses I have seen on a football field."

Equally triumphal was the Daily Express front page which carried pictures of all four Wolves goals under the headline "Wolves fans go crazy after Spartak are routed." A policeman told the paper the town had known nothing like it since VE day as fans sang and danced on their way from Molineux. Many followed the Wolves team coach to the Victoria Hotel in the town centre where a banquet was held for the victors and their Soviet visitors. Another headline, on Desmond Hackett's story underneath the pictures, proclaimed: "The tough manager has tears of joy." Hackett said that Cullis was so emotional in the dressing room after the game that he could not speak but just went from player to player to shake their hands. Said Hackett: "The tough sergeant-major soccer boss had tears in his eyes when he talked to reporters. In a voice hoarse from shouting, he said 'It is the proudest moment of my life. I am happy because I feel we have done something for British prestige.'"

The Wembley game against West Germany was just two weeks away and among the watching England squad at Molineux was Chelsea striker Roy Bentley, who said afterwards: "This success by Wolves was a wonderful tonic for English football. I sat with the rest of the England party who were all grateful to Wolves for this inspiring show. It is not news that our confidence when playing against the Continentals has been shaken in recent years, but this success shows that with spirit the English football system can still win through. It was a proud night for us all."

An interesting footnote to the win was Cullis's reluctance to send on Roy Pritchard when Eddie Stuart was groggy after an acrobatic leap to keep out a Spartak shot. The Soviets had sent on Anatoli Issaev when Aleksei Paramonov was hurt but Cullis did not follow suit even though Pritchard had taken off his tracksuit in anticipation. The boss explained: "It is against British tradition to have substitutes and I was determined tonight, no matter what the result, to try to play the same eleven right through the game. I thought Stuart was only dazed and I was prepared to have him off for five minutes and play only ten men rather than bring on a substitute."

Teams at Molineux Grounds, Wolverhampton, on Tuesday, November 16, 1954:

Wolves: Williams; Stuart, Shorthouse; Slater, Wright, Flowers; Hancocks, Broadbent, Swinbourne, Wilshaw, Smith.

Spartak: Piraev; Ogonkov, Sedov; Parchine, Bachachkine, Netto; Tatouchine, Paramonov (Issaev), Simonian, Vorichilov, Ilyin.

By the time Spartak came to town, Wolves had smoothly moved to the top of the First Division with every prospect of retaining their title. The only personnel change from the side who had at last made Wolves champions of England was at outside-left where Cullis had been faced with the tough decision to omit his former teammate Jimmy Mullen, a member of England's World Cup squad in Switzerland just a few months earlier. Les Smith had deputised when Mullen was injured but had played so well that Cullis realised he could not be dropped. So it was that Smith, not Mullen, played against Spartak and in, arguably, Wolves' most famous match – against Honved.

Before then there was a Molineux match which would in due course have great significance even though Wolves fans might have thought at the time that it was merely a blip. Against a Chelsea side who had just started to find a bit of form after four successive defeats, Wolves fought back to level after being 2-1 down. Then, a goal five minutes from time – a Johnny Hancocks penalty – ought to have been enough for victory but within two more minutes 3-2 had become 3-4 as first Les Stubbs and then Roy Bentley struck for the Londoners. Last time Chelsea had won at Molineux, Cullis had been playing – that day in 1936 when fans invaded the pitch, angry at Major Buckley's transfer policy. The shock win on the first Saturday in December, 1954, hardly seemed a result that would be decisive in the title race. Little did anyone know. However, in nine days' time Wolves fans would forget the Chelsea defeat as Cullis's men became the toast of English football.

The Honved game has been written about many times and its repercussions would lead to the founding of the European Cup. After the 3-2 win over the Hungarians, who included six men who had helped humiliate England, it was a Cullis remark that proved the catalyst for the competition now known as the Champions League. "There they are, the champions of the world," he told pressmen in the dressing room after the game. Such claims had to be justified by a proper tournament, it was reasoned, and most forceful in this view were Gabriel Hanot and Jacques Ferrari of French sports paper, L'Equipe. Their call for a knockout competition did not go unheeded and the European Cup arrived a season later, predictably to be initially shunned by the English football authorities. The story of the match is well documented, Honved led 2-0 after only 14 minutes through Sandor Kocsis and Ferenc Machos but Wolves stormed back to a 3-2 victory thanks to goals from Johnny Hancocks (49 minutes, penalty) and Swinbourne (76 and 77). Wolves fans rejoiced and a nation of TV viewers rejoiced.

Typical of the euphoria were the words of Desmond Hackett in the Daily Express: "Wolverhampton Wanderers became Wolverhampton Wondermen, club champions of Europe, heroes of fighting football, when they outfought and finally outplayed the star-spangled Hungarians at Molineux last night. If Wolverhampton do not strike a gold medal for these men in gold shirts I shall be disappointed. Broadbent became a more effective inside forward than either the pudgy Puskas or the gipsy Kocsis. And Roy Swinbourne . . . you were England's No1 centre-forward. But in the end it was British courage, British fight and British football that left Honved beaten, exhausted, puzzled. One torturing minute from time Czibor shot from six yards. But Williams – neither he nor I will ever know how – saved and Slater swept the ball for a corner across his own goal. So ended the greatest club match I have ever seen with the players taking a bow amid a canonade (sic) of cheers to complete a piece of football history."

Cullis took a leaf out of Major Buckley's book in preparing for the game, as Ron Atkinson well remembers. Atkinson, later to find fame as manager of West Bromwich Albion and Manchester United, was a ground staff boy at Molineux when Honved visited. "It pelted down most of the day," recalled Atkinson, "then, in the middle of the afternoon, Stan told me and the other ground staff boys to turn the hosepipes on and virtually waterlog the Molineux pitch. Its effect was obvious. At the start the Honved players were full of flicks and tricks. Then, as the pitch got heavier, the Hungarians literally became bogged down in the mud and the powerful Wolves players ploughed their way to victory."

Teams at Molineux Grounds, Wolverhampton, on Monday, December 13, 1954:

Wolves: Williams; Stuart, Shorthouse; Slater, Wright, Flowers; Hancocks, Broadbent, Swinbourne, Wilshaw, Smith.

Honved: Farago; Rakoczi, Kovaks; Bozsik, Lorant, Banyai; Budai, Kocsis, Machos (Tichy), Puskas, Czibor.

Chapter 17   Fined by the FA

Four league games after the heights of Honved, brought Cullis down to earth. After drawing 2-2 at Sheffield Wednesday, Wolves lost at home and away to Everton over Christmas. The Molineux match was the ground's last Christmas Day League game with a blond-haired centre-forward by the name of Dave Hickson scoring twice in the visitors' 3-1 win. His second goal evoked memories of Cullis v Stubbins as Hickson ran from the halfway line with Billy Wright in hopeless pursuit. Hickson, a childhood hero for theatre impresario Bill Kenwright, Everton's current chairman, scored again the following day when 75,322 at Goodison saw Wolves beaten 3-2. Cullis was not helped by having to re-jig his team as Johnny Hancocks had been injured in the Christmas morning game. It must have brought back painful memories for Cullis when Boxing Day saw Billy Wright knocked out cold in a heading duel which meant a night in a Liverpool hospital. The skipper had to watch from the directors' box on New Year's Day as Wolves, again minus Hancocks and with Peter Russell in the number-five shirt, were held 2-2 at home by Portsmouth.

Cullis could forget the league the following week but found himself in hot water as Wolves survived their tricky FA Cup third-round hurdle against Grimsby Town at Blundell Park. Last time the sides had met in the Cup, Cullis was playing. That was in the 1939 semi-final when Wolves put five goals past the Mariners. They again hit five but only after conceding two to Grimsby in the first 18 minutes. Cullis was clearly unhappy and eventually emerged on the touchline yelling at his players. Let Bob Ferrier take up the story in the Daily Mirror: "Stan Cullis, manager of Wolves, gets fairly excited over this game of football. In his stand seat he fidgets and fusses, calls and comments more than he ever did as a player – and that was plenty. Sometimes he invades the trainer's trackside bench and suffers there. He did just that at the Grimsby Cup tie when Wolves were trailing sensationally 2-0 down in the second half. Stan's commands to his players cut through the crowd noises loud and clear. Eventually referee Jack Hunt, Matlock schoolmaster, stopped the game. Said Mr Hunt: 'Stop coaching your players from the touchline.' Said Mr Cullis 'There is nothing in the rulebook to stop me.' Mr Hunt later refused to say if he would report the incident to the FA. Says Ferrier to all parties: Cullis is right – there is no rule against it."

Despite what Ferrier wrote, there was a directive about coaching and Cullis was duly reported to the FA after Wolves, suitably inspired by Cullis's words from the sidelines, staged a fine recovery to register a 5-2 victory. Coaching from the touchline was not his only misdemeanour it transpired, he had also had words with the referee after the game. The sequel came a few weeks later when the FA fined Cullis £50.

The FA statement read:

"The disciplinary committee at a meeting on February 21, 1955, considered reports and statements concerning Mr S Cullis, manager of Wolverhampton Wanderers as follows:

"(1) His alleged coaching from the touchline during the match; (2) his alleged ungentlemanly conduct towards the referee in the dressing-room after the game.

"From the evidence adduced the committee were satisfied that Mr Cullis was guilty of ungentlemanly conduct towards the referee after the match and that the coaching he gave to his team from the touchline during the game was in contravention of a council instruction of December 14, 1930.

"The committee decided that (1) Mr Cullis be severely cautioned, warned as to his future conduct and fined £50 for ungentlemanly conduct towards the referee after the match (in deciding the penalty to be imposed the committee took into account the previous misconduct of a similar nature by Mr Cullis); (2) Mr Cullis be instructed to give a written undertaking within seven days not to repeat coaching from the boundary lines.

"The FA wish to make it clear that Mr Cullis did not apply in accordance with rule 45 for a personal hearing until he had been notified of the committee's decision. The disciplinary committee have the full powers of the council and their decisions are final and not subject to appeal."

Cullis was far from happy, maintaining he had been fined on a charge of which he had not been notified and on which he therefore had no opportunity to defend himself. It was yet more evidence of the passion of the man, the total commitment to the cause of his team.

Grimsby may have brought the wrong sort of headlines but it was a result that helped Cullis get Wolves back on track and after successive league wins (2-0 at Blackpool and 2-1 at home to Charlton) talk of the Double would raise its head. It followed a visit to Molineux of Cullis's old England colleague, Tommy Lawton. The veteran had been bought by Arsenal in the twilight of his career but it was the home centre-forward who stole the limelight as Roy Swinbourne headed the only goal of the fourth-round FA Cup game from a Les Smith left-wing corner. In the last 16 of the Cup and top of the First Division – Wolves fans had reason to be proud. Alas, it is well known what pride comes before and Wolves were about to take an almighty fall.

Out of the blue, Wolves, mighty conquerors of Spartak and Honved, came crashing down to earth at Burnden Park against mid-table Bolton. Ray Parry did not open the score until the 31st minute and Eric Bell's goal in the first minute of the second half was answered by one from Dennis Wilshaw. There seemed every chance Wolves might get something from the game until Harry Webster and Parry struck in the space of nine minutes. Then Bert Williams, who earlier in the season had regained his England place, was injured as Willie Moir made it 5-1. The goalkeeper had to be carried off on a stretcher.

Emergency keeper Ron Flowers could not prevent Parry completing his hat-trick as Wolves crashed to their heaviest defeat in 20 years, beaten 6-1. To add to a thoroughly bad day at the office, Johnny Hancocks missed a penalty. Wolves had been well and truly humbled without England centre-forward Nat Lofthouse even getting his name on the scoresheet. Sunderland took advantage to go top of the table.

In such situations the good managers do not panic and Cullis knew that the score flattered Bolton, though they had still been the better side. He would have fielded an unchanged team the following week against Huddersfield Town had it not been for an injury to Eddie Stuart which brought a debut for Joe Baillie, a full-back Cullis had signed from Celtic the previous November. For good measure, the team on the receiving end of six goals now scored six themselves on a snow-covered Molineux pitch, starting with one from Johnny Hancocks after 90 seconds. There followed nine more goals, all of them in the second half. After Wolves had gone 4-1 up, Town pegged them back to 4-3 only to go 6-3 down, Hancocks, who had earlier struck from the penalty spot, completing his hat-trick. Jimmy Glazzard had the final say but the 6-4 win saw Wolves again top of the table, as Sunderland were beaten at home by Charlton.

There was still a carpet of snow at Molineux a week later when Dennis Wilshaw's hat-trick helped Wolves brush Charlton aside 4-1 to reach the last eight of the FA Cup. Four days later, Wolves went to Old Trafford and won 4-2 against a youthful Manchester United side who included Roger Byrne, Dennis Viollet, Tommy Taylor and Duncan Edwards, though there were only 15,679 to witness the Wednesday afternoon encounter. With Bill Slater having to put university duties first, Eddie Clamp impressed as his deputy at left-half. Slater had earlier in the season deservedly won his first full England caps and there would have been more representative honours for Wolves played had not the severe weather intervened. Ron Flowers, Roy Swinbourne and Dennis Wilshaw were selected by England for the B international against Scotland at Ibrox. Wilshaw was named captain while the call-up was deserved recognition for Swinbourne, the Honved Hero. The snow in Glasgow had thawed, only to render the pitch waterlogged so the game was called off. Swinbourne duly got his chance when England played West Germany in a B international a few weeks later and scored in a 1-1 draw.

By the beginning of March, Cullis was in the happy position of knowing what his best line-up was and he was able to field Williams, Stuart, Shorthouse, Slater, Wright, Flowers, Hancocks, Broadbent, Swinbourne, Wilshaw and Smith in the home game against Leicester on the first Saturday of the month. They looked like a team, too, as they scored five goals without reply, four of them coming in a 19-minute burst in the second half. Wolves topped the table with 40 points from 31 games, with Sunderland two points behind but having played a game more.

Chelsea had also played 31 games but were fifth in the table and five points adrift of the leaders. Few among a Molineux crowd of 41,661 would have predicted the wheels were about to come off Wolves' season. Cullis was not helped by a succession of obstacles that prevented him being able to keep that winning team together. Against a Sunderland side, who had also been talked of as candidates for the Double, Wolves' hopes of a place in the FA Cup semi-final were in tatters after just four minutes. In a clash between Bill Shorthouse and lightweight Sunderland winger Billy Bingham, the betting would always have been on the Wolves full-back coming off best. Alas, on this occasion, Shorthouse was laid out and carried off the field with concussion. He spent the rest of the afternoon in hospital as ten-man Wolves battled on with Billy Wright at full-back, Ron Flowers at centre-half and Dennis Wilshaw left-half. It was a hopeless task at Roker Park as Sunderland duly won the sixth-round tie 2-0 thanks to goals from Ted Purdon on 61 and 88 minutes. It was déjà vu for Cullis, Sunderland having ended his Cup dreams as a player at the same stage of the competition 18 years earlier.

Shorthouse was a big loss to the team and Cullis would four days later be denied two more key players for the rearranged league game with neighbours West Bromwich Albion at The Hawthorns. Bill Slater and Dennis Wilshaw were both unable to get time off from their academic duties and so missed the game, played in the afternoon, as the Football League had yet to sanction games under floodlights. To make up for Wilshaw's absence, Cullis rearranged his forward line, recalling Jimmy Mullen and playing Les Smith at inside-right. It did not really work and the Baggies won 1-0 thanks to George Lee's goal after 27 minutes. To add to Cullis's worries, Ron Flowers sustained a nose injury and had to have an operation.

Cullis's anxieties were increased by what should have been a cause for pride – the selection of three Wolves players for the England team to meet Scotland at Wembley. Bert Williams, Billy Wright and Dennis Wilshaw were chosen but would therefore be missing from the Wolves side at home to Preston on the same afternoon. The drain on Wolves' resources could have been even greater. When Portsmouth wing-half Len Phillips withdrew from the side, England manager Walter Winterbottom telephoned Cullis wanting to bring Bill Slater into the team. Ironically, Slater had been dropped from the side in order to give a debut to 18-year-old Duncan Edwards. For once, Cullis did not welcome an honour for yet one more of his players and asked Winterbottom if he would look elsewhere. The England boss could have insisted but agreed to Cullis's plea. The Molineux manager may have been secretly pleased that it was Chelsea who then got the call and agreed to let Ken Armstrong win what proved to be his only cap.

Without their three stars Wolves were held 1-1 by Preston at Molineux while Chelsea, who also had Frank Blunstone in the England team, won 4-2 at Tottenham. As well as their England trio, Wolves had also had to play without injured right-back Eddie Stuart, Cullis giving a debut to George Showell. It was no consolation to Wolves that Dennis Wilshaw, one of their trio on England duty at Wembley, wrote his name into football history as England beat Scotland 7-2. He remains the only man to hit four goals in a full international between the countries.

Home draws with Newcastle and Preston either side of a one-goal defeat at Burnley had taken Wolves up to Easter Saturday and the showdown with Chelsea. With Wolves faltering, the London side had crept up on the rails in the title race and now they had a five-point advantage thanks to a seven-game run that had brought five wins and two draws. Wolves may have had three games in hand but, with two points for a win in those days, those games would be of no advantage if Chelsea should win at Stamford Bridge to establish a seven-point gap. Sheffield United had thwarted Chelsea the day before the big game – Good Friday – by holding them 1-1 at home. Could Wolves go one better?

Over 75,000 fans packed into Stamford Bridge with Cullis at least having a full-strength squad from whom to choose, apart from Showell continuing to deputise for Stuart. The title contenders were nip and tuck for 74 minutes until the game's deciding moment arrived. With Bert Williams beaten, Billy Wright decided to fist out a Seamus O'Connell shot to prevent a certain goal. Under today's laws he would have been sent off but not then. Chelsea were awarded a penalty and full-back Peter Sillett blasted the ball low to Williams's right, the shot being too hot for the 'keeper despite him diving the right way. Chelsea were now in the driving seat to win the title, something that seemed unthinkable a month earlier.

To add injury to the insult of defeat, Roy Swinbourne damaged a knee and would miss the final six games of the season. For the first of those, at home to Aston Villa on Easter Monday, Cullis asked Ron Flowers to don the number-nine shirt and, predictably, the wing-half rose to the occasion by scoring the only goal on a day which saw young Colin Booth given his debut. For the next three matches Doug Taylor was tried at centre-forward, the first being at Villa Park where the home side won 4-2 and Cullis knew the game was virtually up as far as retaining the title was concerned. Then Wilshaw took over from Taylor and scored to help Wolves beat Sheffield United at Bramall Lane, but on the same afternoon the other Sheffield side, Wednesday, could not prevent Chelsea clinching the championship with a 3-0 win at Stamford Bridge. For a second season running a team had won the title for a first time.

Cullis must have been scratching that famous bald pate, wondering just why the season had gone wrong. Some might point to the two-defeat Christmas when Everton showed up some Wolves frailties. Yet that twin setback had been survived and Wolves had got their season back on track. Then came that dreadful run that began at the start of March and consisted of five games without a win, three of them defeats. There had been the FA Cup run and injuries to disrupt the side but Cullis could call on some more than useful reserves. Man for man the Wolves team looked far superior to Chelsea yet, in football, thank goodness, the best eleven players do not always add up to the best team. The plain truth was that Wolves should have been champions two seasons running. They had won national acclaim for their floodlit triumphs but had let the title slip through their hands. It must have mystified and angered Cullis. He would congratulate an old pre-war opponent, ex-Arsenal and England man Ted Drake, who was manager of Chelsea, yet Cullis must have been baffled by his side's fade-out. Their last eleven games produced just three wins. That was not the form of champions. In fact, it was worse form than the two relegated sides Leicester and Sheffield Wednesday, who each gained twelve points during that period compared with Wolves' eight.

For the Scotland game at Wembley, Wolves could, if Cullis had been willing, have had four men in an England team for the first time. However, it did happen when England set off on their summer tour at the end of the season. Ron Flowers, still not 21, was named in the side to face France in Paris, joining clubmates Bert Williams, Billy Wright and Dennis Wilshaw. Flowers, playing at right-half, had an uncharacteristically poor game in a 1-0 defeat and, as was the way in those days, was quickly tossed aside. Portsmouth veteran Jimmy Dickinson was recalled for the games against Spain and Portugal rather than give Flowers an extended trial. In time he would prove that he was, indeed, a world class player. If it had not been for his injury, Swinbourne would surely have also been on the tour and would have won his first cap.

Chapter 18 Moscow, then revolution

Before Cullis could turn his thoughts to the 1955-6 season, there was a little matter of a prestigious trip behind the Iron Curtain. Having seen the mighty Spartak humbled at Molineux, the Russians wanted a chance to show that football could flourish under the rule of Communism. Wolves were invited to play Spartak and then Dynamo in the Dynamo Stadium in Moscow. Cullis savoured the chance to see some of the sights of Russia, knowing that his team were ambassadors as well as footballers. They may have lost both games, 3-0 to Spartak and then 3-2 to Dynamo after being three goals down, but they conducted themselves well and flew the flag for Britain. Each game attracted an attendance of 80,000.

While Spartak had looked a different side from the one beaten at Molineux and were well worth there three-goal win it was not such a stroll for Dynamo. They were helped with a bizarre goal a few minutes before half-time. Eddie Stuart mistimed a backpass – you could still pass back to the 'keeper in those days – and the ball beat Bert Williams, hit a post and rolled across the face of the goal for Yuri Kuznetsov to prod home. Wolves rallied well in the second half and Dennis Wilshaw beat the great Lev Yashin with first a shot from the narrowest of angles and then a header after Ron Flowers had nodded a Les Smith cross goalwards. Smith was deputising for the non-flyer Johnny Hancocks. Cullis said of his team: "They played in the best British traditions and were a credit to their country and their club."

Once back in Wolverhampton, Cullis prepared for the new league season knowing that at Manchester United many talented youngsters had replaced the old guard and were about to pay Matt Busby dividends. The changes at Molineux would not be as dramatic as at Old Trafford but Cullis knew he needed to plan a quiet revolution as some of the players who had served him so well were moving ever closer to the end of their careers. Young men like Eddie Clamp and Colin Booth were deserving of a chance but first of all it was one of the old guard who helped put Wolves name into the record books.

On September 3, 1955, the spotlight ought to have been on the Manchester derby which saw United lose 1-0 to City at Maine Road but all the headlines were on Wolves thanks mainly to a wonder show by their oldest outfield player – Jimmy Mullen. Despite Les Smith's fine displays in 1954-5, Mullen was now restored to the team by Cullis. At Ninian Park, the left-winger scored one goal himself and figured in the build-up for eight others as Wolves beat Cardiff City 9-1. It equalled the best ever top-flight away win set by Sunderland at Newcastle in 1908 and has not been matched since. Roy Swinbourne and Johnny Hancocks each grabbed a hat-trick and even the Cardiff consolation came from an ex-Wolves man, Ron Stockin.

Swinbourne was on fire. All the potential to be a great centre-forward seemed to be being realised. He had hit four goals the previous Saturday in a 7-2 home win over Manchester City and grabbed another hat-trick the Saturday after the Cardiff win when Huddersfield were defeated 4-0 at Molineux. It was after his third successive Saturday hat-trick that Swinbourne was the subject of a bit of the Cullis psychology. Towelling down after a shower following training, the centre-forward was casually approached by Cullis who asked him: "How old are you now, Roy?" Swinbourne told him he was twenty-six and there came a swift rejoinder from the manager: "I shall have to be looking for a replacement soon then, won't I?" Swinbourne loved to re-tell that story, an illustration of how Cullis would ensure his players kept their feet on the ground. Alas, Cullis's remark made in jest would soon prove to be true.

It all went wrong at Luton on November 5, 1955. Cullis had seen Peter Broadbent show signs he could play at half-back, having filled in there when players had been injured during a game. So, in an injury crisis, Cullis decided he would play him at left-half from the start at Kenilworth Road and give 19-year-old Bobby Mason his debut at inside-right. Whether the new-look line-up would work became secondary after just three minutes when Swinbourne was injured. The ground was packed and some youngsters had been allowed to sit inside the perimeter fence close to the pitch and it was in trying to avoid crashing into them and the Press photographers that Swinbourne damaged his knee. It was a bad start to an afternoon that got worse for Wolves as they lost 5-1. The centre-forward limped through the rest of the game but he was sidelined for three weeks. Swinbourne had at that stage scored 17 goals in just 13 games. His call-up to the England ranks seemed a formality. Sadly, it was all about to end for a likeable man of great bravery and great talent.

Immediate worry for Cullis was a replacement for Swinbourne for the visit of Moscow Dynamo four days after the Luton shambles. Doug Taylor, a local lad who had been on Albion's books as an amateur, had been tried and found wanting so the manager gambled and decided that promising reserve team striker Jimmy Murray was the man for the job against the much-vaunted Russians. Just past his 20th birthday, Murray, from the same Kent village as Peter Broadbent, was doing his National Service in the Army, stationed at Lichfield. It was there that he learned he was required to make his Wolves debut and was given leave to face a Soviet invasion.

Murray more than justified Cullis's faith in him as Wolves were once again hailed as heroes of English football thanks to a 2-1 win over Dynamo. Bill Slater scored after 14 minutes and it was 2-0 four minutes into the second half thanks to Jimmy Mullen who had missed out on the big nights when Spartak and Honved were the visitors. The legendary Lev Yashin in the Russian goal was not beaten again and Dynamo made sure it would be a tense finish through Vladimir Ilyin's goal on 62 minutes. Indeed, the Russians thought they had equalised through Genrikh Fedosov's header but referee Arthur Ellis ruled him off-side.

The result and Ellis's decision made the front page of the Daily Express, then the country's top morning newspaper. "Wolves, wonderful Wolves, last night successfully championed Britain against the Iron Curtain for the third time in 12 months," said the report under the 2-1 scoreline in large type. It then detailed the dialogue that had transpired between Cullis and Dynamo vice president Kuprianov:

"Mr K: It was definitely a goal. Mr C: I was in a very good position and I could see the whole thing. I am certain Mr Ellis's decision was right. Mr K: We thought he was wrong and told him so. Mr C: If I had done that I'd have been fined £50, I know, I've been fined before. Mr K: We have no complaint against Wolves. They played well. But we think a draw, thanks to that decision, would have been fairer."

On the back page of the Express the inimitable Desmond Hackett paid his own tribute: "Oh the agony of those dying minutes when it looked as though the Russians must bulldoze through – but every time there came a goal threat there arose a golden shirt, hanging wetly on some exhausted player, to keep Wolves one goal ahead. As the players marched off the music of the British Grenadiers rose triumphantly above the roar of a crazily happy crowd. These Dynamos were nothing like Spartak or Hungarian Honved, who had lit up their matches with brilliant football, in the first half but in the second half they were shattering. How Billy Wright held his defence together in the last twenty minutes only he knows. Williams became unbeatable, Stuart and Shorthouse indomitable. Slater was tremendous either as a faultless defender or a surging thoughtful attacker. Jimmy Mullen could walk into any England team on this show. It was Mullen and that wisp of genius Hancocks who made the Wolves forward line sparkle. The boy, Jimmy Murray, a 19-year-old (sic) serviceman playing his first big game, can remember this night with pride."

Teams at Molineux Grounds, Wolverhampton, on Wednesday, November 9, 1955:

Wolves: Williams; Stuart, Shorthouse; Slater, Wright, Clamp; Hancocks, Broadbent, Murray, Wilshaw, Mullen.

Dynamo: Yashin; Rodionov, Krizhevsky, B Kuznetsov; Boykov, Sokolov; Sabov, Fedosov, Y Kuznetsov, Ilyin, Ryzhkin.

There was a sequel to the Dynamo game three days later when Wolves looked distinctly lethargic in the first half of their home game against Charlton. Usually, such a display would have meant a half-time tongue-lashing from Cullis – but not this time. In seven seasons as a manager he had earned a reputation for his passion and for his no-holds-barred rants at half-time and full-time if he was unhappy with his players' performance. Yet to the players' great surprise there was no ear-bashing for a below-par first-half display which had still brought a 1-0 lead.

There was even the trace of a smile as he said: "Keep it up lads" and then made a quick exit from the dressing room. Wolves livened up no end in the second half to win 2-0, the second goal coming from full-back Bill Shorthouse, the only one he ever scored for Wolves. Afterwards Cullis explained his actions: "I know exactly what the tension, excitement and gruelling play of the Dynamo game did to the lads. Even if we had been beaten today I would not have had the heart to say anything. Now they can have two days off – and they deserve more." The headline on the story in the Daily Mirror read: "The day Cullis almost smiled . . ."

Jimmy Murray scored his first league goal to give Wolves a 1-0 win over Everton at the end of November but the good news for Cullis was that Swinbourne was fit to return to the side at Preston on the first Saturday in December. It proved another bad away day – Wolves lost 2-0, a seventh successive defeat on opposition territory – but had an event of a more lasting significance. Swinbourne wrenched his knee and had to leave the field on a stretcher in the last few minutes. His career was over. Attempts at a comeback would fail and Cullis had to accept he had lost one of his finest players. The same match saw Dennis Wilshaw pull a muscle after 16 minutes and he would now face a long spell out. Murray and Colin Booth would get their chance but Wolves had lost vital experience in attack and would not make an impact on the First Division until Manchester United were virtually out of sight at the top.

There would be no FA Cup run this season, Wolves bowing out 2-1 to West Bromwich Albion at a packed Molineux when visiting wingers, Frank Griffin and George Lee, scored early goals. With Jimmy Murray unwell, Cullis had tried Ron Flowers at centre-forward and having scored in a 1-1 draw at Sunderland, he stayed in the number-nine shirt for the cup-tie. By the end of the day three England wing-halves had played in the centre-forward role as Albion had Ray Barlow leading their attack and for the last 20 minutes Bill Slater swopped places with Flowers. Slater caused Albion some problems and scored eleven minutes from time.

At least Cullis could look forward to striking another blow for English football prestige with the impending visit of Spanish Cup holders Athletic Bilbao. Last thing he expected was to have a players' strike on his hands that meant the March date with the Spaniards was cancelled. It happened because Wolves players voted to back the Players' Union (forerunner of the Professional Footballers' Association) in their fight to get overtime payments for floodlit friendlies and televised games. Clubs were raking in extra income as packed houses watched the encounters with foreign invaders yet the players were getting little from it. The union were determined things would change and their secretary Jimmy Guthrie came to Molineux asking Wolves players to back the fight. They agreed.

As he battled in vain to recover from his knee injury, the last thing Roy Swinbourne needed was some off-field aggro but he was the Players' Union representative at Molineux and had the task of telling Cullis that the players were unwilling to play. Swinbourne recalled: "I called a meeting of all the lads in the visitors' dressing room. There were 25 of us, all union members, in that room. We took a vote on a slip of paper. I counted them and it was very close but it was against playing. I had to go up and tell Stan. I walked up the old passageway from the visitors' dressing room, past the home dressing room, the physio's room, the boardroom, the secretary's room – all the way to the top to Stan's office in the corner. I knocked and went in and said 'Stan, we've had a meeting and the vote is that we don't play.' Whoosh! He went at me. He said 'It's a sell-out, we've sold all the tickets. I'm sending for the chairman, Mr Baker. You go back and get Bill Shorthouse and Billy Wright and the three of you come back here and sit in this office.' I said it had all been done democratically. It was a secret ballot and had gone against the club. It was very close. He still said to go and fetch Bill and Billy. So I went back down and said 'He wants to see us.' So we went up and we sat in the office and we waited for Baker to come. It seemed to take hours. Anyway, I think he was sympathetic, old Baker was. He said 'If the Football League said we could pay you a hundred pounds for playing this game, we'd pay you. But we can't, we have to abide by the Football League. The rules say we can't pay you for these extra games. You just get a bonus and that's it. But if the Football League would change the rules and say it's a hundred pounds a game for floodlit games, we'd pay you.' And we knew that, because we always got what we were entitled to – always first class hotels and everything."

Ross Hall, reporting the developments under the headline "Floodlight Black-out", wrote in the Daily Mirror: "This development can only be interpreted as a victory for the union in the first round of their battle for special fees to players appearing on television and in floodlit games. The timing of the ban made Wolves the guinea pigs and the union's position has undoubtedly been strengthened by this demonstration of support from the staff of so powerful and famous a club as Wolves. The Wolves players must have been torn between loyalty to their club and loyalty to the union. Their decision to support the ban is the strongest indication to the League that footballers are determined to get a better deal."

Within a few days the Players' Union called off their ban in return for a promise from the Football League of talks to sort it all out. However, this came too late to save the Wolves game as money was on its way back to the fans and there was too little time to rearrange the match. Both clubs expressed the hope that the visit could take place at a later date but it never happened. The European Cup was in its inaugural season and soon floodlit friendlies would become of little importance.

On the league front, Wolves were trying – and mostly failing – to keep up with the pace set by Blackpool and Manchester United. The Seasiders were, with their ageing squad, doing their best to match United and their exciting youngsters. Stanley Matthews was still proving a highly effective right winger and when Blackpool came to Molineux in January, 1956, Cullis decided to try to curb the Matthews menace by playing Billy Wright at left-back, as Bill Shorthouse had been injured in a 1-1 draw with Sunderland at Roker Park. The move did not really pay off as Wolves lost 3-2 and Cullis must have realised that Wright would probably have been more effective as a central defender trying to tackle the threat of Jackie Mudie and Allan Brown. Instead, George Showell had played at centre-half, the first time he had done so in the First Division,

Soon Cullis's quiet revolution turned to the question of the right wing, for ten years almost the exclusive province of Johnny Hancocks. He would turn 37 by the end of the season and though he still finished as the club's top league goalscorer with 18 goals from 28 games, the time had come to find a replacement. Unhappy at being relegated to the reserves after playing 34 league games the previous season, Les Smith had joined Aston Villa while Tommy McDonald had played a few matches but hardly sparkled, so Cullis needed to act. For the first time in his management career he spent what was for then a big fee and signed Harry Hooper from West Ham United for £25,000. Son of a Sheffield United full-back of some repute, Hooper had played for England B and England under-23 and had been a member of the full England squad. He was an exciting prospect and this rare signing by Cullis of a high profile player fired the fans' enthusiasm. In contrast, McDonald and fellow Scot Joe Baillie would be sold in the summer, yet more additions to the growing list of Cullis signings that did not bear fruit.

On the day Hancocks made what proved to be his final league appearance, a goalless draw away to Aston Villa on Easter Tuesday, Hooper donned the gold shirt for the first time in front of more than 7,000 fans for the reserve team match between Wolves and Villa at Molineux. Hooper did not disappoint, scoring a hat-trick in a 3-2 win. He looked a perfect replacement for Hancocks and even showed that he possessed the little maestro's penalty-taking prowess, one of his goals coming via a spot-kick. Hooper's father, also Harry, had been a penalty expert for Sheffield United. With Colin Booth adding to the inside forward strength and Murray starting to impress at centre-forward, Cullis's quiet revolution was well under way.

While never having a real impact on the title race, Wolves should have finished second to Matt Busby's Manchester United. Blackpool, United's long time pursuers, had failed to stay the course and lost their last four games of the season. In contrast, Wolves had strung together four successive wins and one of them, 5-1 against Tottenham, saw Molineux stage its first ever floodlit league game, Bill Slater scoring with penalties at the end of each half. If they could make it five in a row by winning at relegated Sheffield United, then Wolves would be runners-up for a second successive season.

The game was played four days after the scheduled end of the season, having been postponed in February because of a frozen pitch. The match being on a Wednesday evening (kick-off 6.30) presented a problem for Cullis, anxious to have the in-form Bill Slater in his team. The bid to surmount that problem would provide Slater with a farcical tale he fondly re-told in later years. Slater's duties at Birmingham University meant he could not travel with the team to Sheffield but the plan was for him to catch an especially-hired plane from Elmdon Airport, as Birmingham International Airport was then known. A car was waiting at Lodge Moor airfield, about six miles from Sheffield, but the driver must have been baffled as the plane merely circled the airfield a couple of times. The pilot was misled by the small size of the air field and had not spotted the car. He decided to fly on and by the time the occupants of the car realised what he was doing and began waving frantically it was too late. The plane landed at Worksop some 20 miles away and even if there had been transport awaiting it there it would have been too late to get to Bramall Lane in time for kick-off. The incident ended with Slater arriving at the ground about 15 minutes after the start. Billy Wright had been moved to his old England position of right-half, where he did not look too happy, while travelling reserve George Showell played at centre-half. The Blades did not play like a relegated side and after trailing 3-1, courtesy of a Colin Booth hat-trick, they scored two goals in the three minutes before half-time. It was still 3-3 at the final whistle but Cullis was convinced that a team with Slater in it, minus the last-minute adjustment, would have beaten the Blades, who had at least left the First Division on a note of defiance.

So Wolves finished third in the table on the same points as Blackpool but with a goal average of 1.36 compared with Blackpool's 1.38. Both on 49 points, they were a massive eleven adrift of champions Manchester United. Matt Busby's young team were now the top dogs and the conquerors of Spartak, Honved and Dynamo were yesterday's men.

Slater was required to make another quick exit from Birmingham when Wolves played a friendly against Notts County and this time it was successful. He travelled by road to Meadow Lane and arrived ten minutes before the start of the match arranged to raise funds for the widow of County stalwart Leon Leuty. A member of the Derby County 1946 FA Cup-winning side, Leuty had died from leukaemia in December. County boss, Cullis's old pal George Poyser, the former Wolves coach, had suggested the game and Cullis was happy to oblige. A gate of 11,617 saw Wolves lose 4-2 on an evening when both full-back Gerry Harris and winger Harry Hooper played in the first team for the first time. The latter did enough to show he could be a worthy successor to the great Johnny Hancocks. For one season, at least, it did indeed look that way.

Chapter 19   A Cup shocker

A test of a great manager is whether he can build more than one great side. That was the task facing Cullis as two more stalwarts of the 1954 team, Bert Williams and Bill Shorthouse, would bow out after the 1956-7 season following in the footsteps of Johnny Hancocks and Roy Swinbourne. It all began well with Manchester City beaten 5-1 on the opening day, Jimmy Murray helping himself to four goals. Then Cullis got himself some unwelcome publicity as his volatile temperament landed him in the middle of an unseemly confrontation.

Wolves were beaten 1-0 at Luton thanks to a 34th-minute goal by centre-forward Bob Morton who ran on to a through ball and scored despite looking to be a yard off-side when the pass was made. Desmond Hackett, in the Daily Express, wrote: "Morton moved on to the glory of his goal and just before the ecstatic crowd exploded in a thunderous salute of cheers there was an agonised cry of 'No, no' from Wolves manager Stanley Cullis." Things got worse after the game when Cullis was involved in a spat with Luton director Tom Hodgson. Let the Daily Express again take up the story:

"Wolves manager Stan Cullis and Luton director Tom Hodgson were involved in a row after the game at Luton last night. Cullis protested angrily that the winning goal scored by Bob Morton was off-side. Fists were raised and Mr Hodgson was grabbed by the tie before the pair were separated by 'Ten Goal' Joe Payne, former Luton centre-forward. Said Mr Hodgson: 'We had an exchange of words and I told him not to act like a baby.' During the match Cullis leapt from his seat and told a Luton fan who had criticised a Wolves player: 'Keep your remarks to yourself.' Wolves directors, on arrival at the Luton boardroom for the usual after-match entertainment were told: 'Your manager has been having a bit of trouble.' The directors, Mr John Ireland and Mr Jim Marshall, found manager Cullis in the dressing room and all three returned to the Luton boardroom. Twenty minutes later Mr Cullis and Mr Hodgson came out shaking hands. 'We were just a couple of old professionals having a go at each other,' joked Mr Hodgson. 'I suppose it was a bit rough at the time but now Stan and I have made it up we are the best of friends.'

"Both clubs tried to make light of the incident. Said Mr Percy Mitchell, chairman of Luton: 'So far as this club is concerned, nothing has happened. We have received an apology from Mr Cullis.' There will be no complaint to the Football Association or the Football League.'" A week later there was a gate of 46,781 at Molineux to see the return meeting between the sides and all the fireworks were thankfully on the pitch in one of the most dramatic first halves the ground has witnessed.

A scintillating game featured an eight-goal first half. Two down after nine minutes, Wolves came back to lead 3-2, were then pegged back to 3-3 only to lead 5-3 at the break. Luton got the only goal of the second half on a night which saw left-back Gerry Harris make his league debut as deputy for the injured Bill Shorthouse. A riveted spectator at the match was Malcolm Finlayson, signed that day from Millwall, the man chosen by Cullis to succeed the great Bert Williams. Finlayson marvelled at what he saw that night: "Bert was in one goal and Bernard Streten, another England international, was in the other. These were two cats and they made save after save yet there were still nine goals. I could not believe what I was seeing."

When three days later Wolves beat Everton 2-1 at home it was an anti-climax after the Luton game. New boy Harry Hooper saw little of the ball, which had also been the case against Luton, and that fuelled speculation among many fans that maybe the right-winger was not liked by his new teammates. Bill Holden remarked in the Daily Mirror that the crowd gave "a half-derisory, half-approving cheer each time the ball was sent in Hooper's direction during Wolves' last two home games". He added: "People are asking: 'Why do Wolves leave Hooper out in the cold? Why do they waste him?'" Cullis was quick to react: "It's almost laughable to hear such stupid suggestions. Hooper gets on very well with the lads. There is no thought at all of freezing him out. There is nothing in any way deliberate in the fact he hasn't seen as much of the ball as Mullen, his opposite winger. Certain technical reasons have combined to produce the effect of concentrating more on the left recently." Holden said Cullis had explained what those technical reasons were but was speaking off the record as he did not want such information becoming available to Wolves' opponents. It was a storm in a teacup and Hooper soon began to justify his transfer fee, scoring goals and making them for others.

Malcolm Finlayson duly made his First Division debut when Bert Williams was injured and did so against newly-promoted Leeds United at Molineux. It was the nearest thing to a one-man team ever seen at the ground, thanks to John Charles, a player discovered, like Cullis, by Major Buckley. He had burst on to the football scene during Buckley's stint as boss at Elland Road. Charles, known as "The Gentle Giant", was outstanding whether playing centre-half or as a striker. On that day at Molineux the Welshman scored his side's two goals and then dropped back into defence to help restrict Wolves to just one goal in reply.

Second game for Finlayson was at Bolton where Wolves won 3-0 after being two up at half-time, and he found out just how demanding Cullis could be. Recalled Finlayson: "At half-time we were leading three nil (sic). There was a long corridor running parallel to the track and as I came up I could hear this voice going on and on – angry. I came in and he (Stan) was going on at Jimmy Mullen and Johnny Hancocks saying: 'Three up (sic)? We should be six up.' And I thought: 'What's happening here? Three up against Nat Lofthouse and the rest, away from home and he's like this.' We won the game 3-0 but he was going mad at half-time, he really was."

As Cullis continued to look to the future and blood more young players, there was no shortage of goals. Colin Booth was among the younger element and earned an England under-23 cap against France at Ashton Gate, Bristol, coming on as sub after Doncaster star Alick Jeffrey had sustained a broken leg in the goalless draw. Booth's displays were demanding a regular place in the team and he hit four goals as Arsenal were beaten 5-2. Two weeks later came another seven-goal game at Molineux when the drama bettered even that Luton epic. Wolves trailed Preston 3-0 early in the second half but scored three times in the last ten minutes to win 4-3, Harry Hooper completing a hat-trick.

Johnny Hancocks, the man Hooper had succeeded, made a cameo farewell appearance in a floodlight friendly against Hungarian side Red Banner, who included Nandor Hidegkuti, one of England's tormentors at Wembley. The game ended 1-1, Hancocks earning the biggest cheer of the night from a crowd of over 43,000 when he came on for the last nine minutes to replace the injured Jimmy Murray. The game had been fitted into the Red Banner schedule with proceeds going to the relief fund set up following the Hungarian revolution. Wolves' ninth-minute equaliser to an early goal by Peter Palotas came from Pat Neil, an amateur formerly with Portsmouth. Neil then played four league games as deputy to injured left-winger Jimmy Mullen. He was thus the last amateur player to appear for Wolves.

In his search for a centre-forward in the Swinbourne mould, Cullis decided to give a run in the team to bustling Barnsley boy, Joe Bonson. Alas, his similarity to Swinbourne was virtually restricted to his Yorkshire birth but he did score a couple of goals when Swansea were beaten 5-3 in the third round of the FA Cup to raise hopes of another decent run in the competition. Cullis would have relished that but was in for a rude awakening. In the fourth round Third Division Bournemouth were the visitors and created one of the great Cup giantkillings by winning 1-0, thanks to a goal after 40 minutes from Reg Cutler. The left-winger had made his mark on the game after just six minutes when he collided with the side netting of the goals at the South Bank end and snapped one of the uprights. There was a seven-minute delay while the frame was repaired. Before they met Wolves, Bournemouth and Boscombe Athletic, as they were then known, had beaten Burton Albion, Swindon Town and Accrington Stanley. They would claim another First Division scalp when they beat Tottenham 3-1 at Dean Court in the fifth round only to fall to Manchester United in the sixth. For some of us it is difficult in 2016 to accept that should Wolves meet Bournemouth in the FA Cup now, it would only be an upset if Wolves won.

Not much was left for Wolves who were well out of the league shake-up though they did finish sixth. The floodlit friendlies continued, though they were of diminishing importance with the European Cup now well established and boosted by the inclusion of Manchester United. The visit of Spaniards Valencia enabled a 20-year-old Scot, Bobby Thomson, to score twice on his Wolves debut in a 3-0 win. He also scored on his First Division debut three days later in a 2-0 defeat of Newcastle.

Two games and three goals – yet he was never given another league game by Cullis. Thomson has mixed memories of his time under Cullis as he revealed in his autobiography, The Real Bobby Dazzler.

Thomson said of the manager: "Cullis wasn't really a nice man. He was ignorant, but as a manager he was brilliant and the sort of boss I would have wanted to be if I was ever going to become a manager. He didn't take crap off any of the players, and he had no favourites. He would give anyone a bollocking, even the international players, and would drop anyone who wasn't playing well, regardless of who you were. If you got on the wrong side of him, you had the Cullis treatment. If you didn't do as you're told and didn't put the effort in, you'd be out the team the very next week. He had such power over the players in those days because they were on such a low wage and there was a conveyer belt of players to choose from, so he could be like that." Thomson also testified to the intense fitness regime under Cullis. "I will always remember the Cullis routine for training – running, running and more running. The first day I was there I remember doing 24 laps of the track in the morning and was told to come back at 2pm, only to do another 18 laps."

Ignorant was one thing Cullis was not but the Thomson view is revealing. Perhaps it says as much about the Scot as it does about Cullis. Thomson was not the sort to conform to Wolves' standards of behaviour. Thomson, who would later have a useful career with Aston Villa and then Birmingham City, admits in his book that he paid scant attention to club rules about going out on Thursday and Friday nights and clearly he was not one to obey the strict demands of the manager. Such players would not find favour with Cullis and usually were sent on their way. Others were happy to conform and did not share the Thomson verdict on Cullis. Three such men, Williams, Shorthouse and Swinbourne, were honoured by a presentation and dinner organised by a group of fans at the end of the 1956-7 season. The trio had brought triumphs to the club yet their successors would take Wolves to even more. The foundations for the most successful three years in the club's history were about to be laid in a far-off land.

Chapter 20   Out of Africa

Cullis now had only Billy Wright and Jimmy Mullen left from the team who had won the FA Cup eight years earlier and he had the re-shaping of the team well under way. Malcolm Finlayson had shown he was more than up to the daunting task of taking over from Williams; Gerry Harris had made the left-back position his; Eddie Clamp had added to the half-back strength of Ron Flowers and Bill Slater; Jimmy Murray had proved to be a natural goalscorer; Bobby Mason and Colin Booth were rivals for an inside forward place with Dennis Wilshaw more and more anxious to pursue his academic career; and then there was Peter Broadbent. At 26, the man from the mining village of Elvington, near Dover, was now in his prime. Admired by the young George Best, Broadbent was a supremely gifted player, who would become revered by the fans who saw him revel in Wolves' impending dominance of the First Division.

Another key to Wolves' success was the off-field team Cullis had helped to assemble, most of them men steeped in the traditions of Molineux. Joe Gardiner, officially the club trainer, was assistant manager in all but name and just as vital to Cullis as Brian Taylor was to Clough or Jimmy Murphy to Busby. The backroom staff also included two other former players in Bill Shorthouse and Jack Dowen and Wolves had an astute and forward-thinking secretary in Jack Howley, who had started with Wolves as an office boy. Cullis had also recruited athletics coach Frank Morris to ensure the players' fitness levels were tip-top, with the recently-opened Aldersley Stadium athletics track an ideal venue for sprint training.

The foundations for the 1957-8 season were laid in South Africa, where Cullis had played his last matches in the old gold shirt six years earlier. Once again Wolves went through their tour with a 100 per cent win record, this time in eight games. Malcolm Finlayson said South African newspapers rated Wolves the best side that had visited the country since the war. Finlayson explained: "The others had gone out for holidays, sort of thing. Wolves didn't. It was made quite clear to us that we were out there to win matches; the locals had not come to see us draw with the local side. So we won all our matches and that was the start of a good side, because we all played together and knew how each other played. We did not have to be running and screaming at each other." It all began well with Jimmy Murray hitting five goals as Southern Transvaal were beaten 5-2 in Johannesburg but Cullis found himself having to defend his team after an astonishing attack in a report in the city's evening paper, The Star. It accused them of bullying tactics, wild appealing, robust play and cursing on the field.

It went on: "The appealing and attempted intimidation of players, and of the referee, took the glamour away from the touring team. The Southern Transvaal players said after the match they were provoked throughout the game. Referee Wilf Lubbe confirmed this. We saw it last year when the FA tourists started their nonsense at the Rand Stadium but we never expected it from the Wolves, one of the proudest teams in Division 1, who are managed by a disciplinarian in Mr Stanley Cullis."

The manager was quick to defend himself the following day when he spoke to an Express & Star representative in Johannesburg: "I was astonished when I read the report. I should say this was one of the tamest games we ever played in South Africa. There certainly was no robust play or wild appealing and as to bullying tactics, I do not know what the writer means. The game was played in a proper sporting spirit, without the slightest sign of viciousness." South African FA president Fred Fell also defended the tourists, saying: "Wolves gave a brilliant exhibition of soccer and there were no incidents which one could take exception to. I was amazed when I read the report." Referee Lubbe denied he had told the South African paper that Wolves players had cursed and provoked the home players. "I wish to dissociate myself from the report," he said.

The brief diversion over, Cullis and directors Jim Marshall and John Ireland took the team to Pretoria where a Murray goal late in the game gave them a 1-0 win over North East Transvaal. Cullis made three substitutions in the game. At half-time he substituted Booth and Mullen for Clamp and Deeley respectively. Ten minutes later he had to send Deeley back on after Harry Hooper was carried off with an ankle injury. Deeley did well on the right wing and stayed there for the next game, a 5-1 win over Natal in Durban. He scored twice that day and Peter Broadbent went one better. In the days of five-man forward lines, Broadbent and Deeley looked a promising right-wing pairing.

So the wins went on – Western Province (6-0), a South African XI (4-1), Southern Transvaal President's XI (7-3), Southern Rhodesia (10-1) and Northern Rhodesia (11-1). Billy Wright, having been required for England World Cup qualifying games against the Republic of Ireland, home and away, and Denmark in Copenhagen, joined the squad for the two games in Rhodesia. Norman Deeley hit hat-tricks in the last two matches and had shown he was a more than adequate substitute for Harry Hooper if required – and, unexpectedly, he would be. Cullis returned home not only with some revised ideas about his line-up for the new season but also with a new player. A two-goal star for the Southern Transvaal President's XI in Johannesburg was a stocky inside-forward named Cliff Durandt. Cullis said he could tell after ten minutes that the 17-year-old had a football brain and promptly signed him.

While Durandt's time was to come, it seemed time was up for Harry Hooper. Cullis had paid a then club record fee for the winger but things happened on tour that meant a fall-out between player and manager. In addition, it appeared that Norman Deeley had at last found his best position after starting out as a wing-half and then being tried at inside-forward. Hooper had been top scorer with 19 goals in his first season, had played for the Football League against the Scottish League and had become a fans' favourite. That mattered not, Cullis did not want him in the team and so Deeley got the vote for the opening game of the 1957-8 season. Wolves were beaten 1-0 at Everton but Deeley kept his place and was soon impressing the fans with four goals in three games. Two of those games brought big home wins over Bolton (6-1) and Sunderland (5-0). The club's nemesis, Luton, beat them 3-1 at Kenilworth Road, but four wins followed before Matt Busby brought to town his Manchester United side who were seeking to make it three title wins in a row. Both Wolves and United had won six and drawn one of their opening nine games and were lying handily placed behind early pacesetters, the newly-promoted Nottingham Forest, managed by another of the game's legends, one-time Villa and England forward Billy Walker.

What neither Busby nor Cullis could have anticipated before their showdown meeting was that a flu epidemic would affect the line-ups. Cullis was laid low and so was Eddie Stuart but United were minus Roger Byrne, Eddie Colman, Liam Whelan and Dennis Viollet after having fielded the same team in each of their first nine games. After a goalless first half Norman Deeley struck twice in the space of five minutes and Dennis Wilshaw made it three before John Doherty's last-minute goal for United. With Forest losing at home to Albion, Wolves were level with them on 15 points from ten games but in second place on goal average.

Wilshaw had returned to the team a couple of games earlier but the 31-year-old was the subject of transfer talk. Birmingham City and Stoke City were said to be interested and the latter were favourites as Wilshaw's teaching job was in the Potteries. Wilshaw's Molineux day was not quite yet done – he would figure in another famous floodlit win – but Cullis knew he had ready-made candidates to replace him in the ever-improving Bobby Mason and the reliable Colin Booth. Four days after the United game, Wolves went to the top of the table when they beat Tottenham, the previous season's runners-up, hitting four goals without reply. The future looked bright in more ways than one as this was the first match under the club's new £25,000 floodlighting system. It was after the Spurs match that Wolves announced that the visit of European Cup holders Real Madrid would be all-ticket, with prices raised to counter the fee demanded by the Spaniards. This was a high-profile encounter and one to test the standing of Wolves as First Division leaders.

Top: The team who brought home the league title in the closing weeks of 1954. Back (left to right): trainer Joe Gardiner, Slater, Shorthouse, Williams, Flowers Stuart; front: Hancocks, Broadbent, Swinbourne, Wright, Wilshaw, Mullen.

Bottom: Seated Cullis turns to watch Billy Wright and Ferenc Puskas lead out their sides for the epic Wolves-Honved clash at Molineux in December, 1954.

Top: It's all over. . . Bert Williams leaves the field at the end of the Honved match while Eddie Stuart shakes hands with Puskas.

Middle and bottom: Key moment in the 1955 title showdown as Billy Wright leaps to punch a shot from Chelsea's Seamus O'Connell over the bar at Stamford Bridge. The sequel to Wright's 'save' as Chelsea full-back Peter Sillett fires home the resultant penalty for the game's only goal.

Top: A Wolves party set off from the Victoria Hotel for an away game. In doorway of the Don Evcrall coach is Bert Williams. Other players (left to right) are Clamp, Deeley, Showell, Jones, Mullen, Broadbent, Slater, Wright, Flowers and Murray.

Bottom left: Cullis looks on as trainer Joe Gardiner gives some advice to Peter Broadbent

Bottom right: Taking a good look at one of the Kremlin's chandeliers on Wolves' 1955 Moscow trip are (left to right) Joe Gardiner, Ron Flowers, Cullis and Bill Slater.

Top: Roy Swinbourne cheekily backheels a goal during Wolves' historic 9-1 win at Cardiff in 1955.

Bottom: In vest and shorts, Cullis lines up with the Wolves squad who toured South Africa in 1957. Back (left-right) Cullis, Mullen, Jones, Broadbent, Finlayson, Murray, Dwyer, Harris, Flowers, trainer Joe Gardiner; front: Showell, Hooper, Booth, Stuart, Mason, Deeley, Clamp, Tether.

Top left: End of a great career . . . Billy Wright waves to the crowd after bowing out in the pre-season practice match. Top right: Bobby Mason fires in the only goal of Wolves' opening game of the 1959-60 season, against Birmingham at St Andrew's, but the campaign would not end happily for the inside-forward who was dropped by Cullis for the FA Cup final.

Bottom: Ever the opportunist, Norman Deeley fires the ball past Villa's Nigel Sims for the only goal of the 1960 FA Cup semi-final at The Hawthorns.

Top: Cullis waits as the FA president, the Duke of Gloucester, is introduced by skipper Bill Slater to Norman Deeley before the 1960 Cup Final.

Bottom left: A video still of the unfortunate incident when Blackburn full-back Dave Whelan broke his leg when trying to dispossess Norman Deeley. Despite Whelan's allegations many years later, there was clearly no over-the-top tackle by the Wolves winger.

Bottom right: Bill Slater descends the famous Wembley steps in 1960 after collecting the FA Cup, the fifth major trophy of Cullis's Molineux reign.

Top: Joe Gardiner – more than just a trainer, he was Cullis's right-hand man.
Cullis personified . . . intensity written all over his face as he watches a game.

Bottom: Ted Farmer beats Everton 'keeper Albert Dunlop for the 21st goal of his Wolves
career in his 21st game on January 21st, 1961, his 21st birthday.

Top: Going down Memory Lane . . . Dennis Wilshaw listens as Roy Swinbourne talks of the time he had to tell Cullis the players were going on strike. Cullis seems deep in reflection as Billy Wright chats to him before the official opening of the Stan Cullis stand.

Bottom: Lining up on the occasion of the official opening of the Billy Wright stand are (left to right) Norman Deeley, former Blackburn Rovers skipper Ronnie Clayton, Peter Broadbent and Cullis.

They tuned up with a 5-1 win at Birmingham City but Cullis had to make a significant change for the visit of the European champions. Billy Wright was with the England squad, preparing for the Home International against Wales, and so missed the big game. Cullis would have to play George Showell to mark Real's star man Alfredo di Stefano, whom the manager considered the best balanced player he had seen. Showell had deputised six times for Wright during the past two seasons and he did not let the side down on this occasion as Wolves gained a famous 3-2 victory, coming from behind just as they had against Honved. Ramon Marsal gave Real a 14th-minute lead which they held until seven minutes after half-time. Peter Broadbent equalised and Jimmy Murray put Wolves into the lead eight minutes later. Hector Rial made it 2-2 before that goal poacher supreme Dennis Wilshaw won the game ten minutes from time when he cleverly hooked a Jimmy Mullen pass over a defender and Argentinian goalkeeper Rogelio Dominguez into the net. It was Wilshaw's last goal for the club and he could hardly have ended his scoring on a higher note. There was no "There they are, the champions of the world" quote from Cullis after the game but he was glowing with pride once more after another triumph for English football, this time over the official champions of Europe.

Teams at Molineux Grounds, Wolverhampton, on Thursday, October 17, 1957:

Wolves: Finlayson; Stuart, Harris; Clamp, Showell, Flowers; Deeley, Broadbent, Murray, Wilshaw, Mullen.

Real Madrid: Dominguez; Atienza (Marquitos), Lesmes; Santisteban, Santamaria, Zarraga (Ruiz); Joseito, Kopa, di Stefano, Marsal, Gento (Rial).

While champions Manchester United were faltering, Wolves pressed on and the chasing group were by mid-November headed by West Bromwich Albion. It was shades of 1954 and their first showdown of the season was at Molineux where 55,428 saw Albion test Wolves' new-found strength despite an injury to Joe Kennedy early in the game which saw him move into the forward line while Bobby Robson switched to left-half and Ray Barlow to centre-half. It took a Derek Kevan goal nine minutes after half-time to spark Wolves into life but they did not equalise until five minutes from time, thanks to an Eddie Clamp penalty.

The Albion game was Dennis Wilshaw's last for Wolves. Cullis, it was, who brought him back from his loan spell at Walsall and he had served the club well, even though the relationship between manager and player did not always run smoothly. Talking to Wilshaw many years later I suggested Cullis might not have been the easiest of characters with whom to work. The instant reply was: "I think the team spirit in the Wolves team stemmed from the fact we all hated his guts."

Admittedly, he then qualified the statement somewhat: "That's probably being a bit too severe but I think we were all united because we felt the same about the manager. But he certainly was a very good motivator, there is no question or doubt about that." Wilshaw had been top scorer when Wolves first won the title and figured prominently in the great floodlit wins over Spartak, Honved, Dynamo and now Real Madrid. His sale to Stoke would make life easier for him and he would serve the Potters well until a broken leg sustained in a cup-tie against Newcastle brought an end to his career in 1961.

Four days after the Albion game, Cullis took his team to Brussels to face RFC Anderlecht and it proved to be the last game for another high profile Wolves man – Harry Hooper. He and Bobby Thomson were paired on the left wing though Hooper switched with right-winger Norman Deeley after half an hour. Thomson was replaced by Colin Booth at the start of the second half. By that stage Wolves trailed to two goals scored in the opening 15 minutes. The 2-0 defeat was the end of Hooper's brief Molineux career and Cullis sold him to Birmingham City before November was out. In contrast, others were prospering. Evidence of the success of the youngsters introduced into the side by Cullis came when Gerry Harris was chosen for the England under-23 team while Jimmy Murray was named as a reserve for the full England side's game against France at Wembley.

Wolves' next excursion into Europe was far more successful – the return game with Real Madrid. On a rainy Spanish night Wolves drew 2-2 with the European champions and, by common consent, were unlucky not to win. A bullet-like header from Bobby Mason gave Wolves the lead after 30 minutes and Wolves seemed hard done by when Enrique Mateos, looking to be four yards off-side, put Real level nine minutes into the second half. Hector Rial put the home side ahead with ten minutes to go but the goal was immediately cancelled out by Jimmy Mullen whose centre was diverted into the net by a defender. A proud Cullis said afterwards: "I would like to strike a medal for all of them." Perhaps that was why the manager turned a blind eye to his players' decision to celebrate their win with a night out in Madrid. At the official banquet after the game, Cullis sent a note to the players saying: "Bus waiting outside to take you back to hotel." They ignored it and sneaked off to see a show at a night club they had been told about. Next day he learned why they had not boarded the team coach and his only complaint was: "Why didn't you tell me? I'd have come as well." Billy Wright told him that if he'd got wind of what they were up to he would surely have stopped it. Wright years later recalled: "Stan continued to protest that he would have come but to this day I am quite sure our manager would have stopped us had he got wind of our intentions. However, nothing more was heard. Stan Cullis is a disciplinarian with a heart of gold."

As in 1954, the backbone of Wolves' season was an 18-game unbeaten league run and it came to an end on Boxing Day, 1957, when Tottenham beat them 1-0 at White Hart Lane through Bobby Smith's eighth-minute goal. By the new year, there was talk of the Double as Wolves began an FA Cup run with a 1-0 win at Lincoln and then a 5-1 home defeat of a Portsmouth side who included two future Wolves strikers, Ray Crawford and Derek Dougan.

A 3-2 defeat at Blackpool was a mere hiccup and when Wolves beat Leicester 5-1 at Molineux on February 1, 1958, they led the First Division by five points from Preston. Wolves had 42 points, Preston 37 and a revived Manchester United 36. All had played 28 games and now Cullis was about to lock horns once more with his old rival Matt Busby in a match which could either open up the title race or tilt it even more in Wolves' favour. Cullis took his team to Blackpool to prepare for the Old Trafford showdown. Alas, the game scheduled for February 8, 1958, did not happen. Two days before the appointed day, United's plane, bringing the team back from their European Cup game with Red Star Belgrade, crashed when trying to take off from snowbound Munich Airport. Seven players were among the dead. The great Duncan Edwards would die two weeks later. What had been a happy day, celebrating Billy Wright's 34th birthday, was overshadowed by this awful tragedy. On the day the teams should have met in Manchester, Cullis and his players were at Molineux joining the rest of the country's football community in observing a minute's silence.

Wolves' next action was in the FA Cup in front of 55,778 against Third Division North side Darlington who in the fourth round had beaten Chelsea 4-1 in a replay. They failed to trouble Wolves, however, and were soundly beaten 6-1. It mattered little that Eddie Clamp missed from the penalty spot, his third failure in a row. Top of the league and in the last eight of the Cup but the Double dream was about to end. The sixth-round exit to Bolton at Burnden Park was a frustrating afternoon for Cullis as his side created chance after chance, failed to take them and bowed out 2-1. It was clearly not Wolves' day, as Jimmy Murray's shot hit the underside of the bar, one from Norman Deeley rebounded from the foot of a post and Bolton's winning goal from Ray Parry came from a bizarrely-gained free kick. Malcolm Finlayson bravely dived at the feet of Nat Lofthouse but on a muddy pitch slid out of the penalty area with the ball still in his hands. The league was now Wolves' target and there was soon evidence that Cullis could be a lucky manager, when he decided to rest Gerry Harris for the midweek trip to Chelsea, a fixture postponed because of the FA Cup run. Harris's deputy turned out to be the night's unlikely hero.

Cullis played George Showell at left-back, only for him to suffer slight concussion after being hit by the ball smack in the face. Cullis moved Eddie Clamp to left-back and Peter Broadbent to right-half with Showell, after some minutes on the sidelines, playing first on the left wing and then on the right. So it was that seven minutes from time when a Jimmy Mullen cross came over from the left it was Showell who volleyed the ball, left-footed, into the corner of the net to give Wolves a vital 2-1 win. That was Wolves' fifth successive league win and they made it six when they won impressively, 4-1, at Nottingham Forest, where Jimmy Murray scored three times.

The succession of wins was ended when Wolves were held 3-3 at home by a Manchester City side on their way to scoring a century of goals and also conceding a hundred. Despite Eddie Stuart misplacing an intended back-pass for an own goal after only 50 seconds, Wolves led 2-1 at half-time. It would have been 3-1 had not a saga of penalty misses continued. Eddie Clamp had failed with three in a row so Bill Slater was given the task this time only for veteran 'keeper Bert Trautmann to save his kick. The topsy-turvy display was merely the prelude to one of Wolves' best of the season as they went to The Hawthorns and beat third-placed Albion 3-0 with the sort of direct attacking football that Cullis had been striving for. As "Commentator" – Phil Morgan – reported in the Express & Star: "Their merciless, and often impertinent, drubbing of West Bromwich Albion, much more pronounced than the 3-0 scoreline can possibly indicate, was a reminder to everybody, and particularly the sceptics on the fringe of their own following, that they are one of the great teams of modern times." To emphasise their superiority, several Wolves players played keep-ball near the end of the game, adjourning to a corner of the pitch and denying Albion possession for what seemed like an age with a bout of short passing

The title was clinched with two games to spare when Wolves beat nearest rivals Preston 2-0 at Molineux, a game Billy Wright and Bill Slater missed through being on duty for England against Scotland at Hampden. The tension of the build-up to the game was too much for Cullis who had been battling against flu and the Express & Star reported: "Far from well during the last fortnight, Mr Stanley Cullis, Wolves' manager, has gone to one of the West Country resorts for a few days." He was back for the big day, however, but when a huge contingent invaded the pitch at the final whistle it was stand-in skipper Eddie Stuart who addressed the fans, followed by chairman James Baker. In the boardroom afterwards, as the champagne flowed, an emotional Cullis did say a few words: "These lads have thoroughly deserved the title. I have never seen a set of players work so hard. I am very proud of them and I think everybody in Wolverhampton must be." Cullis, too, had every right to be proud as he had now assembled not one, but two title-winning sides.

Among the telegrams of congratulation one of Cullis's most treasured was from Manchester United boss Matt Busby, at last on the mend after the life-threatening injuries sustained at Munich. There would be another magnificent gesture from Busby and his assistant Jimmy Murphy a couple of days after Wolves had clinched the championship. When the match postponed because of Munich took place at Old Trafford, United made sure they were out first so they could form two rows and applaud Wolves as they ran between them on to the pitch. It was the old champions paying tribute to the new. Busby had been discharged from hospital in Germany only four days earlier. Wolves beat United 4-0, Peter Broadbent blasting home the final goal from the spot as the reinstated penalty-taker, Eddie Clamp, was limping at the time. However, Clamp had scored in the 60th minute a momentous goal as it brought up Wolves' century of league goals for the season. Cullis had earlier had a minor crisis when goalkeeper Malcolm Finlayson was taken ill on the coach journey to Manchester. Fortunately, reserve Noel Dwyer was found having a leisurely game of golf and rushed by car in time for kick-off. Perhaps he was told: "Forget the greens, you're facing the Reds!"

If there had been no Munich Disaster, would United have made it a hat-trick of First Division titles? Some felt that would have been the case but the reality suggests otherwise. Assuming Wolves would have had the same results, apart from the game at Old Trafford, United would have needed to win their last 14 games to overhaul them. No team had ever won 14 successive games in First Division history. In no way should the tragedy that befell United be allowed to undermine Wolves' triumph.

A win in the final game of the season would have taken Wolves' points total to 66, equalling the First Division record set by Arsenal in 1931. They missed out, losing 2-1 to Sheffield Wednesday at Hillsborough. As Wolves were already champions and Wednesday already relegated, Cullis could field his latest venture into the transfer market. Into the team came Scotland international Jackie Henderson, signed in March for about £16,000 from Portsmouth. The deal perplexed many. Henderson could play centre-forward or left-wing and maybe Cullis saw him as the successor to Jimmy Mullen. However, they say "If it ain't broke, don't fix it" and Wolves had just won the championship in some style. There were young players in the Central League side pushing for selection and the addition of Henderson was a gamble.

While the champagne flowed at Molineux on the day Preston were beaten, beer was the order of the day at a Birmingham hotel where six men chatted around an old oak table.

Alan Williams explained in the Daily Express: "These men look just like any other group of chaps just back from the match. Then the man at the head of the table says: 'Let's get down to work. What did you see today?' The court of King Soccer Scout George Noakes was in session. These were the band of men who had drafted in seven of the side that had just beaten Preston to clinch the title. The men who have found many of the players who have given Wolves the Central League championship and virtually tied up the Birmingham League and Worcestershire Combination titles this season. Men dedicated to search every corner of junior football."

Ironically, in the not-too-distant future that scouting system unearthed a future England World Cup winner yet the coaches decided after lengthy trials that he was not big enough or strong enough to make the grade. The same had wrongly been said of Billy Wright by Major Buckley some twenty years early. Yet that was the reason given to Alan Ball after he had enthusiastically spent weekends and half terms on trial with Wolves only to learn of his rejection in a letter signed by Cullis. Ball would have his World Cup day gloriously at Wembley in 1966, eight years after four Wolves men had figured in the finals in Sweden. Eddie Clamp, Billy Wright and Bill Slater formed the half-back line in three of England's matches and Peter Broadbent was given a dramatic debut in the group play-off game against the USSR. The Wolves forward was a star performer in that game but England bowed out 1-0. Three more Molineux men had been in the preliminary squad of forty players named for the finals – Gerry Harris, Ron Flowers and Norman Deeley,

Chapter 21 Hit for six – but not out

Nineteen-fifty-seven-eight had been a great season throughout the club as they had won the First Division title, the Central League, Birmingham League and Worcestershire Combination as well as the Worcestershire Combination Cup. The icing on the cake came from the youngsters who ended Manchester United's five-year domination of the FA Youth Cup, beating them in the semi-final and then Chelsea in what remains an historic final.

At Old Trafford, the Wolves lads led the holders through a Ted Farmer goal just before half-time, only for Tom Spratt to grab a last-minute equaliser. The same player put United ahead in the second leg at Molineux where Cullis rallied his youngsters for the second half, Farmer quickly putting Wolves level. Goals from wingers Des Horne and Gerry Mannion in the last ten minutes ended United's reign and paved the way for a dramatic final. Wolves trailed Chelsea 5-1 from the first leg but turned it round with a 6-1 triumph at Molineux. That remains the biggest recovery ever made in the competition's final. Cullis missed the second leg, however, as he had taken the first team to play Grasshoppers in Zurich and maybe his absence helped the youth team.

A blast from Cullis might have had the right effect on senior players but not on youngsters. That was the view of Ted Farmer, centre-forward in that youth team. In his autobiography, The Heartbreak Game, Farmer said that the team had been given an ear-bashing at half-time in the first leg when they trailed 2-1 at Stamford Bridge. "We had to bear the wrath of Mr Cullis who could see a dream disappearing," wrote Farmer. "I did not think then, or indeed now, that 18-year-olds should have been subjected to derisive comments so vehemently put. Surely encouragement and constructive advice, firmly given, would have been a better ploy." With Cullis absent for the second leg, coach Bill Shorthouse was in charge of the team and Farmer recalled: "I am certain that with Mr Cullis out of the way a great deal of mental pressure was eradicated from the more nervous members of the team." Farmer certainly showed no nerves in the second leg at Molineux, scoring four goals by half-time to put the teams level on aggregate and then Cullis's South African recruit Cliff Durandt added two more in the second half before Jimmy Greaves struck late on for Chelsea. "Fantastic, wonderful, marvellous, that was Wolves," blared the headline in the Express & Star which just about summed up the team's performance. Cullis sent a message from Switzerland: "Tell them we are proud of them."

Teams at Molineux Grounds, Wolverhampton, on Thursday, May 1, 1958:

Wolves: Cullen; Kelly, Yates; Kirkham, Palin, Cocker; Read, Hall, Farmer, Durandt, Horne.

Chelsea: Smart; Shellito, Legg; Bradbury, Scott, Long; Block, Cliss, Bridges, Greaves, Harrison.

There appeared to be a lot of talent at Molineux in the Central League side and the youth team yet Jackie Henderson had been brought in to present an obstacle to the youngsters' hopes of progress. Somewhat surprisingly, Jimmy Murray, scorer of 29 league goals the previous season, was the first man to make way for Henderson. Most Wolves fans thought the newcomer would play in place of the veteran Jimmy Mullen but 18-year-old Des Horne was given his chance on the left wing on the opening day of the 1958-9 season. There was always a feeling that Cullis wanted a striker in the Roy Swinbourne mould and had reservations about Murray as a centre-forward. The slightly-built Murray was no Swinbourne but he was still very effective in his own way. He had that natural knack, which all the great strikers have, of being in the right place at the right time to put the ball in the back of the net. It's a priceless asset. His goals were not often spectacular but they continued to flow season after season, 20 or more four campaigns in a row. So it seemed harsh that he should be the man to make way for Henderson.

For the first four games of the season, Henderson wore the number-nine shirt – and failed to score. Having won their opening game 5-1 against Nottingham Forest at Molineux, Wolves were brought down to earth in dramatic style. They were beaten 2-0 by newly-promoted West Ham and did well to scrape a 1-1 draw in the return game at Molineux. In between those two games against the Hammers came an almighty wake-up call to Cullis – Chelsea's young side beat Wolves 6-2 at Stamford Bridge. Wolves just could not cope with the pace of the Londoners and 18-year-old Jimmy Greaves helped himself to five goals. The London-based national Press had a field day as the team dubbed "Drake's Ducklings" gave the mighty Wolves a football lesson. Most reports wrote off Wolves and suggested Billy Wright, in particular, was over the hill. Robert Findlay's verdict in the Daily Express was typical: "It was sad to see Billy Wright so outplayed, to see our champions made to look such tired old men." He added a comment from Cullis: "Now they know they'll have to play for their places – every one of them." Wright recalled a few years later: "The substance of almost every report on the match was that Wolves, the league champions, were a spent force. More than that, many football writers hinted darkly it was time I called it a day. Billy Wright was slow, cumbersome, leaden-footed, over the top, an old man . . . I had the full treatment."

Yet Wright would go on to prove he could still cut it at the highest level and Cullis knew enough about football not to panic. The manager knew his team had been well beaten but he preferred to look on it as a bad day at the office. There were no panic changes to the side beaten by Chelsea, the only alteration being a recall for Colin Booth as Bobby Mason was injured. It was only after the drawn game with West Ham at Molineux that Cullis shuffled his forward line, bringing back Jimmy Murray at centre-forward and playing Henderson on the left wing. The result was four wins in a row. The third of these saw Wolves win 2-1 at Blackburn Rovers but brought Cullis some more unwanted headlines. He was accused of swearing.

A national newspaper claimed he had used bad language at Ewood Park and three women spectators had been so offended that they complained to Rovers officials. The complaints got short shrift from both Wolves and their hosts, however, as one thing Cullis never did was swear. Rovers said they would not be taking the matter any further and "Commentator" wrote in the Express & Star: "Mr Cullis may get excited; he may even give his neighbour a hefty nudge now and then but, along with all the others who have spent many days in his company, and have sat with him through football matches all over the place, I have never once heard him use bad language."

After the quartet of wins came a shock 3-1 home defeat by Newcastle and a 2-1 loss at Tottenham before Wolves faced Manchester United in a game at Molineux that made history. Cullis and the Wolves directors, led by chairman James Baker, had a positive view about television and football and believed it could be a force for good, in contrast to the view of the Football League and the FA who were wary of the influence it might have on attendances. It was with TV in mind that Wolves persuaded United to stage a first Saturday evening game at Molineux. Cullis and his board wanted the game to be screened on national TV but their plans were scuppered by the Football League. The authorities were not prepared even to give it a trial run. The game still went ahead as an evening fixture and was won 4-0 by Wolves who gave a league debut to Cliff Durandt as Peter Broadbent was on duty with England in Belfast, as was Billy Wright. United boss Matt Busby said afterwards he was not sure there could be any additional benefit from Saturday night football, adding: "We would have preferred an afternoon kick-off but were quite happy to oblige when Wolves made the offer. Anyway, we can only learn by making mistakes."

Far from thinking televised football was a mistake, Cullis was adamant it should be part of the game's fabric. In his autobiography, he wrote: "Other countries have solved satisfactorily how best to utilise television without killing the sport it is intended to help. I am sure that in England, one league match could be televised every week, providing it was not played on a Saturday afternoon." His suggestion was to bring a league game forward to Friday night so it could be televised live. Not even Cullis could have predicted how much TV would come to control the game but at least he had the realisation that it could be a friend of football rather than its foe.

One man who did not feature in the Saturday night experiment was Jackie Henderson. After just nine appearances he had been sold to Arsenal the day before, making his debut for them and scoring twice against Albion on the same day as the Wolves-United match. The Scotland international had not settled at Molineux. Some said he could not accept the rigorous training regime, others that he did not like being played at centre-forward. His departure had no adverse effect, quite the reverse in fact. Jimmy Mullen came back into the team on the left wing and showed he could still cut it at the highest level even though he was well past 35 – and results picked up.

While Cullis had no objection to Henderson leaving, he was far from happy to read reports that Middlesbrough wanted to sign wing-half Ron Flowers, who at the time was in the reserves. In due course Cullis received an offer of £20,000 in writing from Boro boss Bob Dennison but told him there was no way he would put that offer before the board. Cullis said: "How would they feel if the position was reversed and they read in the papers that I was making an offer for Brian Clough? Flowers is not for sale at any price." Before 1958 was out, Flowers would be back playing for both Wolves and England.

Henderson could have had an early reunion with Cullis when Wolves travelled to Highbury but he was chosen for the Scotland side to meet Wales in Cardiff. He was one of five Arsenal men involved in the game at Ninian Park as the Scots had also called up Tommy Docherty and David Herd while Wales included goalkeeper Jack Kelsey and half-back Dave Bowen. Yet the Gunners still held Wolves to a 1-1 draw, the visitors' goal coming from a shock Cullis selection at centre-forward. Jimmy Murray's return to the side had been halted by injury and the manager decided to try George Showell in the number-nine shirt. His second-half goal wiped out the third-minute lead given the Londoners by reserve striker Tony Biggs. The under-strength home side, clearly missing their absent internationals, thus dropped their first home point of the season. Before that they had won six out of six at Highbury, averaging more than four goals a game.

Showell's goal was followed by another a week later in a 3-1 home win over Birmingham City but his new role lasted just two more games. Cullis knew he needed a recognised forward in that position but sprung another surprise when Wolves made their debut in the European Cup. Having created the catalyst for the competition by dint of their high-profile friendlies, Wolves dearly wanted to make an impact in their first European campaign. The home win and away draw with holders Real Madrid the previous season had fuelled the fans' expectations. Sadly, the first-round game against Schalke '04 found Wolves without a settled forward combination. Cullis did not turn to fit-again Jimmy Murray but decided to give Alan Jackson his chance in the first leg at Molineux. Jackson's previous two first-team games had been on the left wing as deputy to Jimmy Mullen. The Germans led early on but Wolves came back to lead thanks to two goals from Peter Broadbent before Willi Koslowski snatched a draw for Schalke three minutes from time. Wolves had enough chances to have won well and Jackson was among those who wasted good opportunities.

Yet he stayed in the team, duly scored against Burnley and was retained for the second leg of the European tie in Gelsenkirchen. He scored again but the Germans won 2-1 to go through 4-3 on aggregate. Again chances were missed and Wolves' hopes of European glory had disappeared. Jackson would soon disappear, too, playing just one more league game before being relegated to the reserves once more. He was sold to Bury the following summer.

Jimmy Murray was recalled for the visit to Luton where Jimmy Mullen scored his last ever Wolves goal and Malcolm Finlayson saved a George Cummins penalty in a 1-0 win but injury to the centre-forward led Cullis to give yet another new look to his front line. He moved Peter Broadbent to centre-forward, recalled Colin Booth at inside-left, switched Bobby Mason to inside-right and gave Des Horne another chance on the left wing. The side won 3-1 at Nottingham Forest and on Boxing Day, 1958, won 5-3 at Portsmouth thanks to a Broadbent hat-trick. The victory took Wolves to the top of the First Division and they celebrated in dramatic style the following day when Portsmouth came to Molineux for the return fixture. It was only 1-0 to Wolves at half-time but in the last 29 minutes Wolves scored six times to triumph 7-0, Booth and Norman Deeley collecting hat-tricks. Wolves, it seemed, had turned the corner. They had not. They lost at home to Chelsea in the league, then beat Barrow 4-2 away in the FA Cup only to bow out for the second season running to Bolton, this time 2-1 at a snow-covered Molineux. Cullis had to re-think his attacking options yet again and this time he found the magic formula.

For the visit of Blackburn, out went Colin Booth and Des Horne. Jimmy Murray was reinstated as centre-forward, allowing Broadbent to revert to his recognised inside-forward role but now on the left with Deeley. Most significantly, Cullis decided to give a chance to Micky Lill at outside-right. The Barking-born player had scored at Preston in the first minute of his debut the previous season but had been chosen only once since – as deputy for Norman Deeley. Now he would grab his opportunity to such an extent that before the end of the season he was being talked of as a future England player. Cullis also realised that his best option for centre-forward was still Murray, if only he could recapture the form of 1957-8. He could. In 17 games to the end of the season he scored no fewer than 16 times.

The new line-up clicked immediately with a 5-0 win over Blackburn followed by a 4-3 win at Newcastle and a 6-2 victory over Leeds – 15 goals in three games. Once again Wolves were setting the pace at the top of the table with Manchester United and Arsenal in pursuit. United beat Wolves 2-1 at Old Trafford but Wolves would not lose any of their final 13 league games. When the Gunners then had an eight-game unbeaten run they thought they might have a look-in but they got an almighty shock. It was supposed to be a top-of-the-table showdown at Molineux with both Wolves and Arsenal on 41 points, though Wolves from 31 games and Arsenal 32.

Title showdowns are usually close-run affairs, this was a total destruction. A Gunners team who included two future Molineux managers, Tommy Docherty and John Barnwell, were brushed aside 6-1. Wolves were magnificent that day and the pattern was established in only the second minute. Wingers Micky Lill and Norman Deeley combined for the latter to score and by 28 minutes it was game over as Wolves were three up. Three goals in the space of eight second-half minutes clinched the win, Joe Haverty scoring for the visitors four minutes from time.

Teams at Molineux Grounds, Wolverhampton, on Saturday, March 7, 1959:

Wolves: Finlayson; Stuart, Harris; Clamp, Wright, Flowers; Lill, Mason, Murray, Broadbent, Deeley.

Goals: Deeley (2, 63), Broadbent (14, 71), Lill (28), Murray (67).

Arsenal: Standen; Wills, Evans; Docherty, Dodgin, Bowen; Clapton, Ward, Herd, Barnwell, Haverty.

Goal: Haverty (86).

There was an unexpected reaction to the defeat from Arsenal manager George Swindin who said: "We were powered out of the game." That prompted a swift rebuttal by Cullis: "How can he say they were 'powered' out of it? It's nonsense to suggest it. They were footballed out of it. Jimmy Murray, the heaviest of my forwards, is 11st 9lb, Peter Broadbent is 11st and all the others are under that. Arsenal were unlucky to meet us on a day when our boys were great. They played the best football I have seen from them this season." In the Daily Mirror, Bill Holden also rejected the Arsenal criticism: "It was sheer soccer brilliance allied to amazing fitness which gave Wolves victory. There was no suspicion of 'get stuck in' toughness about their play. They baffled Arsenal with their ball control and left them standing when it came to speed."

Desmond Hackett, in the Daily Express, agreed with that verdict: "Bluntly, Arsenal were publicly thrashed by a Wolverhampton team possessing confidence to a degree of arrogance, talent beyond resistance and a team spirit that made Arsenal look like a bunch of quitters. Just one Wolverhampton forward, Peter Broadbent, displayed more ability than the entire Arsenal attack. He tormented and tamed battling Tommy Docherty into a humiliation Tommy can never have previously endured."

There was hardly any stopping Wolves after that as Lill grabbed a hat-trick in a 5-2 home win over Albion followed by both goals in the 2-1 win at Preston. That made it eleven goals in ten games since his recall to the team. Wolves nearly lost their unbeaten run when Burnley led 3-1 at Molineux only to draw the match 3-3 thanks to Gerry Harris's first goal for the club 13 minutes from time. It was the day after that game that the England team to face Scotland was announced, confirming that Billy Wright would become the first man in football history to play in 100 internationals.

Cullis had nothing but praise for the man who had helped pack the kit for Wolves' ill-fated Wembley trip 20 years earlier. Now Wright was going to the famous old stadium to make history and in the team with him were club colleagues Ron Flowers and Peter Broadbent. To complete a special day England won 1-0 thanks to a Bobby Charlton headed goal.

It said much for Wolves' reserve strength that on the day of the England-Scotland game they could still fulfil their league fixture at Bolton and earn a 2-2 draw. Cullis was able to bring in experienced men like Bill Slater, George Showell and Colin Booth. With Eddie Stuart injured and Phil Kelly making his debut at right-back, Cullis gave the captaincy for the day to Eddie Clamp. Wolves at one stage led 2-0 against a Bolton side who had goalkeeper Eddie Hopkinson and winger Doug Holden playing in the Wembley match. The second Wolves goal, scored by Booth, took the Wolves goals total into three figures for a second season running. Yet at the halfway stage of the season, they had managed only 39 from 21 games. Such was the effect of Cullis's changes that Wolves averaged over three goals a game for the second half of the season and their final total of 110 was the best by top flight champions since Arsenal's 115 in 1934-5.

A couple of games after the draw at Bolton Wolves beat Luton 5-0 at Molineux and though Manchester United could in theory catch them on points, the goal average advantage was impossible to overturn. Matt Busby, for one, had no doubts and a telegram of congratulation duly arrived from Old Trafford after the game. The fans had no doubts either, and invaded the pitch. They did not disperse until the players made an appearance in the front row of the directors' box 25 minutes after the final whistle. Cullis stayed in the background as Billy Wright thanked the fans for their wonderful reception and said he hoped they would all be back at Molineux on Wednesday for the game against Leicester. In fact, there were a few hundred more there when the job was duly completed with a 3-0 win and Billy Wright received the First Division trophy. He proudly showed it to the crowd, most of whom had again invaded the pitch. The tracksuited skipper smiled happily as he held the famous old trophy. Wolves were on top of the English football world but Wright had played his last game for the club.

Chapter 22 No Double, Just the Cup!

After his historic game against Scotland, Billy Wright had played five more internationals, the second of them against world champions Brazil in Rio di Janeiro alongside teammates Ron Flowers, Peter Broadbent and Norman Deeley, the second time Wolves had supplied four players to an England side. It was a tough South American tour for Wright and for England, whose 2-0 defeat by the Brazilians was followed by others at the hands of Peru (4-1) and Mexico (2-1) before an 8-1 win over the USA. There was much speculation about Wright's future as an England player after a magnificent career which had seen him play in all but three of his country's post-war internationals. Yet his position in the Wolves side was secure – or was it? Cullis had in fact decided he could not guarantee Wright a place in the team during the coming season. He felt that George Showell should be given his chance. Maybe Wright could no longer cut it at international level but Cullis seemed a bit premature in writing him off at club level. Wright was 35 but he was fit and his wealth of experience and his ability to "read" a game more than made up for any loss of pace. Yet for the public practice match two weeks before the beginning of the 1959-60 league season, he was named by Cullis in the "Whites" team with Showell in the "Colours". In other words, Wright would line up with the reserves. Then on the eve of the match, Wright announced he had decided to retire.

Wright in subsequent interviews and in his final autobiography always maintained the decision to retire was entirely his. He said he had found pre-season training tough and had also received sound advice from former Conservative politician R A "Rab" Butler that it was far better to bow out when still at the top. Nevertheless, many of us suspect Cullis may have played a part in Wright's surprise decision. Wright had never played in the reserves during Cullis's reign as manager and if Showell was in the first team, then the England skipper would inevitably have been expected to turn out in the Central League. This would have been humiliating for a football legend. It is my firm belief that the prospect gave Wright little choice but to end his career. Once informed by Wright of his intentions, Cullis did restore him to the first team to make an emotional farewell in the unreal atmosphere of the public practice match. George Showell was by 1959 a better centre-half than Billy Wright – that was obviously the verdict of Stan Cullis. The Bilston-born player would serve Wolves well in coming seasons, but not as a centre-half. He was, in truth, not up to the task. Cullis had got it wrong.

Before the league season began, Wolves created more history when they arranged with Cup-holders Nottingham Forest to play the Charity Shield game as a pre-season appetizer. A tradition was created and the match, eventually moved to Wembley and later renamed the Community Shield, continues to be played as the prelude to a new league season. Eddie Stuart was given the captaincy by Cullis and duly collected the shield after Forest were beaten 3-1 at Molineux. Cullis had chosen a new centre-half and a new captain yet he would be forced to reconsider both decisions.

Things initially looked to be going well for Cullis, his new centre-half and new captain as Wolves started the season unbeaten in their first five games despite having Peter Broadbent injured in the opening-day win over Birmingham City at St Andrew's. Then at the height of his powers, Broadbent was still missing when Wolves suffered their first defeat of 1959-60, going down 3-1 to newly-promoted Fulham at Craven Cottage. Centre-half George Showell, the man in whom Cullis had placed his faith, had a difficult evening in contrast to his opposite number, the veteran Roy Bentley. A centre-forward who had helped wrest the title from Wolves in 1955, Bentley was a poacher turned gamekeeper, having successfully switched to a central defensive role. Bob Pennington summed it up in the Daily Express: "John Doherty (Fulham's centre-forward) exposed the limitations of Wolves centre-half George Showell. Old master Bentley, by contrast, was just a wonderful mixture of majesty and menace in the best centre-half performance I have seen this season, maybe making Cullis think that his own Billy Wright's retirement was at least nine months premature."

The Londoners' chairman was popular comedian Tommy Trinder and he revelled in this victory over the champions, no doubt expecting to see his team embarrass Wolves again when the sides met at Molineux a week later. A report in the Wolverhampton Chronicle proved prophetic: "While Fulham chairman Tommy Trinder wore a mile-long smile and wise-cracked with delighted spectators, Stan Cullis suffered in passionate exasperation. Only drastic changes, if not cheque book action, will give his team the chance of honours this season – so said the painful pundits yesterday morning after the Fulham reverse." It went on: "Memories are short. Last season Wolves hit a bad patch and were lagging in the league up to the new year. Perhaps the prophets of gloom have already forgotten that they finished top. We say – wait for next Wednesday. Fulham come to Molineux. Will Trinder be wise-cracking then? Or will the wolfish grin be on Cullis's face?" The answers to those questions posed in the Chronicle were an emphatic "No" and "Yes" respectively.

After getting quite a drubbing from the Press, as they had after the defeat by Chelsea early in the previous season, Wolves got back on track with a 3-1 home win over Blackburn Rovers and then gave Cullis plenty of reason to grin when Fulham came to Wolverhampton. His team laid on one of the most scintillating displays of his managerial reign and the Londoners were swept aside as Wolves hit nine goals without reply. Significantly, Broadbent was fit again to mastermind a performance highlighted by four goals from Norman Deeley and a venomous shot from long range with which Ron Flowers put Wolves three ahead by half-time. Such was the fans' appetite for humiliation rather then mere revenge that they groaned when a minute from time Bobby Mason missed the chance to take the score into double figures, scooping a Gerry Harris cross over the bar from just two or three yards out. Express man Pennington had to change his tune now, writing: "Never have I seen such a cold-blooded, calculated, magnificent act of revenge. They even got a pep talk from Stan Cullis for leaving it at 3-0 at half-time." Fulham boss Bedford Jezzard was generous in defeat: "Wolves played some fantastic football. They were like tigers. Few teams could have lived with them in this mood."

Soon on the agenda for Cullis was the European Cup in which he was determined his side would do better than in their first participation. At least he had a more settled attack than the previous season and a tough preliminary round was negotiated with a 2-0 win over ASK Vorwaerts at Molineux after losing the first leg 2-1 in Berlin. In between the European games, Wolves won 5-1 at Luton only to lose by a similar score at Tottenham a week later, Bobby Smith scoring four times. That win saw Spurs move two points ahead of Wolves at the top of the table, unbeaten with 18 points from 12 games. George Showell had been injured against Vorwaerts and so Ron Flowers played centre-half at White Hart Lane. In Showell's continued absence for four more games, Cullis played Eddie Stuart at centre-half. However, the manager's problems at this time lay more in attack than in defence. Micky Lill, whose displays in the second half of the previous season had done much to enable Wolves to retain the title, had not recaptured that sparkling form. Cullis's answer was to switch Norman Deeley to the right and to give Des Horne his chance on the left wing. Lill, briefly a darling of the crowd, was sold to Everton before the season was out.

It was around this time that Cullis made what would prove another fruitless venture into the transfer market. He signed 21-year-old centre-forward Joe McBride for £12,000 from Kilmarnock in late November, 1959. The player had impressed Scottish scouts, though he had scored only six goals in 13 league games that season, and Cullis bought him without ever having seen him play. Birmingham City were rivals for his signature and would have put him straight into their first team whereas at Molineux he would have to play in the reserves and fight for a place in the First Division side.

McBride never did get past the second team and must have known he was not going to do so when Peter Broadbent went down with tonsillitis and there was speculation McBride would get his chance. Instead, Cullis chose Cliff Durandt. It was no surprise when McBride was sold to Luton Town in February, 1960, but what was surprising was that Cullis signed him in the first place. So what went wrong? Maybe he did not measure up to the Cullis standard of behaviour or he did not fancy the tough training regime or he did not settle down in Wolverhampton. It is pure conjecture but possibly the simple truth was that Cullis just did not rate him. Yet the player eventually proved he could cut it at the top level. He would later return to Scotland to play for Partick Thistle and then Motherwell before Jock Stein took him to Celtic where he would almost certainly have played in the "Lisbon lions" team who won the European Cup in 1967 had he not sustained a knee injury. McBride figured in two championship-winning sides for Celtic, was twice a League Cup winner with them, and scored 86 goals in 94 appearances. He was also twice capped by Scotland.

The McBride incident might have been a fruitless venture but Cullis sold him for the same fee he paid Kilmarnock and this meant he had sold six forwards since the previous July for a profit of £56,000, the others being Bobby Thomson (to Villa for £8,000), Alan Jackson (Bury £8,000), Harry Middleton (Scunthorpe £5,000), Colin Booth (Nottingham Forest £15,000) and Micky Lill (Everton £20,000). After selling McBride, Cullis told the Press: "We are always watching good players but there'll be no panic signings."

After an impressive second-round showing in the European Cup, drawing 1-1 with Red Star Belgrade away and winning the return 3-0, Cullis saw the league campaign stutter with three defeats in four games. The first was 3-0 at home to Leicester City, with the visitors two up in five minutes, the opening goal coming from Tommy McDonald, the winger Cullis had discarded three years earlier. Then Bolton, a real bogey team to Wolves at this time, beat them home and away over Christmas. A bizarre injury to skipper Eddie Stuart forced Cullis to reshape his defence and it would eventually prove the making of Wolves' season. George Showell was injured in the 2-1 Boxing Day defeat at Bolton so Bill Slater deputised in the return game, at Molineux two days later. Brian Birch – not the same Brian Birch who had played for Wolves a few years earlier – put Bolton ahead with what proved the game's only goal and Wolves' troubles were increased by an injury to goalkeeper Malcolm Finlayson which meant Stuart had to take goal kicks. The South African contrived to injure himself taking one of the kicks and had to be helped from the field eighteen minutes from time.

With Stuart out of action, Cullis decided to keep Slater at centre-half and use Showell at full-back, a position he had filled several times in the past. It soon became clear that Slater was the true successor to Billy Wright and that Showell looked far more at home as a full-back. Slater's displays got better with each game and after a 4-2 home win over Manchester City in January, the Express & Star's Phil Morgan, still disguised as "Commentator", was prompted to write: "Outstanding among the individual players was undoubtedly Bill Slater, with his fourth successive star performance at centre-half, a display that drew spontaneous applause in recognition of the intelligent way he so often made look easy situations that could so easily have been embarrassing." If Slater's star was in the ascendant, the opposite was true of Eddie Stuart. The club captain was struggling and when, with Gerry Harris unfit, he readily agreed to play in the unfamiliar position of left-back in the 3-2 home win over Luton he did not have the best of games. To make matters worse he got some stick from his own fans as Phil Morgan reported: "There is nothing worse than a player being pilloried by the home spectators and it certainly did not help Stuart." A loyal clubman, Stuart did not deserve such treatment but Cullis had to do what was best for the team. George Showell looked a more assured player at full-back and Slater was proving a revelation at centre-half. Cullis had found the new Billy Wright but more by accident than design.

An improvement in Wolves' league form coincided with the start of an FA Cup run. A 2-2 draw at Newcastle was followed by a 4-2 replay win and then a 2-1 fourth-round win over Charlton at Molineux where visiting 'keeper Willie Duff kept the score respectable, crowning his performance by saving an Eddie Clamp penalty late in the game. Before Wolves could make further progress in the competition, they got a rude awakening that Cullis – nor few others, for that matter – could have foreseen.

Trying to emulate Manchester United by reaching the semi-finals of the European Cup, Wolves knew they faced a tough task. They were paired with Spanish champions Barcelona in the quarter-finals. Amazingly, Cullis had to go into the first leg at the Nou Camp without the man who had galvanised his team's defence – Bill Slater. Birmingham University could not release him from his duties, not even when his team were carrying England's hopes in Europe's major club competition. George Showell moved temporarily back to centre-half against an all-star forward line of world stars, five men from five different countries – Martinez (Paraguay), Kubala (Hungary), Evaristo (Brazil), Suarez (Spain) and Villaverde (Uruguay). Even then, Barca were able to omit Kocsis and Czibor, members of the great Hungary side of a few years earlier. Wolves just could not live with Barca that night and even though they faced virtually ten men for almost an hour. Full-back Flotats was injured in the 34th minute and, it being in pre-substitute days, had to spend the rest of the game a virtual cripple on the right wing. To goals by Villaverde (eight minutes) and Kubala (15) were added second-half efforts from Evaristo (64) and Villaverde (81). There were no excuses from Cullis afterwards: "I can have no complaints. We were beaten by a better side."

Three weeks later, the Spaniards came to Molineux and this time had Sandor Kocsis in their line-up. A scorer when Honved were defeated there in 1954, he was this time on target four times as Barcelona won 5-2. The aggregate was 9-2 and it was an accurate reflection of the gap between the sides.

Teams in the second leg at Molineux Grounds, Wolverhampton, on Wednesday, March 2, 1960:

Wolves: Sidebottom; Showell, Harris; Clamp, Slater, Flowers; Deeley, Broadbent, Murray, Mason, Horne.

Goals: Murray (35), Mason (78).

Barcelona: Ramallets; Olivella, Rodriguez, Gracia; Segarra, Gensana; Coll, Kocsis, Martinez, Suarez, Villaverde.

Goals: Kocsis (29, 42, 60, 74), Villaverde (79).

Attendance: 55,535.

The inquest after the humiliation – not too strong a word – of England's champions was almost as soul-searching as that which followed Hungary's win at Wembley in 1953. The best team in England for the past two seasons had been beaten with some ease and it was an indictment not just of Wolves but of the game in this country. Yet Barcelona did not even make the final, being beaten relatively easily 3-1 home and away by a Real Madrid side on their way to a fifth straight European Cup triumph which would be climaxed by a wonderful exhibition of football when Eintracht Frankfurt were beaten in the final 7-3 at Hampden Park.

Among those who joined in the debate on English football which followed Wolves' exit was Cullis himself. At the time, he had a regular column in the Daily Express and two days after the Molineux mauling he wrote: "It is so painfully obvious we are behind the times. To many people it must be bewildering that Wolves, playing as hard as they possibly could, and lacking absolutely nothing in spirit and endeavour, should be so outplayed. But there are many lessons to be learned. Most striking feature of Barcelona's play, apart from ball skills, was the superb positional sense of so many of their players. No amount of coaching and training would give players the highly developed positional sense shown by these men. In Britain we have to mould our training and tactics to the material available. If players cannot show instinctive positional sense you will coach them only to a certain level. Anything achieved beyond that level depends on the players themselves. And that brings me back to my oft-repeated argument that we must catch them young. It would be interesting to find out the boyhood pursuits of the present Barcelona players. I am convinced their current ball skill can be traced back to the long hours of practice they had when they were ten years of age. In this way they gained an early mastery of the sort of fundamental skills which we find ourselves having to drum into players at the age of 17 and 18. In other words, we are seven years too late."

Cullis, so often ahead of his time, also advocated the use of foreign players: "The introduction of star foreign players would be a shot in the arm for English soccer. There might be objections from the Football Association, and certainly from the Ministry of Labour, who would refuse work permits for players. Signings could not be made without altering the league wage structure. Top players would not come here for £20 a week. But the public would appreciate foreign stars – just as they appreciate foreign entertainers." This view, expressed over fifty years ago, was spot on.

In between the two emphatic defeats in the European Cup quarter-finals, Wolves had moved smoothly into the same stage of the FA Cup, winning 4-1 at Luton, where Bobby Mason was twice on target. After the home drubbing by Barcelona, Wolves bounced back with a 2-0 league win over Manchester United at Old Trafford, where Cullis gave debuts to Gerry Mannion, a 19-year-old right-winger, and Barry Stobart as deputies for the injured Des Horne and Jimmy Murray. Stobart was 21 and had played many seasons in the reserves. He marked his debut with a goal after Norman Deeley, switched to the left wing, had put Wolves in front early in the second half.

A week later Horne was back for the FA Cup sixth-round visit to Leicester but Stobart kept his place with Murray still sidelined. Wolves won the game 2-1 to put themselves one game from Wembley, eleven years after their last visit. The game was dour and came at a time when most football writers seemed to be looking for a stick with which to beat the English game. It gave them plenty of ammunition and Ken Jones wrote in the Daily Mirror: "This match was soccer at its lowest. I am convinced that the FA Cup, British football's No 1 glamour competition, is becoming the game's worst advert. For the whole 90 minutes it was crash-bang soccer with hardly one breath of imagination or intelligence to break the monotony of crash tackles and aimless passing." Ian Woolridge, then with the News Chronicle, said: "The result was little more edifying than an all-in wrestling match between two gross women in a mud-bath which I once watched in a German night club." Denis Compton, a wartime England teammate of Cullis, wrote in the Sunday Express: "This was a grim, savage and relentless battle. Wolves won simply because they were tougher than Leicester. Certainly neither side were particularly interested in playing football."

Despite the criticism, Cullis was again chasing the Double. Wolves were three points behind First Division leaders Tottenham with a game in hand. That was played four days after the Cup quarter-final when Preston visited Molineux and were let off the hook. Wolves led 3-1 at half-time and their lead would have been unassailable had not Eddie Clamp sent a penalty kick in the general direction of Bushbury. Wolves then eased off in the last quarter of an hour and the visitors earned a 3-3 draw. The equaliser came in the 85th minute from Sammy Taylor who had also been a scorer at Deepdale earlier in the season when North End won 4-3 after trailing 2-1 at half-time. Wolves ought to have won the Molineux fixture comfortably and the point tossed away would prove costly.

Before the FA Cup semi-final against Aston Villa, Wolves dropped more vital points when Leicester gained revenge for the cup-tie defeat by winning 2-1 at Filbert Street. Jimmy Murray, fit again and playing at inside-right for the injured Bobby Mason, had given the visitors the lead but Leicester scored twice in the space of six minutes before half-time. It was a setback in the league campaign but now Cullis had to turn his attention to the semi-final at The Hawthorns and there were some big calls to make. Malcolm Finlayson had damaged his shoulder in the game against Barcelona at the Nou Camp and Geoff Sidebottom had proved an able deputy in nine matches since. Now the Scot had declared himself fit and Cullis decided to gamble on the more experienced man for the big game. Cullis trusted his instinct when it came to his attack. He gave Gerry Mannion his FA Cup debut, feeling sure he would not be fazed by the occasion. There were echoes of 1939 when Major Buckley had played 16-year-old Jimmy Mullen in the semi-final against Grimsby. It was also in 1939 that Wolves had beaten Everton in the Cup and opposing Cullis that day was Joe Mercer. The two Ellesmere Port lads would now be in opposition again as Mercer was manager of Aston Villa, relegated the previous season but well on their way to bouncing straight back. Villa, too, had the chance of a double, promotion and FA Cup in the same season, a feat accomplished only by Albion in 1931.

Teams did not usually walk out side by side in those days – except for the Wembley final – and Joe Mercer would have been well aware of Cullis's pre-match tactic of always letting the opposition go out first. It was a piece of psychology whereby the other team would start the game with cheers for Wolves ringing in their ears. Of who went out first at The Hawthorns there is no record but one can only imagine the near-comic sight of first Cullis and then Mercer poking their heads outside the dressing room door and looking down the corridor to see if there was any sign of the other team going out on to the field.

Both selection gambles by Cullis paid off. Villa were beaten thanks to a 32nd-minute goal from Norman Deeley with a nerveless Gerry Mannion figuring in the build-up. His cross saw Jimmy Murray bring a fine save from ex-Wolves man Nigel Sims only for the ball to run free for Deeley to pounce. Finlayson also rose to the occasion with a typically brave display, the highlight being his dive at the feet of ex-Wolves man Bobby Thomson late in the match when an equaliser looked on the cards. Wolves were in the final and attention quickly turned back to the league as four days later championship rivals Burnley were at Molineux.

As top-of-the-table showdowns go, the game mirrored that against Arsenal just a year earlier – Wolves blew away the opposition 6-1. The game against Villa had taken its toll on Malcolm Finlayson and Geoff Sidebottom deputised again but he was hardly needed as Wolves put on a superb show. It was a display to make the critics who had slammed them after the Leicester cup-tie eat their words.

The headline in the Express & Star roared "WOLVES *MUST* GO FOR THE DOUBLE AFTER THIS!" with the word "must" in italics to emphasise the point. Cullis would have been the last to put priority on one competition ahead of the other but things got better three days later when Wolves won 3-0 at Leeds. Having scored twice against Burnley, Gerry Mannion now hit a hat-trick on a day Spurs were surprisingly held 1-1 at home by Luton Town. Wolves and Tottenham were now both on 47 points with the Londoners top on goal average. Burnley were four points adrift with two games in hand but a goal average far poorer than that of Wolves. If only Wolves had not thrown a point away in the home game with Preston. It meant a fascinating run-in lay ahead and the next step would see Wolves create a piece of Football League history.

Bill Slater's displays had been of such quality that he was recalled to the England team to face Scotland at Hampden Park. Ron Flowers was now a fixture in the national side so Wolves would be minus two key players for the game against West Ham. Clubs were obliged by the FA to release players for England but there was no such compulsion where the players of Scotland, Wales and Northern Ireland were concerned. So Tottenham chose to deny Scotland the use of goalkeeper Bill Brown, half-back Dave Mackay and midfield maestro John White. Cullis rightly felt this put his team at a disadvantage and the club protested to the Football League, asking to re-schedule their game against West Ham. Times were changing and the League officials looked favourably on Wolves' request and let them move the Hammers game back two days. It was the first time the League had agreed to postpone a game because of international calls. Had it gone ahead on the Saturday Wolves would have been three regulars down as Peter Broadbent also got the call to Glasgow when Johnny Haynes dropped out through injury. The Hampden clash ended 1-1.

There was a certain sense of justice when Spurs, despite parading their three Scotland stars, were beaten 2-1 by Everton at Goodison. Wolves, able to include Flowers, Slater and Broadbent, then cashed in with a Monday night spectacular as West Ham were beaten 5-0 before a gate of 48,086. Now Wolves led Spurs by two points and Burnley by four, though the Lancashire side still had two games in hand. There were twists and turns ahead as the following Saturday Wolves were beaten at Newcastle where Len White scored the only goal of the game. Two days later, Easter Monday, Wolves beat Nottingham Forest 3-1 at Molineux while Burnley lost 2-1 at Leicester and Spurs were beaten 1-0 at home by Chelsea, their third defeat in four games. When full-back Joe McDonald put through his own goal for Wolves' third goal against Forest it meant Cullis's side had reached a century of league goals for a third season running, a feat achieved in the Football League only by Coventry City in Division Three South in 1931-2-3-4.

Cullis must have felt destiny was on his side as the return game with Forest a day later saw Jim Iley fire wide from the penalty spot on 17 minutes as Wolves held out for a goalless draw. Bill Slater, who missed that game, was two days later named Footballer of the Year by the Football Writers' Association. It was some achievement for a man who began the season in his club's reserve team. The title was Wolves' to lose – and lose it they did. Yet the odds seemed on Cullis's side when in their final home game they hosted a Tottenham team who had virtually thrown away their title chance. Spurs, in Bill Nicholson's first full season as manager, had won only one of their previous seven games, losing four times. That powerhouse of a half-back Dave Mackay had missed the Chelsea game but was now fit again. However, Nicholson decided to play him for the first time in his Spurs career at inside-left with Tony Marchi staying at left-half. It proved a master stroke as Mackay nullified the Wolves midfield and it was his header that put Spurs 2-1 ahead after Peter Broadbent had wiped out a headed goal from Bobby Smith. A third headed goal – from Cliff Jones – sealed a 3-1 away win and the last Saturday arrived with Burnley in the driving seat. They had 52 points, the same as Wolves and one ahead of Tottenham but with two games still to play while their rivals had one. Ideally, the final day of a season should see every side play their last game but Burnley were allowed by the Football League to play theirs – away to Manchester City – two days after the scheduled finish.

To keep the race alive, Cullis knew Wolves had to win their last match – against Chelsea at Stamford Bridge. Gerry Mannion and Bobby Mason had looked below par in the crucial defeat by Spurs. They were not alone but Cullis decided his forward line needed re-shaping. He dropped Mannion and Mason, switched Norman Deeley to the right wing so Des Horne could return on the left and gave the number-eight shirt to Barry Stobart. Not even Cullis could have imagined his changes would be such a success. For Chelsea were beaten 5-1, ample revenge for the 6-2 drubbing in London the previous season. Burnley were held to a goalless draw by Fulham at Turf Moor but, crucially, were only a point behind Wolves and had that game in hand. It was played on the Monday of Cup Final week.

Having agreed to do a "Diary of a Wembley Manager" for the Daily Express, Cullis wrote on the morning of the City-Burnley game: "Yesterday morning I went, as usual, to church. Then on to my office and my biggest concern – the form of my junior teams. I spent quite a while sifting through the reports and found that David Woodfield, a 16-year-old ground-staff lad, had pleased his trainers on his Central League debut at centre-half. The reserves won 3-0. After that pleasing report, I started arranging a series of trials for the start of next season – you can't stand still in soccer just because you happen to be in the Cup Final and at the top of the First Division.

"At Wolves we always believe in thinking five years ahead. So when I finished my work and went home to spend the rest of the day quietly, my chief scout George Noakes stayed on. He had nearly a dozen of his scouts with him and they talked and talked about young players. We must wait and see if these young men can make the grade. We must also wait, I'm sorry to say, to find out if we have won the championship for a third successive year. I'm going to Maine Road to see how Burnley fare because I could not endure the tension waiting for a telephone call to give me the result."

The Master of Molineux could only look on from the stand at Maine Road as Burnley duly beat Manchester City 2-1 to become champions. All the scoring came in the first half, Burnley going ahead after only four minutes as City's veteran 'keeper Bert Trautmann misjudged a Brian Pilkington centre which deflected off him into the net. City were level eight minutes later when Joe Hayes, looking a yard off-side, prodded home a chipped free-kick from Ken Barnes. Reserve winger Trevor Meredith hit what proved to be the winner on the half-hour when he volleyed home a misplaced clearance by full-back Ken Branagan. City did their best to turn things round in the second half and Burnley goalkeeper Adam Blacklaw made several fine saves, including one from Alan Oakes in the dying seconds.

Once again, Cullis had been close to the Double and had been denied; now he had to turn his attention to the side to face Blackburn Rovers in the FA Cup final. After the Chelsea game, Phil Morgan had written in the Sporting Star: "The big problem now is what Mr Cullis will do for his Wembley side. It may be hard luck on those who were outside today, but for my money this lot, playing as they played today, would be good enough. They were not only brilliant, they were supremely confident and that means such a tremendous lot." Desmond Hackett, writing in the Daily Express, also had no doubts: "Martinet of Molineux, the incredible, unpredictable Stanley Cullis, will sit down at his roll-topped desk on Thursday and fill in his Wembley team, which looks like being his most audacious gamble. I confidently predict that in the grim ordeal by soccer against Blackburn Rovers next Saturday he will play 21-year-old Yorkshire lad Barry Stobart, who became a first-team player on March 5." Both Morgan and Hackett would prove spot on.

Just like 1949, Cullis had to decide whether to play in the final a man who had served him well or a man in form. As he had done with Lawrie Kelly eleven years earlier, Cullis chose the latter option. Bobby Mason, who had played in every game leading up to the final, was omitted and Cullis, two days before the Wembley date, announced an unchanged side. In truth, his mind had been virtually made up soon after the final whistle at Stamford Bridge. "I pick my team on current form and nothing else," Cullis told Bill Holden in the Daily Mirror, "but I can tell you it was difficult and a painful experience to tell players they weren't in the Cup team."

Cullis added that others who had figured in the Cup run, Eddie Stuart, Gerry Mannion and Geoff Sidebottom, would join Mason in travelling with the team to their pre-final headquarters. They would, he said, be able to watch the final from a special touchline bench. Such a dubious honour was scant consolation for not playing.

Once again, Cullis had made the right decision and on a sunny Saturday at Wembley Wolves were just too good for Blackburn Rovers. Stobart more than justified his selection and it was his cross that Mick McGrath turned into his own net to give Wolves the lead. A few minutes later Rovers full-back Dave Whelan broke his leg in an innocuous tussle for the ball with Norman Deeley. No-one, not even Blackburn skipper Ronnie Clayton, deemed the injury as anything but purely accidental. Whelan, who became a millionaire and raised Wigan Athletic to great heights, claimed many years later he had been the victim of an over-the-top tackle. It was, of course, nothing of the sort as video recordings of the incident clearly confirm. Deeley scored two goals in the second half and against ten men it was all too easy for Wolves. That might not have been the case for Cullis who, as ever, went through agonies on the touchline as the sun blazed down on Wembley.

While the Rovers side were sporting in congratulating the victors, many of their supporters were unhappy and Wolves were pelted with orange peel and paper as they left the field. This led some newspapers to dub the match the "Dustbin Final". Sadly, over the years the nickname has been repeated and seems to have been interpreted as a summing-up of the game itself. Those of us who saw the match know that Wolves played well and were definitely in command when Whelan sustained his unfortunate injury.

Teams at Wembley Stadium, London, on Saturday, May 7, 1960:

Wolves: Finlayson; Showell, Harris; Clamp, Slater, Flowers; Deeley, Stobart, Murray, Broadbent, Horne.

Blackburn Rovers: Leyland; Bray, Whelan; Clayton, Woods, McGrath; Bimpson, Dobing, Dougan, Douglas, McLeod.

When Cullis spoke from the Town Hall balcony to the huge crowd who welcomed the team back to Wolverhampton the day after the final, he said: "We are glad to be home and at least it is a refreshing change not to be pelted with orange peel." Before coming back to Wolverhampton, there had been a post-match banquet at the Café Royal in London and there Cullis could not resist a blast at those who had criticised Wolves: "For a team devoid of skill we haven't done too badly to finish second in the league, to win the Cup and reach the quarter-finals of the European Cup."

Cullis had reason to be satisfied yet the club could so easily have become the first team in the 20th Century to do the Double and only the third to be First Division champions three years running. The question has to be asked whether he was right to decide at the start of the season that George Showell should have the number-five shirt. Despite all his protestations to the contrary, Billy Wright was surely backed into a corner. His choice was reserve team football or go out at the top. No-one can blame him for choosing the latter. Also . . . should Cullis have realised sooner that a better successor to Wright would have been Bill Slater? When Slater deputised for the injured Showell against Chelsea at the end of November, Phil Morgan said in the Express & Star: "Bill Slater, having his first top-class game at centre-half just got on with the job. It was his distribution of the ball, carried on by the wing-halves too, that put the team so often on the attack." Here was an indication that Cullis had a better man for the job but he did not immediately see it.

Tom Duckworth of the Birmingham Evening Mail had no doubts. Writing in the paper's Sports Argus Annual, he said: "Had Bill Slater taken over the centre-half berth immediately following Billy Wright's retirement at the start of the season, there seems little doubt Wolves would have achieved the Double." He added: "George Showell, earmarked as Wright's successor, did not settle at centre-half. Wolves' revival began when Slater took over the position regularly."

Chapter 23 Spend, spend, spend

Three trophies in three seasons, Wolves were still a power in the land. However, the team had peaked and the four seasons that followed would be testing ones for Cullis. He had established himself as "Master of Molineux". Perhaps he could also have been correctly labelled the "Midas of Molineux" as he had unearthed some nuggets of gold thanks to his scouting staff. Having created two fine teams, it would be asking a lot for Cullis to create a third and though he resorted to the cheque book in a way he had never done before he could not quite pull it off.

Not that there was any sign of a crisis at the start of the 1960-1 season. It began with Wolves drawing 2-2 at Burnley to share the Charity Shield. John Connelly seemed to have won it for the home side with a goal four minutes from time, only for Jimmy Murray to head home a Gerry Mannion corner two minutes later. Barry Stobart played at Turf Moor but the spurned Bobby Mason was restored to the side when the new league season began. It seemed business as usual for Cullis, Wolves collecting five wins and a draw in their opening six games. However, the national spotlight had switched to North London. Bill Nicholson had featured in the Tottenham side who won the Second Division and First Division titles in successive seasons at the start of the 1950s with their trademark "push and run" brand of football. Now, as boss at White Hart Lane, he had assembled a special blend of players who would go down in history as one of football's greatest sides. They had made most of the running in 1959-60 only to be overtaken by Wolves and then Burnley as they faltered on the run-in. It was different in 1960-1 as they reeled off ten successive wins at the start of the season before arriving at Molineux to see if they could make it eleven out of eleven.

This was supposed to be Spurs' toughest test yet, but they did what Barcelona had done and beat Cullis's side with embarrassing ease. At the time I was in the under-15 rugby XV at Tettenhall College and we were at home that day. After our match, I and two other Wolves fans in the team determined to get to Molineux, plenty of mud still clinging to our knees, in time for the last stages of the big match. We would be able to squeeze in as in those days the gates would be opened 20 minutes from the end for those who wished to leave early. I and my pals, changed quickly, not bothering to shower and caught the trolleybus to town, dashed down Waterloo Road and eventually could see the huge South Bank crammed with fans – the gate was 53,036 – and yet there was no noise. A dribble of early leavers had begun and we asked the score. Wolves were 3-0 down. So that was why there was no noise. We went inside the ground in time to see Terry Dyson make it 4-0 and Spurs had written their name into English football history with their record start. Dyson was one of only three players in the Spurs side who had not cost a fee – full-backs Peter Baker and Ron Henry were the others.

While the spotlight was on Spurs, Sheffield Wednesday had also made an unbeaten start to the season but when they came to Molineux boasting nine wins and three draws from their opening 12 games, they got a rude awakening. Cullis had recalled Eddie Stuart to the side to deputise for Bill Slater and now, with Slater fit again, he moved Stuart to his old right-back spot with George Showell switching to the left to the exclusion of Gerry Harris. The defence looked solid and blunted the Wednesday attack while the home forwards got off to a dream start. Norman Deeley scored after 30 seconds and two goals from Jimmy Murray meant Wolves were three up after just ten minutes. Keith Ellis pulled one back for the shell-shocked visitors but Peter Broadbent completed a 4-1 win. Significantly, Slater outshone Wednesday's Peter Swan, the man who had succeeded him as England centre-half.

The Wednesday win saw the fifth appearance of a young man whom Cullis had kept waiting in the wings. Ted Farmer was the hero of Wolves' remarkable FA Youth Cup win two years earlier but only now was given his chance. Although he failed to score against Wednesday his previous four games had brought him five goals, beginning with two in a 3-1 win over Manchester United at Old Trafford. His seven games after the Wednesday win would bring him eleven goals. Cullis had unearthed a gem and Farmer's arrival meant Jimmy Murray could move to inside-right where he was able to feed off Farmer. Murray hit a hat-trick when Chelsea were beaten 6-1 at Molineux on the last day of 1960 but eleven days later the FA Cup holders' defence of the trophy was over. They were held 1-1 at home by Second Division Huddersfield and lost the replay 2-1.

A few weeks before Christmas Cullis had signed a midfield player, Ken Wimshurst, from Gateshead, a club who the previous season had gone out of the Football League when they failed to gain re-election. At 22, Wimshurst was thought of as a useful acquisition but – shades of Joe McBride – he never got past the Central League side. Wimshurst was sold in the summer of 1961 to Southampton where he had five useful seasons, helping them gain promotion to the top flight in 1966. Wimshurst goes down as yet another failed Cullis transfer deal.

The goals kept flowing from Farmer and when he scored in the 4-1 home win over Everton it brought about one of football's quirkiest stats – it was his 21st goal, on his 21st first-team appearance and on his 21st birthday. For good measure, the game was played on January 21. By this time another member of the FA Youth Cup winners, Cliff Durandt, had replaced his fellow South African Des Horne on the left-wing and Cullis soon sold Horne to Blackpool.

By then Wolves had negotiated the opening round of the newly-founded European Cup-winners Cup, beating FK Austria 5-0 at Molineux after losing 2-0 in Vienna, where five times they saw shots strike the woodwork. In the Prater Stadium, Wolves fell foul of West German referee Andre Deutsch who penalised what in England would have been accepted as legitimate tackles yet took no action against the home side's bodychecking. It prompted Cullis to go into the referee's room at half-time to protest about the official's interpretation of the laws. Bill Holden in the Daily Mirror, reported: "I have never seen Cullis so angry as he was after the end of this match." Fortunately, there was a Swiss referee in charge for the second leg which provided a fairytale story for reserve half-back Johnny Kirkham. When Ron Flowers cried off with a bad cold on the day of the game, the Wednesbury lad was drafted in and scored in the first minute and the 26th to wipe out the deficit and Bobby Mason put Wolves ahead on 35 minutes with a gift goal. Austria goalkeeper Herbert Gartner threw the ball straight to him and Mason promptly lobbed it back over his head into the net. Two Peter Broadbent goals in the space of two minutes midway through the second half completed a fine win. That put Wolves into the semi-final as the competition's inaugural season had brought only ten entries.

Wolves' opponents in the semis were Rangers, one of four teams who had to play in the preliminary round. After beating Ferencvaros 5-4 on aggregate the Glasgow giants powered past Borussia Moenchengladbach 11-0 in the quarter-final, winning 8-0 at Ibrox. Now Wolves would have to go to that Scottish cauldron where the gate was 79,229 and Cullis was hampered by an injury which ruled out Peter Broadbent, such a vital figure in the team for the past three seasons. Yet Wolves looked like emerging from a difficult first leg just a goal down. Then, six minutes from time, one of Cullis's most reliable lieutenants, Eddie Clamp, made a rare mistake. He could have passed to his goalkeeper or booted the ball into touch. Instead he tried a crossfield pass which was blown off course and headed forward for Ralph Brand to make it 2-0. Broadbent was back for the return leg, when 10,000 Rangers fans virtually took over Wolverhampton for a day, and he managed to cancel out Alex Scott's 34th-minute goal. However, a 1-1 draw meant Wolves were out and Rangers would go on to the final where they lost to Fiorentina.

Then Cullis was denied the services of Ted Farmer after the match against Manchester City at Molineux, when the youngster continued a feud with City's legendary goalkeeper Bert Trautmann begun earlier in the season. The return match saw the pair booked after a race for the ball ended with the 'keeper grabbing the centre-forward's legs to prompt a scuffle. After the only goal of the match, by Jimmy Murray six minutes from time, Farmer stood over Trautmann clapping his hands in mock applause. It prompted Bill Slater to run half the length of the field to pull Farmer away.

If the inevitable wrath of Cullis afterwards was not enough, Farmer then found himself in hospital. He had been involved in some tough tussles with City's rugged centre-half Dave Ewing and twice needed treatment. He was taken ill the following day and admitted to hospital with internal bleeding and would miss the final five games of the season. Farmer had amassed 28 goals from 27 league games, Cullis pointed out that Trautmann had kicked at Farmer but added: "I agree the clapping was quite ridiculous and I shall speak to Farmer about it – but he's one of the nicest lads you could meet." Farmer's recollection of the incident, told many years later in his autobiography, did not do Cullis any favours. At half-time Farmer had gone to the toilet and discovered he was passing blood in his urine. Cullis was told this by the club doctor but, according to Farmer, told the medical man: "Wait 'til it comes through his backside before you take him off!"

With Farmer sidelined for the last five games of the season, Barry Stobart deputised and figured on the scoresheet twice as Wolves won 5-1 at Arsenal in their penultimate fixture. The fourth goal, scored by Bobby Mason, wrote Wolves' name into the record books. For a fourth successive season they had scored a century of league goals and no team have ever come close to emulating that feat. Those free-scoring four seasons had produced a total of 422 league goals. Jimmy Murray was responsible for 102 of them with 62 from Peter Broadbent and 61 from Norman Deeley. Other notable contributions came from Bobby Mason 39, Farmer with his 28 and Eddie Clamp 21.

With Sheffield Wednesday losing their final game of the season 4-1 away to Aston Villa, Wolves could have grabbed the runners-up spot but they failed to take advantage. They were unexpectedly beaten 4-2 at home by a Fulham side who had been battling to avoid relegation for almost all of the season. Those of us who always felt Peter Broadbent was a better player than England skipper Johnny Haynes had to admit that on this day the Fulham man looked a class act.

Cullis was left to reflect on a 1960-1 season that had still seen Wolves among the big guns of the top flight yet he must have known that they were not quite the force they once were. Some new names had come through the ranks but now the manager would be forced to try to do something he had not done before – build a team by bringing in established players from other clubs. When the opening seven games of the 1961-2 season brought only one win and Wolves were bottom-but-one in the table, the manager spent £27,500 on Queen's Park Rangers outside-right Mark Lazarus, having earlier sold the once bright hope, Gerry Mannion, to Norwich City. It proved an ill-fated purchase, especially as there was already a promising right-winger on the books – Terry Wharton. When the teenager Wharton was given his debut against Ipswich he and Alan Hinton, another teenager on the left wing, scored the goals that brought a 2-0 win.

There were signs of better form but things were far from settled and the team were not playing well. Typical of this was a 1-0 win at Fulham when Wolves struggled to beat a team reduced to virtually ten men for the whole of the second half. An injury to goalkeeper Tony Macedo meant that full-back Jim Langley had to play in goal but he was not beaten until Jimmy Murray struck five minutes from time. Ted Farmer had been recalled to the side for that game, having scored three goals for England under-23s in a 5-2 win over the Netherlands in Rotterdam. If he was pleased with himself after that performance, Farmer was soon brought down to earth by the manager. Farmer recalled: "I had just scored a hat-trick for the under-23s but he warned me not to play any 'FA academic football' at Wolves." Farmer's return was brief as Cullis promptly dropped him along with Murray, Peter Broadbent and full-backs George Showell and Gerry Harris. Farmer's verdict on Cullis: "He was a great manager of a great side but could not manage any type of failure."

By then Mark Lazarus had been played at centre-forward for three games and was later played at inside-right for a couple of games. It was after the second of those, a 1-0 home defeat by Sheffield United, that Cullis dropped him. Lazarus was far from happy and immediately asked for a transfer. He stuck it out for a couple more months before being sold back to QPR. Bobby Mason was also out of favour and he too slapped in a transfer request, though his was refused. It all indicated an unhappy ship.

If one venture into the transfer market seemed an error of judgement by Cullis, so too did his decision to sell the tried and trusted Eddie Clamp to Arsenal. Johnny Kirkham had turned in some useful displays when he had deputised for Clamp or Ron Flowers and Cullis reckoned the 20-year-old deserved his chance even though Clamp was still only 27. Just over a week after his transfer, Clamp was back at Molineux and skipper for the day as Arsenal won 3-2. Kirkham was eventually dropped after a 2-0 home defeat by Blackburn and for the trip to Blackpool, Cullis recalled George Showell to centre-half with Bill Slater switching to his old position of right-half. The changes did not work – Blackpool won 7-2, with centre-forward Ray Charnley on target four times. Those goals made Charnley the First Division's leading scorer with 22 goals, two ahead of Ipswich duo Ray Crawford and Ted Phillips. Five league games had brought Wolves four defeats and a draw. Not since a game against Arsenal at Highbury in December, 1934, had Wolves conceded seven goals.

Cullis made it clear that, like all managers, he could only do so much and the rest was up to the players. He told the Express & Star: "I have never been a man to rush into print but neither have I been one to deny a player a fair chance. The players have had that and only they, on the field, can make the effort to get back to their better form. Their prestige is as much at stake as that of the club."

After so many seasons of his side challenging for honours, Cullis was now in a relegation fight. Chelsea were bottom with 19 points, the same as Fulham who were above them on goal average. Then came Manchester City and Wolves on 21. Could Wolves survive? Indeed, could Cullis survive? For the first time in ten years, Cullis's position must have been in doubt. As in 1952, his directors decided to stand by him and showed enough faith in him to allow him to have money to spend on new players.

Two days after the seaside slamming, Cullis spent £30,000 to sign Aston Villa's Irish international winger Peter McParland but he was not eligible to play in the FA Cup fourth-round clash with Albion a few days later. Yet the match at Molineux did see three Wolves debuts as Cullis boldly brought in goalkeeper Fred Davies, aged 22, full-back Bobby Thomson, 18, and half-back Freddie Goodwin, 18. All played well but Wolves were beaten 2-1. Cullis was not finished buying, however, and two days after the Cup exit he spent £28,000 to bring in Blackburn Rovers inside-forward Chris Crowe.

Never before in his 13-year managerial career had Cullis splashed out such money on two players in the space of a week. He needed the deals to pay quick dividends and, fortunately for him, they did. Davies and Thomson kept their places on the day Crowe and McParland made their debuts but Goodwin made way for Johnny Kirkham. Visitors at Molineux were Double winners Tottenham, who were lying second in the table while Wolves were just two points above the relegation zone. Form was turned upside down that day as both new signings scored in a 3-1 win. The first six games with Crowe and McParland in the team brought five wins and a draw. The pressure had been eased but it was soon clear to see that Cullis had merely papered over the cracks. The last ten games of the season brought just one win and there was an embarrassing 5-1 home defeat at the hands of local rivals Albion. Wolves finished 18th in the table, their lowest position for 29 years.

Soon after the Albion mauling there was a pleasant diversion from the stress of management when Cullis went along to Aldersley Stadium in Wolverhampton for a re-match between the Wolves and Leicester sides who had contested the 1949 FA Cup final. All but three players from the Wembley game were still around for the re-enactment and Cullis and Johnny Duncan led out their sides just as they had done 13 years earlier. Ironically, there was a place in the Wolves side this time for Lawrie Kelly as Terry Springthorpe had emigrated to the USA and once again Wolves were winners, this time 6-1.

Amid the big signings, Norman Deeley had been sold to Second Division side Leyton Orient. Deeley, like Clamp, was a link with the greatest period in the club's history. Others from that era were also on their way. The loyal hard-working Bobby Mason, still only 26, moved to Chelmsford City, though he, too, would eventually join Leyton Orient. Eddie Stuart joined Stoke in the close season and would skipper the Potters when, with Stanley Matthews back in their ranks, they won promotion to the First Division. Malcolm Finlayson, at 32, was ready to concentrate on his expanding business interests. The old order changeth – but would the new one bring more success for Cullis?

The answer to that question was an emphatic yes, if only for a few months, as Cullis put his faith in youth and it paid dividends. During Wolves' greatest days, Cullis had prided himself on the fact that most of those in his teams were players discovered by the club and at the start of the 1962-3 season, whether by accident or design, he found himself naming a team for the opening game that included ten players nurtured at Molineux. With Bill Slater nearing the end of his playing days, David Woodfield was named at centre-half for the visit of Manchester City, Freddie Goodwin was recalled at half-back and the youngsters Terry Wharton and Alan Hinton were given the wing berths. Peter Broadbent was injured and so Chris Crowe was the only player in the team who had cost a fee. Cullis also recalled centre-forward Ted Farmer, having played him in the reserves for much of the previous season even though he had shone for the England under-23 side.

With Farmer scoring four times, Manchester City were beaten 8-1 on the opening day of the season. It was the third time a Wolves centre-forward had scored four goals against City. When this rousing win was followed by away wins at West Ham (4-1) and Blackpool (2-0) the "Cullis Cubs", skippered by Ron Flowers, a veteran at 28, were the talk of English football. After the game at Upton Park, Desmond Hackett waxed lyrical in the Daily Express: "Manager Stan Cullis is entitled to swagger around and call himself Diamond Stan, because he has brought off one of the boldest gambles of all time. He cast out his established stars and brought in kids like defenders Bob Thomson, Fred Goodwin and David Woodfield and had another teenager, Alan Hinton, at outside-left." Highlight of Wolves' eleven-game unbeaten start to the season, was undoubtedly the 2-1 win over mighty Tottenham at White Hart Lane. A feature of the team's success was their willingness to shoot from any range and Spurs were floored by long range efforts from Terry Wharton and Chris Crowe. Cullis's direct methods had triumphed over the more studied approach of Bill Nicholson's team.

Such was the form of the team that Crowe and Hinton were chosen along with Flowers for England's first ever game in the European Nations Cup, forerunner of the European Championship. One newspaper even suggested the whole Wolves forward line should be selected. That might not have been a bad idea as there was little sparkle from England in a 1-1 draw at Hillsborough. Flowers scored England's goal from the penalty spot.

Three days after the England game, the Wolves bubble burst as eventual champions Everton came to Molineux and won 2-0. In contrast to Wolves, the Everton side had been assembled largely thanks to the cheque book. Only defenders Mick Meagan and Brian Labone were home-grown. It was no surprise that the Merseysiders went on to win the title that season but what was surprising was Wolves' subsequent collapse. The eleven-game unbeaten start was followed by six defeats and a draw. Among those defeats was one by the odd goal in nine when Cullis locked managerial horns for the first time with Billy Wright. After a spell in the England coaching set-up, Wright, a boyhood Arsenal fan, had been tempted to succeed George Swindin as boss at Highbury. It looked as though this first meeting between two men who had shared 20 years at Molineux would end in Cullis's favour when Wolves, who had trailed 2-0 and 3-2, went 4-3 up through Peter Broadbent with 16 minutes left. Two Arsenal goals quickly followed and it was first blood to Wright – 5-4. The return later in the season went in Cullis's favour, Terry Wharton scoring the only goal of the game at Molineux.

Cullis could do nothing about Ted Farmer getting injured but he did take action to try to revive the side's fortunes by recalling Johnny Kirkham and Peter Broadbent, the latter having earlier asked for a transfer. Results picked up and Barry Stobart did well at centre-forward in the absence of Farmer. West Bromwich Albion were beaten 7-0 at Molineux and Burnley 7-2, as Wolves finished the season with a flourish, except for the final game, a 5-1 defeat at Blackburn, and ended up a respectable fifth in the table, having totalled 93 goals.

There was no relaxing summer for Cullis as just over a week after the final league game he accompanied his players on a ten-game tour to Canada and USA. He had first drawn up the traditional end-of-season retained list which contained no surprises but marked the end of Bill Slater's Wolves career. He had been appointed deputy director of the National Recreation Centre at Crystal Palace and was given a free transfer. He went with Cullis's blessing and gratitude for seeking out Molineux when he had desired to continue his football career on moving to the Midlands in 1952. Chairman Jim Marshall, vice-chairman John Ireland, and directors Wilf Sproson and Cliff Everall were among the tour party, as well as trainer Joe Gardiner and coach Bill Shorthouse. German side Schalke and Brazilians Bangu were among the opposition as Wolves' unbeaten five-week trip produced nine wins and a draw. When the players started their preparation for the new season, Cullis must have been quietly confident he could build on the progress made by his young side. He was in for a shock despite getting off to an impressive start.

The Cullis-Wright managerial battle was resumed at Highbury on the opening day of the 1963-4 season. Wright, who, like Cullis, ought to have known a bit about centre-half play, had signed Ian Ure from Dundee for £62,500 but his new man in the number-five shirt was given a run-around in a 3-1 defeat by a Wolves team again consisting of ten home-grown players, just as it had done a year earlier. Tottenham brought Wolves down to earth with a 4-1 win at Molineux before a crowd of 51,851 but a home win over a Stoke side skippered by Eddie Stuart, seemed to show Wolves might have a useful season. It was a false omen and soon Cullis would be shopping desperately for reinforcements.

A battling 4-3 loss in the return game with Spurs was the first of five successive defeats. Fourth of those was 5-1 at home to Blackburn who hit four late goals after Wolves had managed to wipe out a first-half deficit. Next up was a trip to Anfield but before then Cullis started to spend the £90,000 which was said to be available to him. He began by signing former England centre-forward Ray Crawford, whose goals had done so much to make Ipswich Town unlikely champions of England in 1962 under the guidance of Alf Ramsey. Cullis watched Crawford in the East Anglians' goalless draw with Everton on the Saturday and then signed him two days later. Cullis told the Press: "I went to the Ipswich match on Saturday to sign Crawford, not to watch him. I already knew about his ability and recognised that he was our type of player." The manager also had lengthy talks with Nottingham Forest wing-half Calvin Palmer but failed to clinch the deal. Reports also said Cullis planned further signings with Dundee's Scotland full-back Alex Hamilton and Hibs winger Jim Scott his main targets. Those deals never materialised.

In between the Crawford transfer and the bid to sign Palmer, Cullis had also to select a team to play Liverpool at Anfield. He made ten changes, five of them positional, as Crawford made a debut to forget – Liverpool won 6-0. Among the changes Cullis made was an enforced one as an injury to Fred Davies meant an unexpected return to league action for Malcolm Finlayson. It proved to be his final First Division appearance and it was a painful one, as well. He sustained a hand injury making one of several brave saves. With Liverpool 4-0 up, Jimmy Murray donned the green jersey. If Finlayson had ended his Wolves career with head held high, Crawford had begun his on a low note. Although Liverpool were well worth their win, the new man missed several clear-cut chances. Wolves had lost five games in a row and the last time that had happened during the Cullis regime was in 1952.

Crawford was too good a player to let a nightmare debut affect his confidence. He had always scored goals during his career and soon started re-paying the faith Cullis had placed in him. Next game he scored twice as Wolves won 2-1 at Blackpool whose goal was scored by Alan Ball, the player who had been rejected by Cullis. That was the start of an eight-game unbeaten run that put the season on an even keel. However, despite all the rumours, Cullis did not at that stage manage to add any more outsiders to the Wolves squad. He did, though, blood a youngster whose talent was obviously of the highest quality and who had come through the Molineux ranks.

Peter Knowles was given his debut when Wolves played Leicester City at Filbert Street. He was named in place of Peter Broadbent, a man on whom he had modelled his game. In time it would become clear that his was a talent that might one day match that of the brilliant Broadbent. Ray Crawford scored the only goal as Knowles had a promising first game. As one Wolves career was beginning another was ending, for Jimmy Murray, played at inside-left that night, was sold to Manchester City at the beginning of November, 1963. A natural goalscorer, Murray had served Cullis well, scoring 155 goals in 273 league games. He made a splendid start for Second Division City with 21 goals in just 19 league games.

Crawford soon found out that Cullis wore his heart on his sleeve and his manner was in stark contrast to the managers the centre-forward had worked for at Ipswich, the studious Alf Ramsey and the mild-mannered Jackie Milburn. Crawford noticed that Cullis would usually storm into the dressing room at half-time, ready to single out a particular player he thought needed a geeing-up. "We could usually hear him approaching the dressing room, especially along the corridor that led to the home dressing room at Molineux," Crawford recalled in his autobiography, Curse of the Jungle Boy. "He always wore metal toe and heel tips on his shoes. You could hear him saying loudly even before he burst into the dressing room 'Where is he? Where is he then?' I remember one game when our winger Chris Crowe, one of our most talented players, was having a nightmare of a game and was in no doubt he would be Stan's half-time victim, so he hid behind a 2ft wide vertical steel girder in the dressing room. As Stan walked around the room asking where he was, Chris moved around the girder and a few of us couldn't help giggling before Stan caught up with him and gave him his usual two-pennyworth. No-one was safe from Stan's half-time rockets."

The first, and probably only, time Crawford got the treatment was against Stoke just before Christmas, 1963. He recalled: "I was sitting in our dressing room at half-time at the Victoria Ground with the score 0-0 when Stan tore in with his usual bustling style. 'Where is he? Where is he then?' Then 'Ah, there he is', pointing directly at me. I'd had a difficult first half up against their rugged centre-half George Kinnell who'd roughed me up quite a bit with some heavy tackles and was winning our duels hands down. I knew I'd had a poor first half but so had most of us. Stan obviously hadn't seen it quite the same way as me. 'Ray,' he said, 'I bought you because I thought you were still the best centre-forward in England but today I think I could get one of the ball boys to play better than you.' After taking the flak I asked Stan what he wanted me to do, to which he just threw his arms in the air in despair and walked out without saying another word." Cullis's brief verbal assault seemed to have the desired effect: "I scored with a header from a Johnny Kirkham centre on the hour and wrapped up the game thirteen minutes later with a vicious cross shot, probably hit with a bit more anger than usual. Stan gave me a big pat on the back at the end of the game (Wolves won 2-0) and all was forgotten. Stan had a soft streak to him and never bore grudges against anyone."

Cullis was proved right in his judgement of Crawford, who scored 26 goals in 34 games for a struggling side who ended the season 16th in the table. By that time, Cullis had done more dealings in the transfer market. The first seemed to be the direct result of a 3-2 home defeat by Nottingham Forest after Wolves had led 2-0 at half-time. Joe Wilson, Forest's tough little full-back who would later become a cult hero at Molineux for a season, paid some particularly uncompromising attention to left-winger Alan Hinton. For the rest of the game Hinton tended to choose discretion rather than valour and if there was one thing Cullis would not tolerate it was what he perceived as cowardice. Less than two weeks later he did a swop deal with Forest which saw Hinton move to the City Ground in exchange for another left-winger Dick Le Flem. Born in Bradford-on-Avon, Le Flem, who grew up in Guernsey, was good enough to win an England under-23 cap, playing against Holland in Rotterdam in 1961 when Ted Farmer scored his hat-trick. Alas, he hardly made a big impact at Molineux. Hinton, however, went on to great things. He would later serve Nottingham Forest and Derby County with distinction and add a couple of England caps to the one he had won while with Wolves. Brian Clough signed him for Derby and Hinton was top scorer with 15 goals, eight of them penalties, when the Rams became First Division champions in 1972.

Hinton had learned from his early days at Molineux that Cullis could be a tough taskmaster: "I always saw Stan as a bit of a bully. He was really hard on me when I was very young and he upset me quite a lot. So one day my dad came down to Molineux with me and we had a meeting with Stan in his office. My dad told him in no uncertain terms that he wasn't getting the best out of me. He told him that one day I would play for England and that proved to be true. Things improved after that meeting but when I left to join Forest the time was right for me and the club. No-one could deny that Stan did a wonderful job for Wolves but by the end he had become a bit of a spent force. The game had moved on. It was becoming a lot more tactical and no longer could teams just rely on superior fitness which was Stan's forte."

About the same time as the Le Flem deal, Cullis also signed another winger, Pat Buckley, from Third Lanark. Not yet 18, he was obviously considered one for the future. Next came two more expensive additions to the squad in the space of two weeks in March. Wing-half Bobby Woodruff was signed from Swindon Town for £37,000 and England international inside-forward Jimmy Melia was bought from Liverpool for £55,000. Something needed to be done to boost a side who were in the middle of a 17-game run that brought only two wins. One of those, 5-1 at home to Birmingham City, saw Ron Flowers score his last goal for the club. It was fortunate for Wolves that Birmingham and Ipswich were well adrift in the relegation places.

Both Melia and Woodruff appeared to be good signings. Woodruff achieved fame for his long throw-ins but there was much more than just that to his game while Melia had played in 24 of the 42 games which would make Liverpool First Division champions that season. One thing that seemed obvious to fans, but not immediately so to Cullis, was that there would not be room for both Melia and Peter Broadbent in the same side. Both were midfield schemers, though both scored their fair share of goals. Melia was in his prime but Broadbent was nearly 31 and it would surely make sense to build a side around the younger man. Cullis eventually realised this and, for the final two games of the season, dropped Broadbent and played Peter Knowles as a striker alongside Ray Crawford. It brought first a 4-0 home win over Fulham and then a 4-0 win at Bolton which sealed the Lancashire side's relegation and enabled Birmingham City to stay up. Knowles scored in both games, while Crawford grabbed a hat-trick at Bolton.

Just before these games Wolves shared six goals with Everton at Goodison Park where the home side included half-back Tony Kay. It would prove to be the England international's last league game. Next day news broke in the Sunday People of bribery allegations involving Kay and two others from his days at Sheffield Wednesday, Peter Swan and David "Bronco" Layne. All three were eventually jailed as were others involved with Jimmy Gauld, the central figure in the match-fixing scandal. It was an unsavoury atmosphere that hung around English football and what better way to get away from it all than a trip to the West Indies. That's what Wolves did but it would prove the lull before the storm for Cullis.

Chapter 24   Sunshine then sorrow

For two weeks in the summer of 1964 Cullis enjoyed a sunshine trip to the West Indies where Wolves and Chelsea played a series of exhibition matches as well as games against Trinidad, Jamaica and Haiti. Chelsea were then in the charge of Tommy Docherty, a young manager whose star was in the ascendant, and met Wolves no fewer than five times in the Caribbean. As luck would have it the opening fixture of the new league season would see the clubs meet yet again, this time at Molineux.

Those final two games of the 1963-4 season should have emphasised to Cullis that a pairing of Crawford and Knowles could profit from the promptings of Melia. However, in the public practice match before the new season began, Knowles had a quiet game while Peter Broadbent turned on the old magic. Cullis decided Broadbent had to be in the team so he omitted Knowles, a player who looked far better suited to a role alongside Crawford. With Le Flem unwell, Cullis gave a debut to young Clive Ford on the left wing but he like the rest was overshadowed by Chelsea's eager young side who won 3-0. "Never have I seen Wolves make such a depressing start to a season," wrote Phil Morgan in the Express & Star and he had covered the club throughout Cullis's reign. "It was almost unbelievable because Wolves had more of the play than Chelsea and yet seldom organised a really effective goal-worthy move or provided a defence well drilled enough to stop the match-winning Chelsea thrusts."

It made sense to bring back Peter Knowles to partner Crawford and this Cullis did for the visit to Leicester City four days later. He did not have to drop Peter Broadbent but moved him to the right-wing with Terry Wharton moving to the left to the exclusion of young Ford. In defence he omitted centre-half David Woodfield, moved Ron Flowers to centre-half and recalled Fred Goodwin. Although Wolves lost 3-2 after Knowles had given them an early lead, it was a much-improved performance, the second Leicester goal coming from an indirect free-kick and the third from the penalty spot. Cullis was happy enough to keep the same line-up for the trip to Leeds three days later but did not make the game. He was taken ill at Molineux the day before the match, when he passed out at his desk. Club doctor Jack Richmond ordered Cullis to have some check-ups and then take a few weeks' rest by the seaside and so the manager eventually decamped to Eastbourne.

Before he returned to his office, Cullis missed five games. It is most probable that he did not get involved with the day-to-day running of the club or team selection during his absence. The Leeds game saw Knowles again give Wolves an early lead and Ray Crawford put Wolves ahead by half-time after Jim Storrie's equaliser. It was another encouraging display but brought only another defeat when Jack Charlton and Storrie scored second-half goals. The better form continued at Molineux when Wolves played the return fixture with Leicester. Ron Flowers was slightly concussed early on and moved to the right wing from where on 35 minutes he managed a centre that Ray Crawford headed home. Frank McLintock levelled seven minutes later with a shot after a free-kick had been pushed to him. That was the way it ended but at least Wolves had their first point. Another battling display brought only a 1-0 home defeat by Arsenal. There then followed two bad away defeats – 5-0 at West Ham and 4-1 at Blackburn.

The record book shows six defeats and a draw in the opening seven games under the managership of Stanley Cullis yet he had not really been in charge of the team for five of those games. Cullis was back at his desk on Monday, September 14, in time for that evening's return game with West Ham, at Molineux. However, by kick-off time he was manager in name only. Cullis later revealed he had been told before the game by chairman John Ireland that the directors had decided he must go. Amazingly, Cullis did not know what was coming when earlier in the day he gave an upbeat interview to the Daily Mirror's Ken Jones which appeared in the following morning's edition.

"Perhaps this will kill all the stories that have been going around about me," he told Jones. "I had a virus complaint and I needed a holiday to get over it. Now I am back. That's the end of it. It's obvious that we have got problems. One point out of seven league matches can hardly be called a good start. I've missed five of those games whilst I've been away. It wouldn't be fair – in fact impossible – for me to try to break down our troubles until I have had a chance to see the team playing again. We have got a lot of work to do. Our problems have got to be sorted out. We must get down to analysing what has been going wrong." It was fighting talk from Cullis and Jones commented: "The determination and dedication that have made Cullis one of the game's great managers was still there." Not long after giving that interview Cullis learned the club were dispensing with his services.

Despite knowing he was out of a job, Cullis took charge of the team for one last time. It would later transpire that the directors had chosen the side for the West Ham game and they decided to drop Jimmy Melia, Cullis's last major signing. It was not until the following morning when he went to confront the manager that Melia learned that it was not Cullis's decision to drop him. Melia commented later that he had only left Liverpool to join Wolves because in Cullis they had a boss of the same stature as Bill Shankly. Melia, who would be on his way before Christmas, said: "Without Cullis I see Wolves as just another average Midland team – Molineux without the magic."

What a farewell the West Ham game turned out to be! It was a memorable one, especially for left-back Gerry Harris. Wolves led 2-1 at the break, goals from Peter Knowles and Ray Crawford having been answered by one from Peter Brabrook, and then Harris stepped into the spotlight. First he managed to put the ball into his own net when trying to clear from Brabrook, then he conceded the penalty from which Johnny Byrne put the Hammers ahead on 61 minutes. After committing two costly errors, Harris almost single-handedly turned the game around with some marauding raids down the left wing. First he sent in a drive of such ferocity that keeper Jim Standen could not hold on to the ball and Crawford was on hand to put it home. Four minutes from time Harris fired the ball into the goalmouth from out on the left and Standen misjudged the flight. The ball flew into the net to give Wolves – and Cullis – a rousing 4-3 victory.

Those of us who saw the game will long remember it and the last thing we expected to hear next day was that Wolves and Cullis had parted company. It was announced on Tuesday, September 15, 1964, 40 days before Cullis's 48th birthday. Cullis said a few days later: "When Mr Ireland informed me I was sacked he suggested that for the sake of my reputation it should be said I was resigning because of a difference of policy or for health reasons. This I refused to do."

Two days after his interview with Cullis, Mirror man Ken Jones was left to reflect on a dismissal that had rocked football: "The sacking, and the way of it, is no credit to Wolves' board. The blow to Cullis must have been bitter after a soccer lifetime spent in the service of this one club. From his home last night he told me: 'Football, like many other professions, is a hard world. One has to be tough. Thirty years is a long time. But this is life and one has to accept it.' Cullis was calm but I detected a note of disillusion. A sad note."

Ted Farmer was still battling against injury during Cullis's last days but was of the opinion that the manager's departure was inevitable. "On the brief occasions I saw him he looked decidedly ill and subdued," wrote Farmer in his autobiography, The Heartbreak Game. "He locked himself away from all the players and staff, thereby having little or no influence on coaching tactics, team talks or possible means of motivation for a rapidly declining team." Farmer maintained: "All first team players were involved in strange fits of temper from the once stable, proud and disciplined man." Farmer believed John Ireland had been brave to take action: "He was criticised and hounded for making a decision that most of the staff knew was inevitable."

Cullis would be a tough act to follow but a new man did not come in until the first week in November. The delay was costly. Wolves played seven games during that time and lost them all. Fifteen games played and just three points – it made survival a virtually impossible task. Even when an appointment was made, it was not a permanent one. Andy Beattie was brought in as a caretaker boss when there must surely have been better candidates. The question had to be: Why sack Cullis if the best you can come up with in his place is Andy Beattie?

It seems the two things are not necessarily connected. A happy ending to the Cullis regime would have been ideal but it was not going to happen. Word was that a senior player had approached the board to say the team had lost confidence in the manager. If that was the case, once the players are no longer motivated by the man in charge then there is usually only one outcome. John Ireland had been chairman a matter of months but he believed something had to be done if Cullis had, to use the modern idiom, "lost the dressing room".

Cullis felt bitter about the way with which he was dealt . . . and no doubt Ted Vizard before him felt the same way. That, alas, is football. There were echoes of Vizard's departure when Cullis said a few days after his dismissal: "I am not ashamed of anything I have done and I see no reason why I should not hold my head up and face the world." That was how Vizard felt.

It was an unsatisfactory exit for the manager who had made Molineux magical. Others among the managerial legends, like Busby, Shankly, Paisley, Ferguson and Clough, bowed out when they felt the time had come and did so with much dignity, even though Clough's farewell ended with Nottingham Forest's relegation. In contrast, Cullis's departure was a far from dignified end to an association that had produced so much.

Ideally, the man who had brought the glory years to Molineux should have left with acclaim and honour. It did not happen and Cullis had reason to feel bitter about his dismissal. He carried with him for years a telephone bill which the club had sent to him just days after his sacking. Accompanying the bill of £3 15s (£3.75) for his line rental was a request for the return of his keys to the club. It was a shabby way to treat a legend, even if the board felt his time was up.

It was only many years later when Sir Jack Hayward took over the club that Cullis was brought back into the fold and the North Bank stand in the rebuilt ground was named after him. That stand was in 2012 replaced by an £18m new one which still carries his name while outside it is the magnificent Cullis statue. The plinth bears the remark that Cullis made to David Harrison:

"In this world you only have one life and I gave mine to Wolves."

Chapter 25 Chairman John a Wolves man

What of the man who was given the task of telling Cullis his reign was over? Chairman John Ireland has had a raw deal over the years. In Jim Holden's biography of Cullis, The Iron Manager, Ireland is described as a "second hand car dealer" which usually has certain connotations. Ireland was, in fact, a well-respected Wolverhampton businessman. Indeed, his die-casting company was a far more important venture than his car business and had some 30 employees, making everything from armaments to car number plates, keeping the factory running 24 hours a day. He was even able to bring his engineering skills to bear on his football activities. When Wolves played those early floodlit games, the linesmen – that's what they were in those days – had flags with a row of lights that could be switched on to signal to the referee and be seen by the crowd. John Ireland was the man who came up with the idea – and he made them himself.

Testimony to Ireland's standing can be found in the book, Centenary Wolves, by football historian Percy M Young who wrote of Ireland's appointment to the board in July 1955: "A well-known amateur footballer and qualified referee, with considerable business experience and at one time a town councillor, Ireland appeared well qualified to undertake duties which were to absorb his interest more and more over the next two decades." Ireland was a prominent member and past president of the local Rotary Club, he was a Mason and had been a town councillor who was once wooed – in vain – to stand for Parliament. Once appointed chairman of Wolves, however, he relegated all other interests and devoted himself to the club, a fact confirmed by his daughters, Shirley Jones, Wendy Swann and Jane Ireland who have always chosen to maintain a dignified silence. Now they shed more light on the man to whom it fell to tell Cullis he must leave.

Wendy Swann said: "Father was a qualified motor engineer. In his teenage years he was apprenticed to Sunbeam Motors and went on to work on special cars being built to set the land speed record. Motor cars were in the family and John's father, John T Ireland, owned the first motor car in Wolverhampton. He also drove the first motorised ambulance in the town. He set up the town's first garage to service and sell cars and this is where father started his working life, later setting up his own motor premises with some prestigious agencies. When he extended his premises to house the die-casting machines, producing motor parts, he even won a contract to produce parts for the first manned moon rockets. So much for the second hand car salesman!"

Ireland certainly did not relish his task of ending Cullis's Wolves career as Shirley Jones revealed: "The board had agreed to it and it was up to father to do the deed. Mother said he hardly slept that weekend - he was walking around the garden in a dreadful state - because we have to remember that sacking a manager did not happen as often as it does today. He told us all what was going to happen. He told us that we should all probably be hounded by the press, particularly him. We should probably have a lot of trouble with the people in Wolverhampton. He told us just to be on our guard. What he said was true. He had nasty letters and there were cars riding around the town with offensive stickers on them about father. A lot of what happened to him he wouldn't tell us until one evening we all went round to see him, my sisters and I, and he said I have to tell you that you have all been threatened. In one phone call the person said: 'We know where you all live and we can find you easily.' They kept having strange cars drive by their house and they had to have police protection. My sisters and I all made sure we had something handy to protect us at home just in case, and wherever we went we always made sure there was someone with us. In no way did father relish sacking Cullis but it had to be done. That is why he fore-warned us what would happen."

If Cullis had given his life to Wolves, then John Ireland had given a large slice of his, too. In fact his association with the club was even lengthier than Cullis's. Ireland, as a ten-year-old, used to inflate footballs for a local firm that had just started to manufacture them and he would take them to the ground. It was his proud boast that never did one of the balls have to be sent back. When he went to Molineux as a young boy he would volunteer for odd jobs, cleaning boots, anything. During the war he did fire-watching at the ground and slept on the premises. As a talented schoolboy footballer, Ireland had played at Molineux and went on to be a more than useful amateur, gaining representative honours. He later became a qualified referee, mainly to ensure he knew the laws of the game.

In time, Wolves president Sir Charles Mander would send Ireland to annual meetings as a proxy holder and later sold him a hundred shares before arranging for him to buy Sir Geoffrey Mander's shares. Ireland became a director in 1955 and took over from Jim Marshall as chairman in 1964. Ireland was a man steeped in gold and black and also one who was determined that if he was going to be chairman he would be hands-on. The family confirmed he would be in touch with club every day, either calling in or on the phone. He felt that if he was chairman he had to know what was going on. He would expect the manager to answer to him. He got involved not just with the club but with the supporters and the players. He used to say 'I have three daughters and 21 lads.' The players used to invite him to their private Christmas party and he was frequently seen at the supporters' club next to the ground.

When he came up with the idea of linesmen's flags with lights on, he sought no credit, said Shirley Jones: "Father made them himself but he never patented the idea. We all said he should but he would not do it. He was just happy to have come up with the idea. He would just giggle about it because he was pleased it had worked." She endorsed Ted Farmer's view that the players' approaching the board was what convinced them Cullis had to go. "Yes, he had lost the dressing room. That puts it in a nutshell. A senior player came to father and the board and said 'We cannot play any more with Cullis as our manager.' It was like Chelsea and Mourinho. I think it was very brave of father to do what he did."

Wolves initially issued a brief statement about Cullis's departure but as a war of words developed and fans vented their anger, a fuller statement was issued: "The decision to terminate Mr Cullis's contract was the unanimous decision of the board and was made only after long and careful consideration. It was with great regret this action had to be taken and that his long association with the club had to end. The directors wish to place on record their appreciation of his valued service to the club as player and manager. The decision was brought about by events and pressure inside the club, particularly covering a period of at least three years but, in view of his long and distinguished record with Wolverhampton Wanderers, the directors were always reluctant to take such action that would meet the many and serious problems which existed within the club. Matters were recently brought to a head by complaints and transfer requests from a number of established players which forced the board to the belief that this position was brought about by the treatment of players, by the manager and who they felt no longer had the confidence and respect of the players. As this state of affairs could no longer be allowed to continue, the directors were faced with a situation that called for drastic and immediate action."

Cullis had come through that bad patch in the early 1950s with Jim Marshall's advocacy swaying directors' opinions but a decade later Marshall, chairman in succession to James Baker, could see that the parting of the ways might now have to come. Indeed, the statement referred to a period of three years, leaving no doubt that Cullis's job must have been on the line when they had that serious flirtation with relegation in 1961-2. Marshall was happy to hand over the reins to Ireland and not be the one who brought the curtain down on one of the great managerial careers. Shirley Jones confirms this: "Oh, I'm quite sure that Jimmy Marshall did not want to do it. He wanted father to be the one to do it."

In time, Ireland, too, would find out that there is no sentiment in football and was ousted in 1976 after he had failed to persuade the board to keep Bill McGarry as boss following the team's relegation. After Ireland was replaced as chairman by Jim Marshall's son Harry, following the sacking of McGarry, Ireland was made president of the club. It was a position that carried little prestige or influence until Derek Dougan became chief executive under the Bhatti Brothers regime six years later.

The Doog, like other former players, had great affection and respect for Ireland. He decided that the Molineux Stand, which had been the first phase in the ill-fated plan to rebuild the ground, would be renamed the John Ireland Stand. Not in the best of health by then, Ireland was a proud club president when he unveiled a plaque which said "This building was designated the John Ireland Stand in honour of his work and distinguished service to Wolverhampton Wanderers Football Club." It caused much hurt to the family when Wolves' owner Sir Jack Hayward, intimated a few years after Ireland's death, that he wanted to rename it the Steve Bull Stand. It was just after Stan Cullis died in 2001 and Shirley had a long conversation with Sir Jack: "I said you can't do that now, at this time. It makes it look as though father had done the wrong thing by sacking Cullis. Well, of course, he had not; he'd done the right thing for the club. So Jack eventually said 'All right, we won't do it' but two years later we heard that he had done it and he had not let us know at all." When the stand was renamed the Steve Bull Stand the plaque that Ireland had unveiled was removed. The family have asked the club about it but its whereabouts is unknown. The family would like to know if the plaque is still in existence and available to them. It would be a treasured possession.

Ironically, it was Ireland who had first tried to get boyhood Wolves fan Sir Jack to get involved with Wolves. They had known each other for years and the family remember Sir Jack visiting the Irelands for lunch and the chairman doing his best to get Sir Jack to join the board. Ireland was also a prime mover in the club buying parcels of land around Molineux to pave the way for its eventual redevelopment. The picture his daughters paint of John Ireland is of a man who was passionate about Wolves and to whom, reluctantly, the task fell of ending Cullis's 30-year association with the club. Wendy Swann adds: "Father always did what he felt was best for the club. In keeping quiet about certain events – and even abuse – he felt it was the right thing to do."

Jane Ireland is even more outspoken. "It is never too late to justify a good name. We have waited many years to have the opportunity to speak out on our father's behalf. To all you who vilified and condemned John Ireland for the decision to sack Stan Cullis – you will never know how close you came to losing Wolverhampton Wanderers FC. The players were refusing to play under the management of Stan Cullis due to his irrational and bullying behaviour. It had to be done – the club was at stake. The players' support was essential and immediate, so Wolves were saved.

"The board duly took the decision that Stan Cullis would have to go. John Ireland was the delegated spokesman for the club and therefore he and our family took the violent fall-out. We were threatened and advised to have police protection. To retain the integrity of Wolverhampton Wanderers FC, John Ireland chose not to speak out, incurring the wrath of the supporters. Finally I can only refer to what Derek Dougan wrote after father's death: 'The man I knew as my 'other' father has gone and not only this club, but the football world, will be the poorer for his passing.' So to all of you still intent on besmirching the name of John Ireland, just thank your lucky stars you had a man of vision and strength at a time when it mattered."

Chapter 26 What others thought

Respected sportswriter **Tony Pawson** in his book, the Football Managers, said of Cullis: "To be near him at a match was to experience total involvement, the torrent of words a meaningless chant to ease the tension. Sitting in front of him once as Wolves overwhelmed Luton in an away Cup-tie was a painful experience as he kicked and tackled his way through the ninety minutes, living every second with his players. Broadbent, the delicately gifted ball-player he had knitted so carefully into a team dedicated to power, was abused for a yellow streak as wide as the pavement. When a director praised a raking pass to the wing, Cullis whipped round on him. 'Good pass? You cannot give a good pass to Deeley. You want to keep the ball away from a useless player like him.' The director should have been on safe ground for he was praising the essence of the Cullis style – long passes to the little winger.

"(Major Frank) Buckley had built the organisation, Cullis refined the tactics. His method suited his temperament, his impatience always to be at his opponent's throat. Midfield there was to be power with the big broad-shouldered men, Flowers, Clamp and Slater, driving upfield. But the ball was to be moved far and fast down the centre or wide to the touchline. Hancocks and Deeley were typical of the wingers so important in the Cullis plan. Both were diminutive men, clever dribblers accurate in their crossing and with a nose for goals. Hancocks, tripping over the field in his tiny boots, was the most powerful shot of his day, lancing the ball in from thirty yards or more. He was also an infallible taker of what he always mispronounced as 'pelaties'.

"There was another facet to the Wolves play. They were the apostles of the modern gospel of work-rate and constant pressure. Whoever lost the ball fought to get it back. Opposing defenders were put under instant challenge. Indeed the ball was sometimes played to them deliberately, with one forward waiting to tackle, another hovering to shoot if it ran loose.

"Fifteen years of achievement was no protection for Cullis when the authoritarian approach, the power play, no longer took the First Division by storm. No club can sustain success indefinitely, but the greater the manager's achievements the more is expected of him. Cullis, a hard judge of others, was just as critical of himself. As Wolves slipped down the table he had no complaint when he was dismissed in September, 1964. It rankled only that there was no word of appreciation for his thirty years' service at Molineux. There is no sentiment in football management: success is the only loyalty."

Long-serving Times football correspondent **Geoffrey Green** wrote in his book, Football in the Fifties: "That the Wolves style, based on his (Cullis's) theories, did not please the press riled him to his very depths. 'All you fellows from London can only see Spurs and Arsenal or Manchester United,' he would growl, giving us the thick edge of his Midlands accent. Yet when all was said and done by the end of the 1950s Wolverhampton could boast a record only a shade behind Manchester United. More important, it was Cullis and his pack of hungry Wolves who first gave back English football its pride and belief in the middle fifties following the humiliating experiences against Hungary.

"Cullis rose to take his place beside Busby as one of the emperors of the game. A hard-hitting competitor with forthright ideas, he lived, breathed and dreamt football. Yet he had a strange secretive quality about him. His wife once told me 'It was only after we got married, having walked out with him for some time when he was in the Army of the war years, that I discovered Stanley's peacetime occupation.' Never once did he tell her he was a professional footballer or that he captained England during that time.

"The Hungarian eye-opener was in due course followed by investigations by technical committees set up by the Football Association. One man, however, proceeded to put his own theories to the test in the best place of all – on the field of play. It was Stanley Cullis. First he disagreed with the opinion that the Hungarian magic at Wembley had been based on close ground passing. His own analysis showed that the Magyar wizards used 94 long passes, most of them in the first hour of the match, by which time they had scored most of their six goals. 'The whole thing was a great Hungarian myth' he said later, and he came to the conclusion that the Hungarians had employed methods which Wolves themselves were trying to use at Molineux. This was to go for goal in a direct, incisive fashion, devoid of frills. The plan was to move the ball from one end to the other in a minimum of passes, using at the same time long crosses from one wing to the other to stretch the opposition defence and open it in the middle. Here Wolverhampton possessed two wingers, Hancocks on the right, a diminutive giant and one of the smallest wingers (of powerful shot too, from all ranges) ever to play for England, and Mullen, another international who could also shoot and centre from the sharpest of angles at full speed. These were the two really dangerous prongs of the Wolves attack in those years.

"To support Wolverhampton in their theories Cullis made use of a certain Wing Commander Reep, stationed nearby at RAF Bridgnorth, only a short journey from Molineux. Reep was a form of human computer who had a system of plotting and recording in detail every move of a football match. The conclusion drawn from these patterns was that the long pass was the most lethal. Using this evidence and capitalising on the speed, shooting and cross-field moves of Hancocks and Mullen, Wolves set out to prove their theories in a series of prestige matches against Continental opposition – this was before the advent of European competition. In the process they succeeded beyond their wildest dreams and in the process lifted English heads.

"Those, indeed, were great days and nights down Molineux way. Analysed between the seasons 1949-50 and 1960-1 Wolverhampton were out of the top three places in the league only three times in all, two of them at the start of the period that almost saw Cullis lose his head. There surely lies a lesson for directors of clubs who expect and demand either instant or continuing success.

"The Wolves strength in those days lay in a number of things – the penetration of Hancocks and Mullen down the wings; the goalscoring of Swinbourne, Wilshaw and, later, Murray through the middle; the subtle prompting from inside-forward by Broadbent; but most of all the power and grit generated by a succession of fine half-backs like Billy Wright, Flowers, Slater and Clamp, all of them internationals. The half-back lines of those years were the backbone of the side; long, swift passing, the avoidance of unnecessary frills and first time shooting gave the whole machine its teeth. There was a hunger about those Wolves."

Distinguished football writer **Ivan Sharpe** painted a vivid picture of the Wolves man in his pomp: "Cullis was all lit up – all aglow, I mean. His concentration was quite exceptional; that is one reason why Major Frank Buckley, when managing Wolves' affairs, predicted the successful career as manager which Cullis has since achieved. As a player, Cullis leaned over the ball so intently that one could almost hear him planning the next move."

Top sportswriter **David Harrison** felt Cullis was often the forgotten man in football managerial history: "Three Football League championships and two FA Cup final triumphs and a string of famous victories over Europe's finest stand as a permanent testimony to Cullis's managerial might. He was the first of the superbosses whose methods and achievements dwarfed the efforts of their teams, predating Busby, Nicholson, Shankly, Revie, Clough, Paisley, Ferguson and the rest. He was a tough dedicated deep-thinking, uncompromising visionary who ruled with a rod of iron. But he was also underrated. It will forever anger those who knew, admired and respected him that whenever the roll of honour is unfurled to commemorate the great managers of all-time, that Cullis's name is invariably missing.

"It is not just Wolves fans like me who believe that. I have been in the company of Brian Clough with Cullis and the irrepressible former Derby and Nottingham Forest boss clearly revered the Molineux master. Much to Cullis's embarrassment, Cloughie would embrace the great man, kiss him on both cheeks and launch into a glowing tribute. 'Stanley is a true gentleman,' he said when they were once guests at a football writers' dinner, 'but I bet he was a right bugger to work with. I can learn more in ten minutes with him than hours with the so-called coaching geniuses of the game. It is a crying shame that his work in football is not more widely recognised.'"

Former Villa and England inside forward **Billy Walker**, who later managed Sheffield Wednesday and Nottingham Forest: "Stanley Cullis was a young man with every confidence in himself and a natural technical and also strategic ability. He was never one to hang back when an opinion had to be expressed and, on the field, he had a command, not only of himself but his colleagues, that would have sat more easily on an older pair of shoulders. Cullis never bothered about that. He was a relentless driver and, even now, when he is manager of the club, he is determined, in his way, of having the team play according to his concept of what a Wolves team should be, as Major Buckley was before him. Stanley Cullis learned in a hard, tough school, and he is as hard and as tough as any of his mentors."

In his 1976 autobiography, Liverpool's **Bill Shankly** paid high tribute to Cullis, saying: "While Stan was volatile and outrageous in what he said, he never swore. And he could be as soft as mash. He would give you his last penny. Stan was 100 per cent Wolverhampton. His blood must have been of old gold. He would have died for Wolverhampton. Above all, Stan is a very clever man who could have been successful at anything. When he left Wolverhampton, I think his heart was broken and he thought the whole world had come down on top of him. All round, as a player, as a manager, and for general intelligence, it would be difficult to name anyone since the game began who could qualify to be in the same class as Stan Cullis."

Manchester United boss **Sir Matt Busby**, who like Cullis steered his side to three First Division titles in the 1950s: "Of all the opposition in my time none strove harder to whack the life out of me than Stan Cullis, a top centre-half who became a top manager. A strong, no-nonsense character, Stan. Yet an interesting sidelight on this tough fellow is that his happiest day was when his son decided to forego better paid professions to become a clergyman. And I know that after the Munich crash Stan's son and daughter prayed for me. For all that, Cullis the professional, who as a player was kind enough to say that I was the only one he modelled his game on, did not, as a manager, allow the crash to stop his Wolves beating United to win the 1957-8 championship. Stan Cullis's Wolverhampton team were like him, honest, unambiguous, uncomplicated, making full use of wingers like Jimmy Mullen and Johnny Hancocks and straightforward players like Billy Wright and Ron Flowers behind them. Under Stan, Wolves won three league championships and the FA Cup twice. He gave a lot to football."

The verdict of **Tommy Lawton**, legendary England centre-forward: "Stan Cullis was out on his own among modern centre-halves. You needed plenty of courage, the penetrative powers of a tank and pace of a racing whippet to beat Stan completely, so what chance had Scotland in the many games he played against them? Cullis rose to the front because he stood out in an era of stopper centre-halves. He brought something of the lost art of centre-half play back into the game.

"Who can forget this burly fellow with his twinkling toes, head with its scanty flock of hair, stretched forward, arms working like flippers, as he started away upfield on one of his great runs through the middle? Or the short pass, worked almost out on a drawing board and with set square, to his wing half or inside forward? Stan was a great player to have on your side, but a menace when opposed to you.

"Stan was like a rock. Nothing worried him. Nothing upset him, but although he was hard and tough, he was a ball player. He could beat his man as cleverly as anyone. And he hardly ever wasted a ball. Very serious about everything he is always ready to discuss some new theory, whether it's sanctions or surrealist art, education or Esperanto – he's an expert at that, by the way, and he talks just as much on the field.

"Always a great believer in vocal encouragement is Stanley Cullis. Another thing Stanley firmly believes in is to learn by his own mistakes. No sooner is a game over than he gets down to analyse where he went wrong, and how he should go about rectifying the errors. I often wonder whether Stanley lies awake at night playing over again a match in which he has figured in the afternoon."

Billy Wright, Cullis's chosen skipper during the great years: "Still recalled with some nostalgia by many football students as one of the most accomplished footballing centre half-backs of all time, Stanley Cullis is often referred to – quite incorrectly – as the last of the attacking centre half-backs. Cullis was not an attacker. He possessed extraordinary dribbling ability and by means of accurate and intelligently placed passes started attacks without actually taking part in them. Where Stanley Cullis had such a pull over his opponents was in body balance. With his arms stretched out like a tightrope walker picking his way along a wire, Stan Cullis had complete control of his body and was seldom caught off balance. All the time he gave colleagues the feeling that he was the man in command. In my opinion it was Stanley Cullis's ability to put the shutters up in the centre of the field, literally becoming king of all he surveyed, which led to him developing into a great constructive centre half-back. The explanation is quite simple. For many other centre half-backs the primary task of stopping their opponents demanded so much concentration they could not find time to turn their attention elsewhere. Cullis was different. He was a soccer genius, a dominating personality, able to take upon himself two jobs at once and still be master of the situation.

"To watch Stanley Cullis in possession of the ball was also an object lesson, always he kept his body between the ball and his opponent. He was one of the most difficult footballers to dispossess. My summing-up of Stanley Cullis: he was a soccer artist and quite the best centre half-back in the game, but before he developed his all-round qualities he concentrated on first becoming a good 'stopper'. After that his constructive ability developed. His ability to read a match and anticipate the moves of the opposition had to be experienced to be fully appreciated. Cullis, too, had that priceless ability to make those surrounding him produce their best form. Mind you, he was a hard man to please; Stan, in fact, was never completely satisfied with himself. And the outcome? Everyone fought hard to reach the highest standard of play – and more often than not succeeded.

"If you did what he wanted then you could not have a better friend but he would not tolerate people ignoring his instructions. I'm not saying he would not listen to your views, because he would and if he thought what you were saying made sense he would put it into practice. He could rant a bit but he would only have a real go if he thought you weren't giving one hundred per cent. If you were just having one of those days, he would forgive you that. He would not allow defenders to play about with the ball and if you played it across the field he would go daft. He reckoned the more you passed the ball the greater the chance of the move breaking down. The more you passed the more time the opposition defenders had to get back and consolidate. I watch games now and the majority of goals still come from three or four passes. We did not play so much a long ball game, we played direct football. We could change the direction of attack with long passes. If Jimmy Mullen had it on the left and was surrounded he would swing the ball over to the right and Johnny Hancocks would be in the clear. Or we could play a long ball up to Roy Swinbourne and know he could hold the ball up which is only what centre-forwards do today."

Three times a First Division championship winner and an FA Cup winner, **Ron Flowers** wrote in his autobiography in 1960: "I do not always agree with him but there is no disputing he has in every way proved himself to be one of the most successful managers in modern football. The Stanley Cullis approach to the problems of modern football always makes interesting hearing, and reading, for he thinks most seriously about all aspects of the game and his reactions often intrigue me. Many managers, when a team is passing through a lean spell, would prefer to sit down and talk over the current problems with his players. But not our chief. As a former player of distinction, he realises that a player knows when he is playing badly and must be worried. He never adds to our worries at such a time by large-scale inquests, and I for one deeply appreciate this approach. Our manager, on the other hand, has very thorough and searching tactical talks when we're doing well, which over the past ten years means we've had plenty of discussions.

"One of the great qualities of Stanley Cullis as a manager is that he knows what he wants. The boss likes to hear our ideas, and encourages us to air our views. But as our manager he'll tell us when he disagrees, and straight from the shoulder say what he requires from us all. On a Saturday, if we have not had a team talk, he will always come to the dressing room before the match to have a word with certain players to discuss the men opposing them. Mr Cullis's advice is always on target. During the course of a season our manager spends as much time as possible watching the teams we will oppose. He makes a mental note of the players we will be meeting and he has what I can only term a photographic mind. If Stanley Cullis tells you that your opponent has certain strong qualities, and weaknesses, you can be certain he is giving you the right advice."

Skipper of the 1960 FA Cup-winning side **Bill Slater**: "Stan portrayed this image of being a hard and demanding manager and the players responded well to that. He would not have any dirty players and I cannot remember a single player being booked or sent off. He did not like us swearing around the club. He also did not like players to fall over each other if we scored a goal. A handshake was enough. He had this idea that scoring goals was what we were supposed to be doing and, if you think about it, he was right. Underneath, I think he really felt for the players and had their interests at heart. I remember once when my wife was in hospital over Christmas, he invited me to his home for Christmas Day lunch. Not many managers would have done that."

Hero of the win over Honved, **Roy Swinbourne**: "He was hard but he was fair or tried to be fair, because it's very difficult when you've got 48 pros on the books and we did have something like 48 in those days. He could get so worked up during a match he would be wet through with sweat and he could lose his rag a bit at half-time. He could say what he liked to us but nobody else could criticise us. If a director came in he'd soon make it clear he could not interfere. He would always stand up for us if anybody else tried to say anything. We played the long-ball game but I liked to play the ball a bit. I'd started as an outside-right but Stan said 'You're big, you're strong . . . if I wanted someone to play ball I'd have signed Ronnie Allen.' So that told me!"

Top-scorer in the 1954 title winning team, **Dennis Wilshaw:** "I had a deep respect for Stan even though we did not always get on. As I look back I realise I must have been very hard to manage. Stan was a long ball advocate but not as a player. I played with Stan a couple of times and he used to hit short balls to Tom Galley or Joe Gardiner or play square balls. If we did this when he was manager then we were in trouble. I remember in one match Tom Galley had received the umpteenth square ball from Stan and he told him 'Stan, kick the next effing ball up field, I'm effing tired'."

South African **Eddie Stuart**, named by Cullis as club skipper after Billy Wright's retirement: "He was a hard man but he certainly got results. I think the secret of his success both as a player and a manager was that he was a perfectionist. He had drive and enthusiasm although when he took over the managerial reins he inherited a good team backed by a fine scouting staff. He was the master of Molineux and his word was virtually law. However, he had a very caring side. He ensured the club looked after me when I was ill and I shall never forget seeing him after the win over Spartak in 1954. I was in tears at the end of the game as we walked off and I saw Stan come on to give Billy Wright a hug and Stan was in tears as well."

Chapter 27 Final Verdict

So where does Stanley Cullis stand in the annals of English football? Firstly, as a player he was without doubt among the greats despite his career at club level being reduced to just four league seasons. What came across time after time in researching this book was just how highly-rated Cullis was as a player. As a centre-half he must have been a commanding figure. Like so many top central defenders he was able to "read" the game and was comfortable on the ball so that he could initiate attacks with a short or long pass to one of his midfield men. He was also a born leader, being made skipper of his club at a young age and captain of England when he was younger than most of his teammates.

He was in many ways the Duncan Edwards of his day, though he had no pretensions to being a goal-scoring midfield player. However, there are similarities between the two. Like the Dudley-born Manchester United legend, Cullis matured quickly. Both were capped for England at an early age and looked like being fixtures in the national side for many years. Through greatly differing circumstances, their clubs were denied their best years. Their league careers were of similar length. Cullis played 152 league games for Wolves, Edwards played 151 for Manchester United.

While England's wartime matches against Scotland and Wales were never given full international status, nothing can be taken away from them as full-blooded contests between some of the best players in a generation. Cullis stood out in these games and it is rare to find him getting a bad rating. My father was fortunate enough to see Cullis playing for club and country and spoke of his unique style in the way he crouched over the ball with arms working furiously and allowing himself time to dwell on the ball if necessary – a luxury he would come to deny most of his players when he became a manager.

Wolves' directors had seen enough of Cullis the player to know that he had all the qualities needed to be a manager – knowledge of the game and ability for man-management and motivation. In addition, he had a will to succeed and a passion for the game of football that was Shankly-like in its intensity. He was not the type to stand for any mavericks among his players. He would not discourage the expression of opinions but once tactics had been agreed upon he would not tolerate any deviation from the plan.

At the 2016 dinner of the Wolves Former Players' Association, Alistair Robertson spoke eloquently of the value of team spirit in football. Robertson, who captained Wolves when they rose from the depths of the Fourth Division in the late 1980s, emphasised that a key factor in football success at any level was "getting the dressing room right".

No matter how good the players might be, if the dressing room was not right, then success would not follow. Robertson said he could not stress this too highly. Cullis also knew the value of team spirit and wanted a certain standard of behaviour from his players. More than one player left Molineux because he did not conform to the Cullis code of conduct. The result was a team who were very much together and when speaking to the great players from that era one was always struck by their modesty, their genuine humility and a camaraderie that had lasted over the years. To put it another way, they all seemed lovely blokes, not a bad apple among them. No wonder, they had got the dressing room right.

A fine judgement in his management team also proved a vital factor in Cullis's success with Wolves. His first lieutenant was his former half-back colleague Joe Gardiner, given the title of "trainer" but being much more than that. He and Cullis made an ideal partnership, Gardiner being the quiet man who could smooth things over if Cullis had ranted and raved as he was sometimes wont to do. Gardiner would move in with a few words of encouragement for any player who had received an ear-bashing from the manager. Gardiner had the players' affection and respect and that combination does not always occur. Another pre-war clubmate, Jack Dowen, was also on the training staff and Bill Shorthouse would be recruited once his playing days were over. Up in Yorkshire there was yet another ex-player Mark Crook running the Wath Wanderers nursery club which proved a valuable source of young talent. All these backroom boys were Wolves men through and through as, of course, was Cullis. Backing them up was chief scout George Noakes, whose scouting network unearthed a succession of fine players.

It must be remembered that football in the fifties was a whole world away from football in 2016, the year that marked the centenary of Cullis's birth. In Cullis's heyday, the manager was paid far more than his players and he was the boss in every sense of the word. Some, like Matt Busby at Manchester United, ruled with a more benevolent attitude, preferring the more subtle, laid-back approach to management. That was not Stanley's Cullis's way and his methods proved just as effective as those of Busby. At the same time as demanding 100 per cent effort and loyalty, Cullis would also give full support in return. He was determined his players would be well looked after by the club and while he might give them a verbal-attack now and then, he would always defend them and would not criticise individuals publicly. He was not one, either, to make excuses if he knew his team had been beaten fairly and squarely. As far as success goes his record from 1948-9 to 1959-60 was better than any other manager on the England scene in terms of major trophies won. This was achieved when there was no elite group of clubs who dominated the top flight. The First Division was in every sense a level playing field with few, if any, easy games in a 42-match season. In those twelve seasons, no fewer than seven clubs won the championship, Wolves and Manchester United heading the list with three title wins each, while Portsmouth could boast two.

Purists might point to the attractive style of Arthur Rowe's 1951 Spurs side yet their push-and-run brand of football was soon found out and they did not build on their title success. Similarly, the title wins of Arsenal (1952-3), Chelsea (1954-5) and Burnley (1959-60) were one-off triumphs. Wolves' direct style endured throughout this period and produced relentless, attractive football that entertained the fans and gave them the thing they love most – goals. What was a fine league record during that time might have been twice as good as Wolves missed out on one title on goal average to Portsmouth, another by just one point to Burnley and, in chasing the elusive Double as well as blazing a trail of floodlit friendly triumphs, handed a third to a run-of-the-mill Chelsea side.

The unique feat of scoring a century of league goals in four successive seasons says everything about Cullis's football philosophy and while he liked strong no-nonsense half-backs he wanted them to be comfortable on the ball. Billy Wright, Ron Flowers, Bill Slater and Eddie Clamp were a quartet of immense talent. Cullis was happy, too, to encourage skilful ball-playing forwards. He liked wingers who were not mere providers but could score goals as well. The contribution of Johnny Hancocks, Jimmy Mullen, Norman Deeley and, if all too briefly, Micky Lill is testimony to this. He also allowed the sublime talents of Peter Broadbent to flourish in midfield and was blessed with natural goalscorers like Jesse Pye, Roy Swinbourne, Dennis Wilshaw and Jimmy Murray. A team are only as good as their weakest links and the contribution of the lesser lights cannot be underestimated. Men like full-backs Eddie Stuart, Gerry Harris and Bill Shorthouse and inside-forwards like Sammy Smyth and Bobby Mason played vital roles in the success of Cullis's sides.

Without doubt, Cullis was fortunate to inherit from his predecessor Ted Vizard the nucleus of a fine team but it was Cullis who took them to a higher level. He then built a new team who proved even more successful than his first one. Among the players already on Wolves books when Cullis became boss, was Bert Williams, without doubt one of football's finest goalkeepers, and the manager chose well when it came to selecting a successor. Malcolm Finlayson differed in style from Williams but proved just as effective and represented one of Cullis's best ventures into the transfer market. Other deals were not so successful and if there has to be criticism of Cullis it could be in his judgement when making signings. Finlayson and Broadbent were obvious exceptions to this but others came and went without being able to make a lasting impression at Molineux. Critics might accuse Cullis of not being able to adjust his methods when the Wolves style no longer proved as effective as in the past. That might be the case, though Cullis never really got the chance to show he could move with the times. The sacking of Cullis was not handled with any great dignity and arguments will continue about the rights and wrongs of it. What cannot be denied is that for a whole generation of Wolves fans the Master of Molineux provided year after year of excitement and success. There were many highs and a few lows but rarely a dull moment. For that, Wolves fans of my age will be eternally grateful.

They played under him

These are the players who played under Stanley Cullis with their League, FA Cup and European Cup appearances made while he was manager. Appearances made under other managers are not included. A reign that began in 1948 embraces 16 full seasons and eight games into the 1964-5 campaign. Figures indicate league appearances with FA Cup and European games in brackets. Appearances in the Charity Shield matches and friendlies are not included.

Baillie, Joe. 1 Signed when 25, the defender had been left-half in the Celtic side who won the Scottish Cup in 1951 but he failed to break into the first team at Molineux, his lone appearance being at right-back against Huddersfield in 1955. He moved to Bristol City then Leicester City and Bradford Park Avenue.

Barron, Jim. 8. Goalkeeper who joined the club as a junior but had to play second fiddle at Molineux to Fred Davies. Moved to Chelsea and then served Oxford United and Nottingham Forest well. Was back at Molineux as part of John Barnwell's coaching staff.

Baxter, Bill. 43 (4), Goals 1. A wing-half at a time when Wolves were spoilt for choice in that department. The Scot was on the club's books before the war but his debut did not come until 1948. Sold to Aston Villa where he was a stalwart for a number of seasons.

Birch, Brian. 3, Goals 1. A young forward of whom great things were expected but did not fulfil promise at Manchester United or Wolves.

Bonson, Joe. 10 (2) Goals 5. A burly Barnsley-born centre-forward given a brief first team chance in the 1956-7 season before joining Cardiff City.

Booth, Colin. 78 (4), Goals 27. Manchester-born, he was reserve for the England schoolboys side before joining Wolves where he seemed to have broken into the first team in 1955-6 and the following season but had to play second fiddle to Bobby Mason in the title winning seasons of 1957-8 and 1958-9. He won an England under-23 cap while with Wolves. Once scored four goals against Arsenal. Was sold to Nottingham Forest, and continued to score regularly for them as he later did for Oxford United and Doncaster Rovers.

Broadbent, Peter. 446 (42), Goals 144. Without doubt, Cullis's best signing when a £10,000 fee to Brentford in 1951 made the 17-year-old the costliest teenager at the time. Arguably the most naturally gifted player in Wolves history, he won First Division championship medals in 1953-4, 1957-8 and 1958-9 as well as an FA Cup winner's medal in 1960. He played seven times for England. Career encompassed 14 of the 16 full seasons Cullis was manager.

Brodie, Chic. 1. Goalkeeper signed from Aldershot who made just one appearance before being sold to Northampton seven months after joining Wolves.

Chatham, Ray. 68. Was on Wolves books as an amateur before becoming a part-time pro in 1946. A former centre-forward, he looked like establishing himself as first-choice centre-half in the early 1950s when Bill Shorthouse switched to full-back but Shorthouse later moved back to central defence to his exclusion. Chatham then joined Notts County in 1954 and played for them well into his thirties.

Clamp, Eddie. 214 (23), Goals 25. Born in Coalville, Leicester, he played in the same England schoolboys team as Johnny Haynes in 1950 and was a tough-tackling wing-half but possessed a great deal of football ability to go with it. With Billy Wright and Bill Slater, he formed an all-Wolves half-back line for England in four games in 1958. A key member of the side who won back-to-back First Division titles in the late 1950s and the FA Cup in 1960. Cullis sold him to Arsenal, believing he had a ready-made successor in Johnny Kirkham.

Clews, Malcolm. 1. Tipton-born forward who made just one appearance despite being on the books for several years. Moved to Lincoln City and then into non-League football.

Cocker, Les. 1. Not to be confused with the Leeds and England trainer of the same name, the England youth international was a member of the 1958 FA Youth Cup-winning side.

Crawford, Ray. 41, Goals 30. He was one of Cullis's last major signings. An England centre-forward and prolific scorer of goals, helping unlikely Ipswich Town to be First Division champions in 1962. He continued to score regularly in his brief spell with Wolves and was still at Molineux when Cullis was sacked. Crawford was eventually sold to West Brom. His career brought him well over 300 goals.

Crook, Alf. 1 (1). A regular in Wolves' reserves for several seasons, he made just one league appearance and one in the FA Cup, though the latter was the memorable 1949 semi-final replay win over Manchester United.

Crook, Bill. 126 (14), Goals 1. Younger brother of Alf, the former Wolverhampton Grammar School boy was the regular first-team right-half in the first four post-war seasons and was a member of the 1949 FA Cup-winning side. He was a part-timer at Molineux, his main employment being as a draughtsman at Rubery Owen. Transferred to Walsall.

Crowe, Chris. 83 (2), Goals 24. Signed by Cullis from Blackburn Rovers in early 1962 at the same time Peter McParland was bought from Aston Villa. The pair helped Wolves' successful relegation fight that season. Crowe was the only player who cost money in the team who got the 1962-3 season off to a flying start, a run which won him a lone England cap.

Davies, Fred. 94 (3). Liverpool-born, he was signed by Cullis from Borough United. In the best traditions of Wolves goalkeepers and had several seasons as first-choice, including the 1966-7 Second Division promotion-winning side. Later played for Cardiff and Bournemouth.

Deeley, Norman. 206 (28), Goals 73. Smallest player ever to win an England schoolboy cap and was at first a wing-half or inside-forward before becoming a highly effective wingman able to play on the left or right. Scored a lot of goals as Wolves won the successive First Division titles at the end of the 1950s and was twice on target when Wolves beat Blackburn 3-0 in the 1960 FA Cup final. Was capped twice by England.

Dunn, Jimmy. 94 (14), Goals 29. Liverpool-born inside-forward, the son of a famous Scottish international of the same name. Played briefly alongside Cullis in the latter's final season. A member of the 1949 FA Cup-winning side, he joined Derby County in 1952 and as a coach he served Albion well in the 1960s.

Durandt, Cliff. 43 (5), Goals 9. Chunky inside-forward from Johannesburg who later became a winger but could not hold down a regular place apart from a spell in the 1960-1 season. Was spotted by Cullis during the club's 1957 tour of South Africa. He was eventually transferred to Charlton before returning to play in South Africa.

Dwyer, Noel. 5. Cullis knew he had a reliable reserve goalkeeper when he signed him from Irish club Ormeau but his five seasons at Molineux saw him make just five league appearances as stand-in for Malcolm Finlayson in 1957-8. Later played for West Ham and Swansea and won 14 caps for the Republic of Ireland.

Farmer, Ted. 57 (5), Goals 44. A member of the FA Youth Cup side who overturned a 5-1 first-leg deficit against Chelsea to win the final 7-6 on aggregate. Farmer scored four goals in the 6-1 second-leg win at Molineux. Had a fine debut season with 28 League goals from 27 games but was later hampered by injuries which brought a premature end to a highly promising career. Won England under-23 caps and looked good enough to play for the full England team.

Finlayson, Malcolm. 179 (22). One of Cullis's best signings when he bought him from Millwall as successor to Bert Williams. A brave goalkeeper who was a member of the 1957-8 and 1958-9 First Division title-winning sides and the 1960 FA Cup winners, making him the club's most decorated 'keeper. Unfortunate not to have been capped by Scotland.

Flowers, Ron. 381 (32), Goals 34. Yorkshire-born wing-half who was a cornerstone of the great Wolves side of the 1950s. Broke into the team in the latter part of the 1953-4 First Division title-winning season and was a member of the 1957-8 and 1958-9 championship sides as well as the 1960 FA Cup winners. Captained England three times in a 49-cap international career during which he made 40 consecutive appearances, a run bettered only by clubmate Billy Wright.

Forbes, Willie. 24 Goals, 7. A Ted Vizard signing from Dunfermline in 1946, he was a useful wing-half or inside forward whom Cullis sold to Preston where he had several good seasons, helping the Lancashire club to the 1954 FA Cup final.

Ford, Clive. 1. The last player to be given a First Division debut by Cullis – on the opening day of the 1964-5 season. Later played for Walsall and Lincoln.

Galley, John. 4 (1), Goals 2. A young centre-forward who made just four league appearances under Cullis but later scored a lot of goals for Rotherham and Bristol City.

Gibbons, Len. 25 (4). A full-back who seemed to have broken into the team in 1951-2 only to lose his place the following season to Roy Pritchard.

Goodwin, Freddie. 43 (2). Cullis memorably gave him his debut in an FA Cup-tie against West Brom along with Fred Davies and Bobby Thomson. Later played for Stockport County.

Guttridge, Bill. 6. Hard-tackling full-back who made just two league appearances in each of three successive seasons before joining Walsall, whom he served with some distinction.

Hancocks, Johnny. 266 (27), Goals 138. Played for Walsall before the war and was signed by Ted Vizard in 1946 so was in the team during Cullis's final playing season. A small man with a mighty shot he helped Wolves win the FA Cup in 1949 and scored 24 goals when the First Division title was won in 1954. His 26 goals in 1954-5, achieved at the age of 35, is a record for a Wolves winger. Would probably have won more than three England caps had it not been for his aversion to flying.

Harris, Gerry. 207 (25), Goals 2. One of the hard men of the side who won back-to-back First Division titles at the end of the 1950s and then the FA Cup in 1960. Good enough to win four England under-23 caps and was also on standby for the England squad in the 1958 World Cup.

Harris, John. 3. The Gornal-born full-back seemed on the brink of successful career but broke his leg in only his second league appearance, Later played for Walsall.

Henderson, Jackie. 9, Goals 3. Cullis signed the versatile Scottish international and saw him as a possible successor to veteran left-winger Jimmy Mullen or as a rival to Jimmy Murray for the centre-forward spot. However, Henderson did not settle at Molineux and was sold to Arsenal.

Hinton, Alan. 75 (3) Goals 29. Cullis did not do his best bit of business when he transferred the Wednesbury-born England international to Nottingham Forest in exchange for Dick Le Flem. The latter stayed only briefly at Molineux while Hinton won two more England caps with Forest and was then a significant member of Derby's 1972 First Division title-winning side.

Hooper, Harry. 39 (2), Goals 19. A Cullis signing that did not work out. Bought from West Ham as successor to Johnny Hancocks and had a fine first season only to fall out of favour with the manager during the club's 1957 tour of South Africa. Later played for Birmingham City and Sunderland.

Horne, Des. 40 (11), Goals 18. A youngster, who arrived from Durban seeking a trial, the left-winger eventually followed in the footsteps of the great Jimmy Mullen. Horne is only Wolves player to win both FA Youth Cup and FA Cup winner's medals. Later joined Blackpool.

Howells, Ron. 9. A member of the side who were runners-up to Manchester United in the first ever FA Youth Cup final, he was with Wolves for six seasons but made few first team appearances as Cullis had several top class wing-halves. He was sold to Portsmouth.

Jackson, Alan. 4 (2), Goals 2. A winger or centre-forward, he failed to break permanently into the first team and was sold to Bury.

Jones, Gwynfor. 21. Welsh full-back whose occasional league appearances came during seven years as a loyal reserve.

Kelly, Lawrie. 39 (5). Full-back whom Cullis decided not to field in the 1949 FA Cup final and later joined Huddersfield Town where in 1953 he was a member of the defence who played in all 42 matches during the Second Division promotion-winning season.

Kelly, Phil. 16 (2). Won Republic of Ireland caps at full-back while at Molineux but not a regular first-team place and moved to Norwich City.

Kirkham, Johnny. 85 (7), Goals 14. Wednesbury-born half-back whom Cullis thought was good enough to replace Eddie Clamp when he sold the latter to Arsenal. Though an England under-23 international, Kirkham failed to live up to expectations. Later played for Peterborough and Exeter.

Knowles, Peter. 19, Goals 7. A gifted player who modelled his game on that of the great Peter Broadbent. Cullis gave him his debut and he looked a certainty to play for England when in 1969 he announced he was quitting football because it was in contradiction with his beliefs as a Jehovah's Witness. Many thought he would return to the game but underestimated the extent of his religious conviction.

Lazarus, Mark. 9, Goals 2.Yet another Cullis signing which did not work out. Bought the winger from QPR and then sold him back to the Londoners whom he helped win the League Cup in 1967.

Le Flem, Dick. 13, Goals 4. A left-winger from Nottingham Forest brought to Molineux in a deal which saw Alan Hinton move in the opposite direction. Made only a few appearances before being sold to Middlesbrough.

Lill, Micky. 30 (3), Goals 16. Cullis made a title-winning decision when he brought the Barking-born winger into the team in the second half of the 1958-9 season. Lill had a purple patch of form and was briefly talked of as a future England player. He was then sold to Everton but never really fulfilled his potential.

McDonald, Tommy. 5 (1), Goals 1. A winger signed from Hibernian as a possible successor to Johnny Hancocks, he was then sold to Leicester City where he had several successful seasons before returning to Scotland with Dunfermline.

McLean, Angus. 72 (6), Goals 1. A well-built Welsh-born full-back who played alongside Cullis in the latter's final season as a player. Cullis played him frequently in his first three seasons as manager, including one game as a centre-forward which brought him one of the two goals he scored while at Molineux.

McParland, Peter. 21, Goals 10. Cullis signed the left-winger from Aston Villa in 1962 and he helped a successful fight against relegation. The man who scored two goals when Villa beat Manchester United in the 1957 FA Cup final, found himself replaced by Alan Hinton as first choice for Wolves in 1962-3. He was sold to Plymouth Argyle.

Mannion, Gerry. 17 (2), Goals 7. Cullis played the 19-year-old in the 1960 FA Cup semi-final and the right-winger briefly looked a star in the making. He won England under-23 caps but never built on his fine start and was sold to Norwich City.

Mason, Bobby. 146 (25), Goals 54, The Tipton-born inside-forward was an unsung hero of the 1957-8 and 1958-9 First Division championship teams but was omitted from the 1960 FA Cup final side after playing in all previous rounds. Later played for Leyton Orient.

Melia, Jimmy. 16, Goals 4. Cullis's last big signing. He bought the England international from Liverpool in 1964 and Melia looked a more than useful acquisition. He had played enough games for the Merseysiders to win a First Division championship medal that same season. Alas for him, Cullis was sacked and not long afterwards Melia also left Molineux. He joined Southampton and in 1965-6 helped them gain promotion to the top flight.

Middleton, Harry. 1. A useful centre-forward in the reserve team but his only first team appearance was as a winger. Later gave good service to Walsall.

Mullen, Jimmy. 365 (33), Goals 89. Played in the same team as Cullis before and after the war and then proved a fine member of the team that Cullis guided to FA Cup success in 1949 and the First Division title in 1954. Was still playing when the title was again won in 1958, and the following season. Won 12 England caps and played in the 1950 and 1954 World Cup final tournaments.

Murray, Jimmy. 273 (23), Goals 164. Cullis was fortunate to have the Dover-born player to fill the gap left by the career-ending injury to Roy Swinbourne. Not a swashbuckling centre forward but a natural goalscorer who top-scored in the two First Division title-winning seasons at the end of the 1950s. Collected an FA Cup winner's medal in 1960. He won a couple of under-23 caps, played once for the Football League and was once named a reserve for the full England side.

Neil, Pat. 4, Goals 1. The left winger's league appearances in 1956-7 made him the last amateur to play for Wolves

Parsons, Dennis. 23 (3). Birmingham-born goalkeeper who served as a deputy for Bert Williams before being sold to Aston Villa.

Pritchard, Roy. 178 (21), Dawley-born full-back broke into the team in 1948-9 in time to gain an FA Cup winner's medal and played 27 games in the 1953-4 First Division title-winning team. Moved to Aston Villa and then Notts County and Port Vale.

Pye, Jesse. 122 (16), Goals 58. Another player Cullis inherited from Ted Vizard's squad. A centre-forward of quality who was equally at home as an inside-forward. Will always be a Wolves hero for his two great goals in the 1949 FA Cup final. His only cap was against the Republic of Ireland when England suffered their first home defeat by non-UK opposition.

Rowley, Ken. 1 (2) Made three appearances for Wolves in 1949-50, two of them in the FA Cup. Moved to Birmingham City and started well but was out of action for a long time after a bad injury.

Russell, Eddie. 30 (4) A wing-half who managed to impress despite having some tough competition. Earned a place on the FA tour to America in 1950. Moved to Middlesbrough and then Leicester City.

Russell, Peter. 3. Looked a good centre-half prospect when, at 19, he impressed in the 1954 Charity Shield game against West Brom but made only three league appearances before joining Notts County.

Short, Jack. 98 (9), Goals 2. First had a Wolves trial as a centre-forward but was turned down. Came back a year later, 1949, and was taken on to the staff as a full-back. Served Cullis well in that position for four seasons, including the 1953-4 First Division title-winning side before losing his place to Eddie Stuart. Played for Stoke City and then his home-town club Barnsley.

Shorthouse, Bill. 314 (27), Goals 1. Eventually took over from Cullis as the club's first-choice centre-half, having joined the club as an amateur in 1941. He was very close to winning an England cap in the early 1950s. Gained an FA Cup winner's medal in 1949 and First Division title medal in 1954. Later a key member of Cullis's backroom staff at Molineux and when Cullis was manager of Birmingham City.

Showell, George. 194 (16), Goals 3. Cullis reckoned he was the man to take over from Billy Wright as Wolves' centre-half but his judgement was wrong and Showell eventually lost his place to Bill Slater. Bounced back, however, and was right-back in the 1960 FA Cup-winning side.

Sidebottom, Geoff. 28 (5) A fine goalkeeping deputy to Malcolm Finlayson for three seasons before being transferred to Aston Villa.

Simpson, Alex. 2. A Scottish wing-half who made just a couple of appearances under Cullis before having a useful career with Notts County, Southampton and Shrewsbury Town.

Sims, Nigel. 38 (1). Well-built goalkeeper who deputised for Bert Williams on many occasions over several seasons and even kept him out of the side briefly. In 1954 was in the Young England XI for the annual pre-FA Cup final game against an England XI. Joined Aston Villa and was in the side who beat Manchester United in the 1957 FA Cup final.

Slater, Bill. 310 (29), Goals 25. Cullis was a lucky man when Slater, still an amateur, opted to join Wolves when he came to work at Birmingham University. A big contributor to Wolves' three First Division title wins and switched to centre-half not only to skipper his side to their FA Cup triumph in 1960 but also to be named Footballer of the Year. Played 12 times for his country, including the 1958 World Cup finals.

Smith, Leslie. 86 (2), Goals 24. A skilful winger whom Cullis could readily call upon as deputy for Johnny Hancocks or Jimmy Mullen, even keeping the latter out of team for most of the 1954-5 season which enabled him to play his part in the famous wins over Honved and Spartak. Joined Aston Villa and was in their 1957 FA Cup-winning team.

Smyth, Sammy. 72 (13), Goals 35, The Irish international wrote his name into Wolves folklore with his goals in the epic 1949 FA Cup semi-finals against Manchester United and then with his splendid individual goal to clinch victory over Leicester City in the final.

Springthorpe, Terry. 24 (2). Another hero of the 1949 FA Cup final triumph, being a controversial choice but thoroughly justifying Cullis's decision to play him at left-back rather than Lawrie Kelly.

Stevenson, Ernie. 2. An inside forward product of the Wath Wanderers nursery whom Cullis soon moved on to Cardiff City. He also played for Southampton and Leeds.

Stobart, Barry. 49 (4), Goals 22. Cullis created a shock when he named him for the 1960 FA Cup final rather than Bobby Mason, who had played in all previous rounds. Stobart justified his selection but his games in his preferred position of centre-forward were limited by the presence of Jimmy Murray then Ted Farmer. He joined Manchester City and later played for Aston Villa and Walsall.

Stockin, Ron. 21 Goals 7. It looked briefly as though Cullis had made a successful sortie into the transfer market when he signed Stockin from Walsall and he gained a place in the first team during the second half of the 1952-3 season. However, he was ousted from the team the following season by Peter Broadbent and joined Cardiff City and then Grimsby Town.

Stuart, Eddie. 287 (32), Goals 1. Cullis had great admiration for the South African full-back who figured in the three 1950s championship teams and made him captain of the club after Billy Wright's retirement. Unfortunate to lose form and missed out on the 1960 FA Cup final success. Moved to Stoke and skippered their 1962-3 Second Division promotion-winning side. Later led Stockport to promotion from the Fourth Division in 1966-7.

Swinbourne, Roy. 211 (18), Goals 112. Cullis knew he had one of the best centre-forwards in the land in the Yorkshire-born player whose 24 goals in 1953-4 helped Wolves become champions of England for the first time. A national hero thanks to his two goals in the win over Honved and would surely have played for England had not injury struck him down at the height of his powers in 1955.

Taylor, Doug. 3. The former West Brom amateur played three games at centre-forward at the end of the 1954-5 season before joining Walsall.

Taylor, John. 10, Goals 1. Not one of Cullis's best signings. A striker bought from Luton Town, where he had won an England B cap. He was given his chance at inside-right at the start of 1952-3 but did not take it, scoring only once, and was transferred to Notts County.

Tether, Colin. 1. There were high hopes for the young full-back and Cullis took him on Wolves' 1957 tour to South Africa but he made only one first team appearance before being moved on to Oxford United.

Thomson, Bobby. 1, Goals 1. The inside forward from Dundee scored three goals in two appearances for Wolves (one of them a friendly against Valencia when he scored twice) but could not make an impact with so many good players on the books. He was sold to Aston Villa whom he served with some distinction. He later played for Birmingham City.

Thomson, Bobby. 106 (3). A Smethwick-born full-back not to be confused with his Scottish namesake. Was thrown in at the deep end by Cullis when given his debut as an 18-year-old in the fourth-round FA Cup tie against West Brom in 1962. He was an immediate success and went on to win eight full England caps as well as skippering the under-23 side.

Thompson, David. 3. Technically the last player to make his debut under Cullis's management, though he was selected when the manager was on sick leave. The right-winger was given his debut ten days before Cullis was sacked. Later played for Southampton, Mansfield Town and Chesterfield.

Walker, Johnny. 37 (7), Goals 26. The Scottish inside-forward joined Wolves just after Cullis retired as a player. Played enough games in 1950-1 to become a fans' favourite. Later had many successful seasons as a wing half with first Southampton and then Reading.

Wharton, Terry. 105 (3), Goals 40. The youngster was given his chance by Cullis and served Wolves well, usually as a right-winger, scoring a lot of goals, several of them from the penalty spot. Made over a hundred appearances for Bolton.

Whitfield, Ken. 9 (1), Goals 4. In Dougan-style, Whitfield scored a hat-trick on his home debut but did not kick on from that. He was more at home at wing-half which was where he later served Brighton well.

Williams, Bert. 304 (28). Signed from Walsall by Ted Vizard and Cullis reaped the benefit of having one of the all-time great goalkeepers to call on for nine seasons. Capped 24 times for England, Williams was a member of the 1949 FA Cup-winning team and the 1953-4 First Division championship side. Played for England in the 1950 World Cup finals.

Wilshaw, Dennis. 211 (7), Goals 113. On becoming manager, Cullis soon recalled him from a loan spell at Walsall. A natural striker, Wilshaw top-scored with 26 goals in 1953-4 when Wolves became champions of England for the first time. Capped 12 times for his country, including games in the 1954 World Cup finals, Wilshaw remains the only man to score four goals in an England-Scotland full international.

Woodfield, David. 72 (1). Cullis gave him his chance as successor at centre-half to Bill Slater and he would serve Wolves well for seven seasons, even playing at centre-forward at one stage.

Woodruff, Bobby. 18. Signed by Cullis in March, 1964, he was one of Swindon Town's crop of talented players. Famous for his long throw-ins but he was also a talented all-round player. Capable of playing up front as well as in midfield.

Wright, Billy. 417 (40), Goals 7. First man in the world to win 100 caps, Wright had two great careers, first as a wing-half and then as central defender. He was an inspiration on the field as a leader and Cullis could not have had a better man to captain his teams. Named Footballer of the Year in 1952, Wright was an FA Cup winner in 1949 and captained Wolves' First Division title-winning sides in 1954, 1958 and 1959.

Cullis career year by year

1934 The 17-year-old from Ellesmere Port signs for Wolves in February.

1935 Debut at right-half against Huddersfield Town at Molineux.

1936 Plays centre-half in the first team at Blackburn in March.

1937 First England cap – against Northern Ireland in Belfast.

1938 Wolves miss out on First Division title when they lose at Sunderland on the last day of the season.

1939 Double disappointment as Wolves again First Division runners-up and are unexpectedly beaten by Portsmouth in the FA Cup final.

1940 Twice sustains head injuries playing in France for the British Army.

1941 Scores his first senior goal as the Army beat an Allied Armies XI 8-2 at Stamford Bridge.

1942 Breaks his leg playing for Fulham at Portsmouth.

1943 Appointed England captain in succession to Eddie Hapgood.

1944 Plays last of his 20 wartime internationals before being posted to Italy.

1945 Dropped by manager Ted Vizard from Wolves side in second leg of FA Cup-tie against Charlton.

1946 Turns down offer to be manager of Hull City.

1947 Announces his retirement before Wolves miss out on title yet again when they needed only to beat Liverpool on the last day of the season. He becomes the club's first ever assistant manager.

1948 Appointed manager of Wolves after Ted Vizard loses his job.

1949 Wolves win the FA Cup to climax Cullis's first season in charge.

1950 Title disappointment again as Wolves finish runners-up on goal average to Portsmouth.

1951 Signs Peter Broadbent. Scores his first ever goal for Wolves when he comes out of retirement during the club's unbeaten tour of South Africa.

1952 First managerial crisis as Wolves slump to 16th in the table. Gives debuts to two future club legends – Ron Flowers and Bill Slater.

1953 An unbeaten 18-game run proves foundation for successful title bid.

1954 Wolves champions at last and then enjoy floodlit triumphs against Spartak and Honved.

1955 Runners-up to Chelsea and lose to Sunderland in FA Cup quarter-final.

1956 Has to apologise after scuffle with Luton director. Signs goalkeeper Malcolm Finlayson as successor to Bert Williams.

1957 Another unbeaten tour of South Africa lays foundation for another successful title challenge. Wolves beat European champions Real Madrid 3-2 at Molineux and draw return game 2-2.

1958 Wolves win First Division title and score a century of goals

1959 Wolves champions again and once more hit century of goals.

1960 Wolves win the FA Cup having been denied the Double as Burnley pip them for the First Division title. Beaten 9-2 on aggregate by Barcelona in European Cup.

1961 For the fourth successive season Wolves score a hundred league goals – a unique feat.

1962 Slump in form prompts signing of Chris Crowe and Peter McParland. Youngsters then give hopes of more success but it proves a false dawn.

1963 Signs Ray Crawford as Wolves face a relegation battle.

1964 Signs Jimmy Melia. Sacked after 30 years with the club.

Wolves' record under Cullis

Season	P	W	D	L	F	A	Pt	Pos	FA Cup
1948-49	42	17	12	13	79	66	46	6th	Winners
1949-50	42	20	13	9	76	49	53	2nd	Round 5
1950-51	42	15	8	19	74	61	38	14th	Semi-final
1951-52	42	12	14	16	73	73	38	16th	Round 4
1952-53	42	19	13	10	86	63	51	3rd	Round 3
1953-54	42	25	7	10	96	56	57	1st	Round 3
1954-55	42	19	10	13	89	70	48	2nd	Round 6
1955-56	42	20	9	13	89	65	49	3rd	Round 3
1956-57	42	20	8	14	94	70	48	6th	Round 4
1957-58	42	28	8	6	103	47	64	1st	Round 6
1958-59	42	28	5	9	110	49	61	1st	Round 4
1959-60	42	24	6	12	106	67	54	2nd	Winners
1960-61	42	25	7	10	103	75	57	3rd	Round 3
1961-62	42	13	10	19	73	86	36	18th	Round 4
1962-63	42	20	10	12	93	65	50	3rd	Round 3
1963-64	42	12	15	15	70	80	39	16th	Round 3
1964-65	8	1	1	6	10	23	3	22nd	

Bibliography

All for the Wolves (Rupert Hart-Davies), Stanley Cullis. 1960.

Arsenal A Complete Record (Breedon Books), Fred Ollier. 1992.

Aston Villa A Complete Record 1874-1988 (Breedon Books), David Goodyear and Tony Matthews. 1988.

The Breedon Book of Football Managers (Breedon Books), Dennis Turner and Alex White. 1993.

Bolton Wanderers FC The Official History 1877-2002 (Yore Publications), Simon Marland. 2002.

British and Irish Special and Intermediate Internationals (SoccerData), Keith Warsop. 2002.

England the Football Facts (Facer Books), Nick Gibbs. 1988.

Everton a Complete Record (Breedon Books), Ian Ross & Gordon Smailes. 1988.

The Essential History of Blackburn Rovers (Headline), Mike Jackman. 2001.

Feet First Again (Corgi Books), Stanley Matthews. 1955.

Findon's Football Handbook (Findon Publications), Matty Watson. 1948.

Football is My Business (Sporting Handbooks), Tommy Lawton. 1946.

The Football League Match by Match 1946/7 (SoccerData), Tony Brown. 2002

The Football Managers (Eyre Methuen), Tony Pawson. 1973.

Footballer's Progress (Sporting Handbooks), Raich Carter. 1950.

For Wolves and England (Stanley Paul), Ron Flowers 1962.

Fulham the Complete Record (Breedon Books), Dennis Turner. 2007.

The Great Ones (Sportsman's Book Club) Joe Mercer, 1966.

The Heartbreak Game (Hillburgh), Ted Farmer. 1987.

Huddersfield Town A Complete Record 1910-1990 (Breedon Books), Terry Frost. 1990.

The Iron Manager (Breedon Books), Jim Holden. 2000.

Kicking and Screaming (Robson Books), Rogan Taylor and Andrew Ward. 1995.

Liverpool the Complete Record (deCoubertin Books), Arnie Baldursson and Gudmundur Magnusson. 2011.

Manchester United A Complete Record (Breedon Books), Ian Morrison and Alan Shury. 1992.

Proud Preston (Carnegie Publishing), Ian Rigby and Mike Payne.1999.

The Real Bobby Dazzler (Derby Books), Bobby Thomson. 2010.

Sheffield United the Complete Record (Derby Books), Andrew Kirkham. 2012.

Sheffield Wednesday The Complete Record (Breedon Books), John Brodie and Jason Dickinson. 2011.

Soccer in the Fifties (Ian Allan), Geoffrey Green. 1974.

Talking with Wolves (Breedon Books), Steve Gordos. 1998.

The Wolves Encyclopaedia 1877-1989 (Paper Plane), Tony Matthews (with Les Smith). 1989.